To Improve the Academy

To Improve the Academy

Resources for Faculty, Instructional, and Organizational Development

Volume 20

Devorah Lieberman, Editor
Portland State University

Catherine Wehlburg, Associate Editor
Stephens College

ANKER PUBLISHING COMPANY, INC.

Bolton, Massachusetts

To Improve the Academy

Resources for Faculty, Instructional, and Organizational Development

Volume 20

ISBN 1-882982-46-0

Composition by Deerfoot Studios
Cover design by Boynton Hue Studio

Anker Publishing Company, Inc.
176 Ballville Road
P.O. Box 249
Bolton, MA 01740-0249 USA

www.ankerpub.com

To Improve the Academy

To Improve the Academy is published annually by the Professional and Organizational Network in Higher Education (POD) through Anker Publishing Company, and is abstracted in ERIC documents and in Higher Education Abstracts.

ORDERING INFORMATION

The annual volume of *To Improve the Academy* is distributed to members at the POD conference in the autumn of each year. To order or to obtain ordering information, contact:

Anker Publishing Company, Inc.
P.O. Box 249
Bolton, MA 01740-0249
voice   (978) 779-6190
fax   (978) 779-6366
email   ankerpub@aol.com
web   www.ankerpub.com

PERMISSION TO COPY

The contents of *To Improve the Academy* are copyrighted to protect the authors. Nevertheless, consistent with the networking and resource-sharing functions of POD, readers are encouraged to reproduce articles and cases from *To Improve the Academy* for educational use, as long as the source is identified.

INSTRUCTIONS TO CONTRIBUTORS
FOR THE NEXT VOLUME

Anyone interested in the issues related to instructional, faculty, and organizational development in higher education may submit manuscripts. Manuscripts are submitted to the current editors in December of each year and sent through a blind review process. Correspondence, including requests for information about guidelines and submission of manuscripts for Volume 21, should be directed to:

Catherine Wehlburg
Department of Psychology
Box 2066
1200 E. Broadway
Stephens College
Columbia, MO 65215
voice   (573) 442-2211
fax   (573) 876-7248
email   cwehlburg@wd.stephens.edu

Professional and Organizational Development Network in Higher Education (POD)

Mission Statement

Approved by the Core Committee on March 24, 1991:

The Professional and Organizational Development Network in Higher Education (POD) fosters human development in higher education through faculty, instructional, and organizational development.

POD believes that people have value, as individuals and as members of groups. The development of students is a fundamental purpose of higher education and requires for its success effective advising, teaching, leadership, and management. Central to POD's philosophy is lifelong, holistic, personal, and professional learning growth, and change for the higher education community.

The three purposes of POD are:

1)   To provide support and services for its members through publications, conferences, consulting, and networking.

2)   To offer services and resources to others interested in faculty development.

3)   To fulfill an advocacy role, nationally, seeking to inform and persuade educational leaders of the value of faculty, instructional, and organizational development in institutions of higher education.

Membership, Conference, and Programs Information

For information contact:
David Graf
POD Network
Nova Southeastern University/FGSEHS
1750 NE 167th Street
N. Miami Beach, FL 33162
voice   (954) 262-8786
email   Grafd@nova.edu

Chapter Contributors

Jim Borgford-Parnell, University of Washington

Stephen D. Brookfield, University of St. Thomas

Barbara Cambridge, American Association for Higher Education

Virleen Carlson, Cornell University

Peter D. Eckel, American Council on Education

Nadia Cordero de Figueroa, University of Puerto Rico, Rio Piedras

Katherine Frank, University of Washington

Fred Hebert, University of Wisconsin-Stevens Point

John P. Hertel, United States Air Force Academy

Wayne Jacobson, University of Washington

Mona B. Kreaden, New York University

Eric W. Kristensen, Orion Educational Development

Amy Lawson, Indiana University

HeeKap Lee, Indiana University

Devorah Lieberman, Portland State University

Marty Loy, University of Wisconsin-Stevens Point

Saundra Y. McGuire, Louisiana State University

Kathleen McKinney, Illinois State University

Joan Middendorf, Indiana University, Bloomington

Barbara J. Millis, United States Air Force Academy

Linda B. Nilson, Clemson University

Robert K. Noyd, United States Air Force Academy

David Pace, Indiana University, Bloomington

Michael Peck, University of Washington

Susan C. Piliero, Cornell University

Lois Reddick, University of Washington

Terrel Rhodes, Portland State University

Pedro A. Sandín-Fremaint, University of Puerto Rico, Rio Piedras

Timothy P. Shea, University of Massachusetts, Dartmouth

Pamela D. Sherer, Providence College

Richard G. Tiberius, University of Toronto

David G. Way, Cornell University

Catherine Wehlburg, Stephens College

Dennis A. Williams, Georgetown University

Table of Contents

Preface

This year's *To Improve the Academy* is reflective of a trend that is occurring across higher education: elements of change throughout an institution. The three sections of this volume reflect these elements by the level and context at which they occur within an institution of higher education: the macro level, the unit level, and the classroom level. Much thought went into the focus of this year's volume, and the chapters best illuminate theory and practice addressing faculty development in each of these contexts. All chapters were selected through a rigorous blind review process. The chapters included in this volume are a delightful combination of theory and application. All chapters met the theme of this volume, the quality of scholarly writing, extensive reviews of literature, a grounding in theory, and an application that can be generalized to the volume's readers. All reviewers are recognized experts in the areas of faculty development, instructional technology, organizational change, and assessment.

Without the effort of many individuals, *To Improve the Academy* (Volume 20) would not be available to you today. Further, the contributions made by the many individuals enhanced the quality of this volume. First, I must thank the authors for contributing the chapters contained within. The quality of their work is of the highest caliber. I am certain that as you read the chapters, you will experience new and renewed insights about your own work in faculty development and higher education. I anticipate that you will copy chapters to share with your colleagues. During an era where we are all encouraged to contribute to the body of literature in higher education, I believe we should stop and praise the authors in this volume, who have devoted their time and effort to produce scholarly works that are grounded in the discipline of faculty development.

Without my colleagues associated with POD, reviewing the chapter submissions would not have yielded the quality you have before you. I would like to thank the following persons for taking time from their own schedules to review and offer feedback to all who submitted chapters to this volume:

Patricia Armstrong, Princeton University
Kenneth Baldwin, University of Maryland, Baltimore County
Jim Borgford-Parnell, University of Washington

Lesley Cafarelli, Collaboration for the Advancement of College Teaching
    & Learning
Cynthia Desrochers, California State University, Northridge
Nancy Diamond, University of Illinois at Urbana-Champaign
Gloria Edwards, Purdue University
Rae Jean Goodman, United States Naval Academy
Alan Kalish, California State University, Sacramento
Tricia Kalivoda, University of Georgia
Ann Kovalchick, Ohio University
George Lueddeke, Southampton Institute, United Kingdom
Sabrina Marschall, University of Maryland University College
Kathleen McKinney, Illinois State University
Judith Miller, Worcester Polytechnic Institute
Ed Nuhfer, University of Colorado, Denver
Daniel Pratt, University of British Columbia
Donna Qualters, University of Massachusetts Medical Center
Laurie Richlin, California State University, San Bernardino
Douglas Robertson, University of Nevada, Las Vegas
D. Lynn Sorenson, Brigham Young University
Catherine Wehlburg, Stephens College
Sheryl Welte-Emch, University of Northern Iowa
Laurel Willingham-McLain, Duquesnue University
Dina Wills, Lehigh University
Alan Wright, Dalhousie University

As scholars we find that time is our most precious commodity. And because we have professional commitments within our own institutions, it is critical that those who rely upon us recognize the importance of devoting time to projects such as serving as editor for *To Improve the Academy*. I offer my heartfelt thanks to Portland State University's leaders and visionaries, President Bernstine and Provost Tetreault, for supporting me in the time I devoted to reviewing, editing, and organizing this year's volume. I could not report to finer administrators. When our own administrators recognize how works such as this one contribute to the body of literature and move forward the areas of faculty development and organizational change, then we, as scholars, are validated for our own scholarship and inspired to continue.

For those who have edited works comparable to this one, you know that if it were not for the assistance of those who work in our offices on a daily basis, the final product would not exist. For this year's *To Improve the*

Academy, I owe my heartfelt appreciation to Andrew Huot in the Portland State University Center for Academic Excellence. Andrew's organizational skills were impeccable, his level of frustration with the project miraculously low, and his ability to keep the project moving uncannily timely. Andrew, thank you so very, very much.

Finally, as every editor knows, the patience level of her family is truly the key to any project. My family's support could not have been greater. Thank you so much, Roger, Alicea Jacova, and Emery Rose.

Devorah Lieberman
Vice Provost & Special Assistant to the President
Portland State University
May 2001

Introduction

The chapters contained in this volume of *To Improve the Academy* reflect the trend in higher education to view the institution from a systems perspective. For a chapter to be included within this volume it must meet specific criteria: 1) the quality of writing must be of the highest standards, 2) the theories and practices put forward must be grounded in the literature, 3) the philosophical basis of the chapter must be reflective of the POD mission, and 4) the chapter should meet a need in the faculty development literature. I am pleased that the 18 chapters contained within all meet the four criteria outlined. POD's contribution to the field of faculty development is apparent from the volume before you.

Chapters in the volume are organized by context and content. There are three primary sections within the volume that focus on the macro level of the institution, the unit level of the institution, and the professor-student level of the institution. The content of each of the chapters suggests how theory and practice within a particular context level (macro, unit, and classroom) can, in some way, impact every other part of the institution.

Section I: The University highlights four chapters that address the broadest thinking about faculty development across the entire university. As you finish reading the chapters in this section, you will be aware that faculty development has an impact on every individual, every unit, and every initiative that encompasses an institution.

Section II: Teaching and Learning Centers features seven chapters that illuminate the importance and role of faculty development centers within an institution. These chapters address the mushrooming services and philosophies of faculty development centers. The authors of the first chapter discuss how they began to imagine and organize a campus-wide faculty development center. Other chapters in this section discuss the role of centers for teaching assistants, measuring impact on center's constituents, requiring faculty development, integrating diversity into center activities, developing a center portfolio, instructional technology, and the role of faculty development.

Section III: The Learner, the Professor, and the Learning Environment brings the reader to the level of the student, the professor, and the environments in which they co-exist. These chapters ground their concrete suggestions for improving and enhancing student learning in theoretical constructs. There is not a chapter within this section that does serve to heighten the importance of understanding the role of the instructor in the learning environment. The reward is that the practical suggestions can be generalized to nearly any face-to-face, hybrid, or asynchronously delivered course content.

Each chapter within this volume ends with the contact information of the chapter authors. In the spirit of POD, if you have further inquiries or questions about a chapter, feel free to contact the author(s) of the chapter.

I am proud to have edited Volume 20 of *To Improve the Academy*. The importance of faculty development in higher education, nationally and internationally, continues to grow and the issues evolve and expand. It is an exciting and much needed time to be a faculty developer.

Devorah Lieberman
Vice Provost & Special Assistant to the President
Portland State University
May 2001

Section I

The University

1

Institutional Transformation and Change: Insights for Faculty Developers

Peter D. Eckel
American Council on Education

This chapter presents a series of insights about the process of institutional change and how leaders might implement it. Since the majority of energy goes into what the institution should do, little attention in higher education is given to how institutions should go about change. Based upon six years of work with 24 diverse institutions working on a range of change agendas in two projects, this chapter presents some conceptualizations of change and offers some language to discuss the type of intended change that might be useful for faculty developers and other campus leaders. It identifies three key elements in the change process and offers insight on strategies to implement them. It then connects these elements to the important role of faculty developers.

INTRODUCTION

Those individuals involved with faculty development and bringing about change and improvement on their campuses are well versed in the reasons for higher education to do things differently, adopt new pedagogies, create new relationships with students and other stakeholders, and think more critically about better serving the public good. They are familiar with the external pressures and the new opportunities that are creating new environments within which higher education must work. Thus, we can quickly move beyond the discussion of key challenges and emerging opportunities.

In many instances, campus leaders know what to do; they have identified the needed changes that will help the institution improve in key
ways. This chapter presents a series of insights about the process of institutional change and how leaders might implement it. Since the majority
of energy goes into what the institution should do, little attention in
higher education is given to how institutions should go about change.
Based upon six years of work with 24 diverse institutions working on a
range of change agendas in two projects, this chapter presents some conceptualizations of change and offers some language to discuss the type of
intended change that might be useful for faculty developers and other
campus leaders. It identifies three key elements in the change process and
offers insight on strategies to implement them. It then connects these elements to the important role of faculty developers.

ACE PROJECTS ON TRANSFORMATION

To assist institutions of higher education as they responded to their
changing environments, the American Council on Education (ACE)
launched the Project on Leadership and Institutional Transformation in
1995 with 26 public and private institutions, including community colleges, liberal arts colleges, comprehensive and doctoral universities, and
research universities. Two institutions elected not to continue in the project's final two-year phase. (Appendix 1.1 lists the 26 participating institutions and their change agendas.)

The participating institutions joined the project with a range of
change agendas. Some were shifting to a student- or learning-centered
culture from a faculty-centered one, or infusing technology across the institution to improve teaching and learning. Others were rethinking faculty responsibilities and roles, implementing new ways of making decisions, or recrafting the curriculum and its purposes. Over time, the
institutions' agendas evolved—some became more complex and challenging, as one change led to another, and others grew more limited in
scope and less profound in their potential effects. The path of change
took twists and turns, sped up and slowed down, and the substance of the
change agendas took on new dimensions over time. The process was
never linear; unexpected events and unintended consequences of predictable occurrences shaped the course of change in every institution.

The goals of the project were to assist institutions on their journeys
of change to help them achieve their goals. We sought to help campus
change leaders (faculty and administrators with the responsibility for

leading institution-wide change) articulate a comprehensive agenda for change. We provided on-campus support through visits by experienced consultants and sponsored meetings of campus teams to share their successes and challenges and to collectively explore issues of institutional change. The project was organized to give institutions a supportive structure and language to think more deeply and intentionally about the complexities and challenges of change. We sought help their institutions develop the capacity for intentional change through reflection and learning. From their experiences we drew a series of insights and now seek to disseminate the learning to administrative and faculty leaders and policy makers.

We further refined our ideas through the Kellogg Forum on Higher Education (KFHET), a partnership to explore and better understand institutional change and transformation involving campus leaders from Alverno College, the Minnesota State College and University System, Olivet College, Portland State University, and the University of Arizona; faculty from The Center for the Study of Higher and Postsecondary Education at the University of Michigan, The Higher Education Research Institute at the University of California–Los Angeles, and The New England Resource Center for Higher Education at the University of Massachusetts–Boston; and staff from the W. K. Kellogg Foundation and ACE.

This partnership sought to combine experiences of leading transformational change with a variety of research and case studies highlighting the process of institutional change and transformation. Through presentations, wide-ranging discussions, papers, and campus visits, the KFHET partners of campus leaders, scholars, and association and foundation staff explored and exchanged ideas about change in higher education. Through this continued refinement, the ideas presented here were tested and refined.

TYPOLOGY OF CHANGE

One of the first insights from the project was the difficulty of talking about change and transformation. We discovered that the terms "change" and "transformation" were problematic in several ways. The terms frequently provoked emotional responses among faculty, staff, and students, leading many institutional leaders to avoid them altogether. Campus leaders were concerned that the terms would elicit resistance and defensiveness, and instead chose the concepts of improvement and enhancement. While some people on campus were excited and energized by the idea of change and transformation, others found it threatening. The notions of change, and particularly, transformation, on many campuses were seen to devalue an institution's and individual's accomplishments and commitments.

Participants also defined the terms differently. In some instances, change meant doing anything differently, no matter how large or small. At other institutions, change was altering a discrete set of activities or creating new structures, and at others, change was about connecting to large-scale modifications and launching new endeavors. The term transformation was also broadly and inconsistently defined. Some institutions used the term loosely, meaning a variety of interrelated changes that added up to something more than adjustments or innovations. Other times, transformation was implied to mean a complete break with the past. These people inferred transformation to be a fundamental shift in institutional identities and purposes, disregarding history and mission to start anew.

Developing a set of common definitions within the project was an important basis for clear communication and common understandings. Differentiating among types of change helped institutional leaders better describe the degree of change they sought, and helped create more intentional and reflective change processes. Institutional leaders could develop change processes consistent with the type and magnitude of the desired change.

Two basic descriptors—depth and pervasiveness—can describe categories of change. Figure 1.1 outlines four types of institutional change—adjustment, isolated change, far-reaching change, and transformational change.

FIGURE 1.1
Typology of Change

Depth

		Low	*High*
	Low	Adjustments (I)	Isolated Change (II)
Pervasiveness			
	High	Far-Reaching Change (III)	Transformational Change (IV)

The first quadrant is adjustment—a change or a series of changes that are modifications to a practice. Changes of this nature are revisions, alterations, or renewals. They occur when current designs or procedures are improved or extended. An adjustment may improve a process or the quality of a service, or it might be something new. Nevertheless, it is not a drastic alteration and does not have deep or far-reaching effects.

The second quadrant, isolated change, is deep but limited to one unit or a particular area; it is not pervasive. Depth focuses on how profoundly a change affects behavior or alters structures. Deep change implies a shift in values and assumptions that underlie the usual way of doing business. It requires people to act and think differently. The deeper a change, the more it is infused into the daily lives of those affected by it. An example of an isolated change is an academic department that decides service is of central importance. In this unit, hiring, promotion, and tenure decisions are heavily based upon faculty service records, students engage in service-learning as a integral part of their course work, the curriculum is rethought around community-based learning, and faculty members are annually recognized for service contributions beyond the campus.

The third quadrant is far-reaching change; it is pervasive but does not affect the organization very deeply. Pervasiveness refers to the extent to which a change is extensive across the institution. The more pervasive a change, the more it crosses unit boundaries and touches different parts of the institution. The use of computers is a familiar example of pervasive change. Computers sit on most faculty members' desks, students have access to computer labs, and many have their own computers. Furthermore, computers are used in university offices across campus for everything from tracking student accounts and inventory in the bookstore to submitting grades and analyzing data for research. However, the effect is limited and does not go deeply into the institution.

The final quadrant is transformational change. Transformation occurs when a change is both deep and pervasive. It is deep, addressing those assumptions about what the institution does, how it behaves, and what produces. In other words, transformation goes to the core of the institution. It is pervasive, a collective, institution-wide phenomenon. It is cultural change, altering the beliefs, values, norms, underlying assumptions, structures, processes, and policies. Transformation does not entail fixing discrete problems or adjusting and refining current activities. Our definition of transformation does not imply that institutions will change completely. Institutions in the projects sought to retain the basic functions of teaching, research, and service, but aimed to alter the ways in which they performed them and rethink the operating principles behind them.

Absent from our definition of transformation is the concept of speed. Because transformation is deep and pervasive, and it alters culture, most American institutions would not show dramatic and far-reaching results quickly. Transformation is most likely to occur through evolutionary rather than revolutionary steps. Specific contexts and internal factors influence the rate of change differently for institutions. Most colleges and universities do not have the cultures, the structures, or sufficient environmental pressures to bring about rapid transformation. We observed that transformation is a five-, ten- (or more) year journey.

Although Figure 1.1 presents the four types of changes as distinct, on most campuses, change is a composite of these types. Rather than change being discrete, within one quadrant, its dimensions may be thought of as overlapping. A change may be more or less pervasive, or it may be more or less deep. As was often the case, the magnitude of the agenda changed over time. Some institutions started out seeking isolated change, but through a cascading effect, the change agenda touched other units. Other institutions began with large hopes of transformation, only to scale back their intended efforts.

THE CHANGE PROCESS: THREE STRAIGHTFORWARD TASKS

The second set of insights from the project focuses on the process of bringing about transformational change. Through six years worth of observations, visits, conversations, reports, and meetings through two projects, we have learned that transformational change is about three fundamental tasks: 1) creating institution-wide momentum and energy for change, 2) removing barriers to change and elements that reinforce the status quo, and 3) helping people to think differently and adopt new mental models. All of the institutions in the ACE projects that made significant progress on their change agendas were able to create processes and strategies to do these three things. However, these tasks are not easily accomplished. The challenge for campus leaders is to determine strategies that will work within their individual contexts and cultures to accomplish these tasks.

These insights reflect the strategies and approaches used by the institutions that made the most progress on their institutional transformation agendas in the two projects. We came to call them "transforming" institutions, because by their own admission, the work of transformational change is never complete. Successes led to new challenges, calling for more change.

Create Institution-Wide Momentum and Energy

Because of higher education's decentralized nature, competing priorities and objectives, norms of autonomy, and individual faculty academic freedom, any change effort requires a tremendous amount of momentum and energy to reach all areas of the institution. Institutions can also too easily rest on past successes without critical self-examination and become complacent. The following strategies were used by institutions that made the most progress on their change agendas to generate the needed institution-wide momentum and energy for change.

Actively made a compelling rationale for change. Transforming institutions had leaders who framed the change agenda in ways that were constructive to their efforts. Leaders articulated in clear and compelling ways why the institution had to undertake the proposed change. These leaders realized that key constituents must recognize the necessity for action before they willingly participate. That need for action must speak personally to faculty, administrators, staff, and other campus stakeholders. Leaders connected the need for change with important institutional and individual values: improving student learning, increasing excellence, and becoming more socially responsible. They positioned the change agenda as essential to a better future, not simply a different one. Leaders used a variety of approaches to make the case compelling. Some successful campuses used a data-driven approach, collecting hard data and conducting studies to assess the extent of the challenges. Other institutions took a softer approach, using qualitative factors—stories, beliefs, anecdotes, assumptions, and aspirations—to make the case for change.

Framing the change agenda constructively also involved explicit dissemination strategies, what one faculty leader called "an internal PR campaign." Regular presentations of data, highly visible ad hoc task forces, widely disseminated reports, periodic columns in campus newspapers, and special newsletters helped convey why the change is important. Leaders also engaged in informal conversations, using unstructured time at the beginning and end of meetings to bring others into the discussion of why the change was needed to improve the institution.

Identified the right timing. Institutions that progressed had leaders who identified the right issues to tackle at the right time in the institution's life. Timing the introduction of the change agenda was important.

For some institutions, the right timing meant not introducing new challenges immediately on the heels of resolving a difficult set of issues or soon after a divisive decision. For others, new challenges provided a catalytic event that infused new energy and enthusiasm after getting through a difficult period. In other instances, leaders built on the positive energy and confidence of a job well done. In each case, the right time meant something different depending upon the institution's historic trajectory.

The timing also had to be right in the rhythms of academic life. Institutions that made progress neither introduced new, complex issues at peak times in the semester, such as when faculty were busy starting their classes, nor did they make decisions over the summer that would affect faculty. Rather, change leaders chose to introduce ideas and start work when they could capture the most attention and time. They also worked to moderate the pace of change. Institutional leaders learned that too much change at once could easily overwhelm the campus.

Created rich opportunities for involvement. The leaders at transforming institutions created a variety of opportunities for people to participate in meaningful ways. These opportunities allowed faculty and staff to choose the timing of their involvement, the length of their commitments, the degree of intensity, and the specific projects. Participation was flexible and people were able to change the ways they participated over the course of time. People could be highly involved at the beginning, take time away, and rejoin in a different capacity. Because opportunities varied, they capitalized on the various strengths of participants. Institutional transformation requires many talented hands, and although passionate leaders are important, they cannot effect transformation by themselves.

Identified champions. Recognizing that change would not occur simply by the effort of a dedicated few, leaders at transforming institutions identified and tapped champions across campus. Because of the depth and pervasiveness of transformational change, people in different units played important roles in leading the change efforts across the institution. Department chairs, senior faculty, and midlevel administrators were essential to make the changes last. Campus change leaders made sure to give the champions the support, assurance, and resources needed to bring about changes in their areas.

Used public deadlines effectively. Campus leaders used public deadlines to keep the change process moving. Sometimes these deadlines were determined by external groups, such as due dates for funding proposals. At other times, internal events, such as board meetings, budget cycles, or the printing of the course catalog, created important deadlines. By making deadlines well known and the potential risks of missing them public, leaders were able to keep the process on track. At the same time, leaders neither created or enforced arbitrary deadlines for quick decisions, nor did they set unrealistic timelines that would lead to premature decisions that later might be overturned or need to be revisited.

Gained external recognition. Institutions successful with change gained energy and momentum through a variety of external relationships with other institutions, funding agencies and philanthropies, and other national projects. These off-campus supporters and collaborators enhanced legitimacy on campus, introduced new ideas and solutions, and helped institutions overcome an insularity that impeded progress. Frequently, they resulted in new resources, sometimes substantial, to contribute to the change efforts. Institutions gained recognition in prestigious journals, and from funders such as the Kellogg Foundation, National Science Foundation, and FIPSE. External recognition and being touted as a leader in higher education strongly benefited on-campus change efforts.

Remove Barriers

Effecting institutional change is as much about removing obstacles as it is about introducing new things. Institutions can easily become tied down and remain stuck in the status quo without recognizing that to do things differently institutions must remove barriers and elements that reinforce the status quo. To accomplish this task, project institution leaders used the following strategies.

Developed new skills and knowledge. Institutional leaders recognized the difficulty of implementing new changes without providing adequate training or faculty development. To do new things requires mastery of new knowledge and skills. Institutions that made progress toward transformation developed intensive and comprehensive development programs for staff, administrators, and faculty. For instance, one institution, to support its change agenda, offered a range of services and programs, including workshops for department chairs, a mentor program for junior faculty, a range of seminars on teaching, learning, assessment, and community-based learning, and workshops and brown bag lunches on the scholarship of teaching. It also runs an orientation for new faculty. Each activity was aligned with the direction and goals of the transformation agenda.

Secured new resources. One of the most common barriers preventing change is inadequate resource. Institutions that made progress found new sources of revenue from private foundations, state legislatures, and increased endowment returns that they invested in change. For example, two institutions were able to secure one-time large investments from their states to launch important projects. This needed money went to purchasing computers and upgrading facilities that would support their changes in teaching and learning. Other times, new funds were created through internal reallocation processes or from savings in other areas. New funds, in addition to providing the resources to do new things, also created a sense of legitimacy for the changes. Faculty and staff saw these as investments as recognition of their good work.

Created new units and positions. Campus leaders recognized that their institutions needed to create new units and positions to support their change agendas. The current organizational chart was insufficient. They created units to provide new services, such as community-university relations and centers for teaching excellence or for computing, technology, and pedagogy. They also created new administrative positions that had key elements of the change agenda in their portfolios. These new positions were frequently filled by faculty leaders on short-term leaves or through course buy-outs. These new positions and offices meant someone was responsible for the issues surrounding the change and sent the message that these issues are important enough to receive staff, budgets, and office space.

Tapped shared governance bodies constructively. The forms and functions of institutional governance, such as faculty senates and joint faculty-administrative planning groups, vary across institutions. Institutions that made progress toward transformation developed processes to tap these decision-making bodies effectively and did not violate well in-grained procedures. They expected governance processes to be constructive and worked to ensure that they were, rather than approaching them as impediments to change. By working constructively with governance leaders and adhering to the expected roles for campus governance, institutional leaders were able to use governance as a facilitator of change. At the same time that these institutions honored the traditional means of decision-making, they were not afraid to create new, ad hoc bodies that met institutionally defined thresholds for legitimacy that could work faster and assemble the necessary leaders better than standing governance committees. They balanced formal governance and its structures and procedures with new, innovative, responsive task forces of faculty and administrators (and, frequently, students).

Help People Think Differently

Transformational change is not only about doing things differently, it is also about thinking differently, both institutionally and individually. Because it is cultural, transformational change forces people to ask what the changes mean for themselves, their activities, and their assumptions. We observed two ways that transforming institutions demonstrated new institutional thinking. In some instances, colleges and universities attached new meanings to familiar language and concepts. For example, one institution recognized that it had redefined what it means to be a good teacher in its new technology-rich environment. No longer was it someone with well-organized lecture notes ready to present information, but a good teacher now was someone who knew how to use the available technology to help students actively engage with the material. Other times, institutions developed new language to describe new activities and changed assumptions and priorities. For example, one institution collectively added the words "customer" and "client" to its collective vocabulary. Faculty and administrators decided that the institution's customers were the companies that hired their graduates, the local community where their graduates lived, and the state legislature that provides the institution with resources. They thought that their students were more accurately described as clients. This new language helped articulate how they thought differently about the ways the institution served its different stakeholders. It helped the campus to differentiate the various ways it was responsible for learning, to whom, and in which ways.

At institutions that made progress on their transformation agendas, leaders created opportunities for people to come together to question the status quo, to explore the ways it had become insufficient, to question assumptions, to tell stories, and to posit new ideas. Institutions that made progress on their change agendas used some of the following strategies that help people to think differently and change their preconceived notions.

Created numerous campus conversations. Ongoing and widespread conversations to clarify and create new meaning rather than to advance or argue positions were major factors in helping individuals and institutions think differently about themselves. Such conversations allowed significant numbers of people to learn about problems and challenges from a broad, institutional perspective, creating a deeper understanding and greater investment in the entire institution. These opportunities allowed faculty and staff to wrestle collectively with ideas, to try out new priorities and ways of thinking, and to align key concepts with new realities. Then they could explore the ways in which they personally could adjust to the emerging future. Through these conversations, institutions developed new common language and a consensus on key ideas.

Benefited from outsiders and their ideas. Institutions that made significant progress on their change agendas benefited from the ideas, comments, suggestions, and confrontations from interested outsiders who challenged key institutional beliefs and assumptions and introduced new ideas. Some institutions invited outside speakers to attend campus retreats or sponsored lecture series. For example, one institution working on diversity and social engagement created a lecture series of national and international speakers including church and civic leaders, social activists, writers, and government officials from the United States and abroad who addressed ideas of social responsibility and the civic role of the university. Some campuses sent groups of faculty and administrators to regional and national conferences. Other campuses sent teams to visit other institutions working on similar issues. Many change leaders widely distributed key readings and discussed them at retreats, during weekly or monthly meetings, or through reading groups specifically organized as professional seminars. In all cases, leaders went beyond simply distributing readings or disseminating ideas: They actively engaged the campus in discussions of ideas.

Created processes to articulate a set of guiding ideas. Change leaders organized processes to develop a set of concrete ideas that would shape the direction of the change agenda and connect it to important institutional values. These ideas typically manifested themselves in documents. Although the documents created often made lasting contributions, the process of creating, drafting, circulating, discussing, rewriting, presenting, and polishing the document helped people to think differently. The process of writing down important ideas got people to talk about their assumptions, engaged them intellectually, and got them to think deeply about difficult issues. These documents became campus compacts, statements, and discussion papers that later shaped institutional direction and, in some cases, informed strategic plans.

Used cross-departmental work groups. Many of the institutions created cross-departmental work teams that helped foster new ways of thinking. These work groups brought together faculty and staff from across the institution who had different perspectives and different assumptions. The tasks they were charged with, their interactions, and their collective explorations led to discussions about beliefs, assumptions, and ideas. The cross-fertilization of ideas helped people see different perspectives, challenge beliefs, and adopt new perspectives.

Gave public presentations. Institutions created numerous opportunities for people to present publicly their ideas and talk about their institution's change agenda. The practicality of putting together and delivering presentations helped unfreeze mental frameworks. Organizing and putting together a presentation for public consumption demanded people to articulate their ideas and assumptions, sometimes helping to highlight inconsistencies. Speaking aloud created another opportunity for individuals or groups of people to catalyze their thoughts. Finally, presentations created an opportunity for feedback and questioning. The cumulative effect of preparing and the act of speaking and responding to questions helped people adopt new ideas and perspectives.

CONCLUSION: IMPLICATIONS FOR FACULTY DEVELOPERS

The insights presented here have direct implications for those involved in faculty development. The chapter began describing a typology of change, with an emphasis on the depth and pervasiveness of a change agenda. The deeper and more pervasive the change, the more it has the potential to be transformational. We learned through our observations that an explicit recognition of how much change is desired is essential to crafting effective change strategies. Without articulating the intended scope and magnitude of the intended change, leaders can identify strategies that leave their efforts far short of intended goals. An important role for faculty developers is to help the institution think about how much change is needed (adjustments, far-reaching change, isolated change, or transformation) and develop appropriate strategies to effect that level and breadth of change. Faculty developers have an important institution-wide perspective to understand the complexity of problems, opportunities, and constraints. They are uniquely positioned to be a conduit between faculty and administrators and have contact with a range of faculty from different departments and disciplines. The nature of their work, and their place within the institution, provide ample opportunities to lead and shape the campus discussion about how much change is needed.

Beyond this role, faculty developers can play active roles in leading change. This chapter suggests three central elements important to effecting transformational change—creating momentum and energy, removing barriers, and getting people to think differently. Within each of these three areas, faculty developers can make vital contributions.

Faculty developers are in central roles to help craft and disseminate a compelling rationale for change. They are often bridges to the external environment and links between departments, and, at universities, across colleges. Because of their contact with faculty in a variety of units, they can help campus leaders better understand the rhythms of campus life. They have a good sense of when timing is wrong to introduce a change agenda, and when faculty are preoccupied with classes, grading, advising, and other important deadlines. They know the highs and lows of campus life and the academic calendar. They have insights about when the institution might best be ready to accept a new large-scale undertaking. Faculty developers, most likely, also know the informal, yet influential, faculty leaders. They can play important roles in identifying champions who will strengthen an institutional change effort. They also know the points of potential resistance and understand how to work around naysayers. Finally, to create momentum and energy needed for change, faculty developers can play important roles in gaining external recognition for campus efforts. They can help secure external grants to support change activities and gain external recognition for campus efforts.

Faculty developers can help remove barriers that reinforce the status quo and prevent the institution from making important improvements. Because of their primary responsibilities, they can help faculty and staff develop new skills and knowledge. By aligning development opportunities with the needs of the change agenda, they can facilitate change. Many of the institutions in the two projects developed extensive faculty and staff development programs specifically to advance the transformation agenda.

Finally, faculty developers can help people think differently. They can create opportunities for facilitated, institution-wide conversations about key elements of change and what it means for faculty and staff. Through formal workshops and symposiums and informal brown bag lunches, faculty developers can clarify ideas and get people to become aware of and reconsider their preconceived notions. Faculty developers can bring in outsider speakers who help the institution thoughtfully explore different ideas and assumptions. Through speaker series and guest lectures and organized campus reading groups, faculty developers can introduce new ideas and develop methods to debate and explore the applicability of ideas to the institution and its future direction. Developers can encourage and facilitate public presentations related to the institutional change agenda. Through the activities sponsored and hosted by faculty developers, opportunities arise for faculty and staff to create and deliver public presentations, both on campus and off, that help to clarify their own thinking and challenge preconceived notions by those attending.

NOTE

Portions of this chapter appear in the *On Change* occasional paper series, produced as part of the American Council on Education (ACE) Project on Leadership and Institutional Transformation. The author acknowledges the ideas and contributions of Madeleine Green and Barbara Hill, coauthors of those papers. The occasional papers are available in PDF files or for purchase from the bookstore of the ACE web site: http://www.acenet.edu.

Contact:

Peter Eckel
Assistant Director, Kellogg Projects on Institutional Transformation
American Council on Education
One Dupont Circle, NW (Suite 800)
Washington, DC 20036
(202) 939-9444
(202) 785-8056 (Fax)
Email: Peter_Eckel@ace.nche.edu

Peter Eckel is assistant director of the Kellogg Projects on Institutional Transformation at the American Council on Education. This work was completed as part of the Kellogg Forum on Higher Education, a partnership to explore and better understand institutional change and transformation involving ACE, the W. K. Kellogg Foundation, Alverno College, The Center for the Study of Higher and Postsecondary Education at the University of Michigan, The Higher Education Research Institute at the University of California–Los Angeles, Minnesota State College and University System, The New England Resource Center for Higher Education at the University of Massachusetts–Boston, Olivet College, Portland State University, and the University of Arizona.

Appendix 1.1
ACE Project on Leadership and Institutional Transformation Participating Institutions and Their Change Initiatives

Ball State University
Redefining relationships with the larger community

Bowie State University
Shared governance, outcomes assessment, and merit-based performance pay

California State Polytechnic University, Pomona
Developing and implementing an integrated strategy for enhancing learning and teaching with technology

Centenary College of Louisiana
Strengthening the academic community without sacrificing academic freedom

The City College of the City University of New York
Maximizing student success

College of DuPage
A transformative planning process

El Paso Community College District
The pathway to the future/El Paso Al Futuro

Kent State University
Moving the strategic plan forward: Cross-unit planning and implementing

Knox College
Faculty life in a changing environment: Family, profession, students, and institutional values

Maricopa County Community College District
Learning@Maricopa.edu

Michigan State University
Enhancing the intensity of the academic environment

Mills College
Reexamine and revitalize the interrelationship between undergraduate women's education and specialized graduate programs for women and men

Northeastern University
Call to action on cooperative education

Olivet College
Creating a culture of individual and social responsibility

Portland State University
Developing faculty for the urban university of the 21st century

Seton Hall University
Transforming the learning environment

State University of New York College at Geneseo
Review, debate, and revision of general education requirements

Stephen F. Austin University
Revitalizing faculty, administration, and staff

University of Arizona
Building academic community: Department heads as catalysts

University of Hartford*
Planning and managing technology

University of Massachusetts–Boston
Assessing student outcomes

University of Minnesota
Improving the collegiate experience for first-year students

University of Puerto Rico, Rio Piedras
Reconceptualizing the baccalaureate degree

University of Wisconsin–La Crosse*
Building community: An institutional approach to academic excellence

Valencia Community College
Becoming a learning-centered college: Improving learning by collaborating to transform core college processes

Wellesley College
Improving the intellectual life of the college

(*Participated in years 1–3)

2

A Brief History of Educational Development: Implications for Teachers and Developers

Richard G. Tiberius
University of Toronto

An historical review of the practice of educational development identified four belief systems about teaching and learning that shape the practice. Each system is characterized by an assumption about the teacher's role: content expert; performer, who makes learning happen; facilitator, who encourages learning through interaction; and helper, whose relationship with learners is a vehicle for learning. The good news is that even teachers who are limited to only one of these belief systems can be successful. On the other hand, developers must have an appreciation for more than one belief system if they are to be successful at helping teachers.

INTRODUCTION

I was honored by the invitation to give a plenary lecture at the 25th anniversary meeting of the Professional and Organizational Development Network in Higher Education (POD). A historical paper should be ideal for this occasion but I was concerned about my lack of professional training in history. My biggest worry was the pitfall of historical determinism. I winced at the prospect of my discovering a hierarchy of historical stages in the practice, leading up to the highest form, which just happened to be my perspective. Developmental theorists seem to place themselves at the top of their hierarchies.

I was encouraged when Bill McKeachie, who lived this history, and Karron Lewis (1996), who wrote a history of the field in the United States, confirmed the trends that I had identified. It was also gratifying to reach conclusions that were not hierarchical, at least for teachers. Indeed, my conclusions echoed those of Daniel Pratt (1998), namely that diversity in teaching roles can be celebrated. That felt right. I would not trust a conclusion that blamed the teachers for their limitations. On the other hand, the implications for developers turned out to be provocative, unpleasant, and risky. There appears to be a hierarchy of faculty developers and I am not at the top of it. That felt right too. I am always suspicious of conclusions that do not wound the pride. With that enticement, let me tell the story. I will argue that there are four belief systems about educational development: content mastery, skilled performance, facilitation of learning, and personal engagement, each with its own historical trajectory—a beginning, a peak, and a decline.

BELIEF SYSTEM I: TEACHING AS CONTENT MASTERY

Imagine that it is the 1950s and you are a university professor who would like to improve your teaching. What would you have found? About half of you would have found some kind of formal in-service program for faculty in your college or university, according to a survey of 1,000, 4-year colleges in the United States. The most active programs were those that helped professors maintain their academic specializations (Many, Ellis, & Abrams, 1969). You might have been given funding for sabbatical leave, travel to professional meetings, research support, or guest speakers. Both the administrators who gave this money and the teachers who received it believed that such funding was an appropriate means of teacher development because they shared a common belief system about the role of teachers, one which I will call "content mastery." This belief system began before WWII and was the dominant belief system in the 1950s. Although it waned in the 1960s, it is still with us in some forms (Figure 2.1).

The beliefs about the teacher's role that dominated this period were the traditional academic folklore captured by the following slogans: teachers are born, not made; teaching is an art, not a science; a professor's classroom is his castle; hire good people and get out of the way (Gaff, 1975). These sayings implied that little could be done to improve the teaching of professors. Teachers were expected to be masters of their specialty and need not be a master of teaching. The teacher-learner relationship was impersonal and formal. The belief system supported the concept of division of labor: "My job is to deliver the lecture and to test the learners. Their job is to learn."

FIGURE 2.1
Belief System #1: Teacher as Content Expert

Researchers		Teachers
General principles	➡️	Generalizable knowledge
In-service programs		
Financial support	➡️	Sabbaticals, travel, research support, funding for speakers

Although educational development was predominantly something administrators did for teachers, educational researchers and developers did exist. Research on college-level teaching during this period used the methods of experimental psychology, mainly tightly controlled experiments, to yield behavioristic principles. Their expectation was that their research would yield a body of general principles that would flow to teachers where it would be applied to their practices. The product of this research was available to teachers but not very accessible. In my experience few teachers read it. There was a radical separation between teachers and researchers during this period.

Indeed, the early 1960s marked the decline of this period and introduced the first faculty development units, beginning with the Center for Research on Learning and Teaching in Michigan in 1962.

During this time, research was published in journals that live on Donald Schön's (1995) high ground where manageable problems lend themselves to solution through the use of research-based theory and technique. Sociology, psychology, and education journals by specialists topped the list, for example, *The Sociology of Education, The Journal of Higher Education, The Journal of General Education, College Teaching,* and *The Bulletin of the Association of American Colleges.*

Toward the end of this period books on university teaching were beginning to appear. These books went beyond providing generalized principles of learning. They addressed specific skills, including sensitivity, relationship enhancement, and small group learning. The following list includes some of the more popular ones: *Teaching Tips: A Guidebook for the Beginning College Teacher* (Wilbert McKeachie, 1951); *College Teaching: A Psychologist's View* (Claude Buxton, 1956); *Two Ends of the Log: Learning and Teaching in Today's College* (Russell Cooper, 1958); *Learning to Work in Groups: A Program Guide for Educational Leaders* (Matthew Miles, 1959); *Handbook of Research on Teaching* (Nate Gage, 1963); *Teaching Methods in Australian Universities* (Australian Vice Chancellors Committee Report, 1963).

Finally, in those early days, a small number of people were engaged directly in the improvement of teaching and learning. They were mostly psychologists who attempted to apply basic research to the teaching and learning process. We did not call ourselves "developers" and our clients were often disappointed. Upon entering the seminar room to attend a typical session that I presented to teachers, you would have seen on the black board the inverted "U" relationship between performance and arousal (from my work in the lab of the motivation psychologist Dan Berlyne). An exuberant young man with jet-black hair would have explained, "You see, students who have too high or too low an arousal level will not learn as well or perform as well as students who have an intermediate arousal level!" The silence that followed I interpreted as thoughtful interest until one teacher asked how he could detect where his students were on the arousal curve and what could he do about it, anyway? My response was to explain that we know the rats' arousal level because we starve them. Eventually I came to realize, along with the rest of the field, that faculty need more than general principles. They need specific skills, contextually grounded.

Although content mastery has become less popular, it is still present.

> Dr. Kontent (not her real name) is the only physician in a geographic area with expertise in child psychiatry. She asked the university department not to send residents to her since she was not interested in teaching. Residents waste her time and she does not get paid for it. Since Dr. Kontent was the only child psychiatrist in town, the residency coordinator sent residents to her site anyway. Residents joined the team at which clinical issues were discussed, interacted among themselves, asked questions, and observed. They learned something in the setting although Dr. Kontent did almost nothing to accommodate them.

Now imagine that it is 1970 and you are a university professor who would like to improve your teaching. In the 1950s you would have been unlikely to find an educational development office or program at your institution, but by 1975 you would have been very likely to find one due to an explosion in faculty development programs in the early 1970s. Although there were fewer than 50 faculty development programs in the United States at the end of the 1960s (Sullivan, 1983), by 1975, 41% of all four-year institutions had faculty development programs (Centra, 1976).

This growth was driven by the campus unrest of the 1960s, an influx of challenging students (older, ethnically diverse), the stagnation in new hiring, and new discoveries about learning and memory by cognitive science. You probably would not have found funding to upgrade your competence in a subject area, but you would likely have found people eager to help you acquire a wide range of competencies, including knowledge, attitudes, values, motivations, skills, and sensitivities. A transformation had taken place in the late 1960s and early 1970s in the normative beliefs about the role of teaching. According to Gerry Gaff (1975), this transformation was characterized by the emergence of a new set of assumptions about the role of teacher: The belief that instructional competencies are learned; that these competencies include a complex set of knowledge, attitudes, values, motivations, skills, and sensitivities; and that teachers had a responsibility to learn the competencies.

The new developers tended to fall into one of two camps identified by their dominant beliefs about the role of the teacher and by the kinds of skills that were the focus of their efforts. Both of these belief systems had been developing in the 1950s and 1960s and would peak in the 1970s and 1980s. One group tended to see teachers as performers who made learning happen and the other tended to see teachers as facilitators who encouraged learning. I will trace each of these belief systems separately.

BELIEF SYSTEM II: TEACHING AS A PERFORMANCE AIMED AT MAKING LEARNING HAPPEN

There were precursors to the performance belief system in the late 1950s and early 1960s epitomized by the programmed learning movement. Proponents of programmed learning believed that the modern science of teaching could be captured in the program (Figure 2.2). It would then be "teacher free."

Administrators not only assumed direct responsibility for financial support, but also heavily supported educational development units as well. The units were increasingly staffed by a new group of researchers and practitioners who could translate research for teachers. We called ourselves "developers." Research was still dominated by the discipline of

FIGURE 2.2
Teaching as Skilled Performance: Mid-1960s to Present

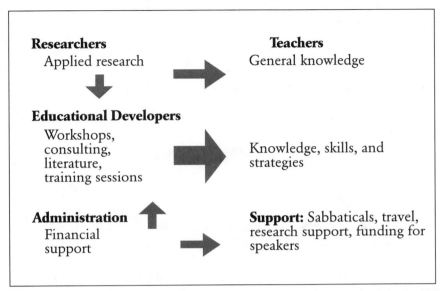

psychology with its experimental methodology, but researchers who viewed teaching as a skilled performance became more focused on knowledge and skills of teaching rather than on the general principles of teaching. Under the performer belief system, teachers could make learning happen by the application of teaching skills to students. Developers could make professors teach better by training them in the skilled performances. And researchers could suggest and evaluate teaching methods that could be taught as specific skills (Figure 2.3).

This belief system held the teacher responsible, not only for mastery of the field, but also for mastery of the skills of teaching. The teacher could make learning happen (Orme, 1977). The teacher's relationship with learners was characterized by the metaphors transfer, shaping, and molding. Learners were vessels to be filled, or clay to be molded into shape. Teachers produced an engineer or medical doctor or provided students with principles of biochemistry. Teachers who were guided by these metaphors were likely to blame failure on flaws in the material, for example, or inert or intractable students. If "the container is not very full, the explanation tends to be in terms of leaky containers" (Fox, 1983, p. 152).

FIGURE 2.3
Teaching as Skilled Performance: Early 1960s to Present

Students	Listen and absorb
⬆	
Teachers	Make learning happen
⬆	
Developers	Make teachers better
⬆	
Researchers	Produce generalizable knowledge

If the teacher's primary role were to transfer information or to shape the student then teachers could focus on the validity of the learning objectives and on the effectiveness of the transmission process. Rather, less attention needed to be paid to the characteristics of individual learners or to the teacher-learner relationships. The teachers' expectations of their learners would be that learners should be attentive and malleable listeners. The learners' expectations of their teachers would be that they should be knowledgeable, set clear goals, and use effective communication methods.

Many books on university teaching appeared during this period, a number of them directed at skills, and more faculty were reading them. Some of the more popular ones included *Teaching Tips: A Guidebook for the Beginning College Teacher,* 6th and 7th editions (Wilbert McKeachie, 1969 & 1978); *Teaching and Learning in Higher Education* (Ruth Beard, 1970); *The Assessment of University Teaching* (Barbara Falk & Kwong Lee Dow, 1971);*What's the Use of Lectures?* (Donald Bligh, 1972). A number of new journals and societies appeared that were devoted directly to teaching in higher education, including *The Chronicle of Higher Education* (1966); Jossey-Bass publishers (1967); ERIC Clearinghouse on Higher Education (1968); *Change: The Magazine of Higher Learning* (1969); *Higher Education* (1971); *Instructional Science* (1972); *Research in Higher Education*

(1973); The Professional and Organizational Development Network in Higher Education (1975); *Studies in Higher Education* (1976).

I remember clearly the days when my faculty development efforts consisted of attempts to help teachers acquire skilled performances. At one workshop, I used to advise teachers to use movement because research has shown that movement is associated with the best lecturers. My advice did liven up some presentations, but just as often teachers would blindly apply the prescription, jumping all over the place but not helping students learn. Their movements were distracting because they were not choreographed with the point they were making (for example, when I step forward and remove my glasses to make a personal comment).

It is easy to find teachers, even today, who believe that the primary role of the teacher lies in such performances.

A patient-educator from the local diabetic organization, Ms. Drama (not her real name), delivered information about diabetes to a roomful of newly diagnosed patients. Her delivery was excellent. She was witty, dramatic, organized, and had lots of attractive slides to accompany her talk. And the patients said they learned a lot from her session even though she disappeared before any questions were asked and did nothing to establish a relationship with them.

Now imagine that it is the 1980s and you are a university professor who would like to improve your teaching. You could still find help developing useful techniques for delivering lectures or for conducting small groups, just as you did in 1970. The skilled performance approach to teaching is still alive and well. But in 1980 you would also be likely to find developers who would be eager to engage you in exploring your attitudes, intuitions, feelings, sensitivities, and values. Developers might attend to your interaction with your learners. They might offer to help you listen and receive feedback as well as explain and give feedback. They might talk about matching your teaching strategies to student needs.

BELIEF SYSTEM III: TEACHING AS FACILITATION OF LEARNING

In 1980, facilitation of learning was challenging skilled performance for the dominant belief system about teaching. This movement toward sensitivity to students also had very early roots. It began in the late 1940s and early 1950s with Lewinian group dynamics and Rogerian nondirective therapy. It blossomed in the mid-1960s and early 1970s with the NTL training sessions and group dynamics workshops that proliferated during the explosion of faculty development units in the 1960s. In the late 1970s and 1980s, student- and group-centered teaching became very popular.

The difference between the two systems can be captured visually by adding two-way arrows to the chart in Figure 2.2. Those who focused on interaction to facilitate learning tended to see their relationships with others as two-way. Developers not only translated research results, they also conducted research and collaborated with researchers. Teachers learned from students too. The teacher was the facilitator of learning whose primary task was to find out about the learner so that interventions could be targeted at specific needs. The teacher needed more than the skills of lecturing, explaining, and providing feedback; the teacher needed the skills of listening, understanding the student, and receiving feedback.

This belief system required a major change in the nature of the teacher's expertise because it changes the task of teaching from one of static expertise to dynamic expertise. Static tasks require little or no improvisation. A static task involves the performance of a specific set of actions, such as a gymnastics routine, playing a concerto, or surgical knot tying. By contrast, dynamic tasks require the practitioner to decide on appropriate strategies and adapt to various contingencies, such as a hockey game, jazz improvisation, or diagnosing a complicated medical case. Dynamic expertise requires continual feedback and adaptation to new situations. The teacher's relationship with learners was characterized by interaction and two-way communication (Figures 2.4 & 2.5). Learners, teachers, developers, and researchers all discovered the wisdom of practice—that knowledge can flow two ways and that teachers too can define significant research problems (Schön, 1995).

This third belief system was accelerated by scholarship. The transfer and shaping metaphors of teaching had come under siege. Fox (1983) argued that the growth metaphors (teaching is like gardening) were gradually superceding transfer metaphors (teaching is like filling a mug) as individual teachers developed and the field progressed. Fernstermacher (1986) attacked the assumption that teachers were responsible for student learning. He argued that the teachers' task is to help students perform the tasks of learning. Indeed, a review of the literature on faculty development concluded that the metaphors of teaching and learning were changing from teaching as transfer of information to teaching and learning as an interaction or conversation (Tiberius, 1986).

FIGURE 2.4
Facilitation of Learning: Mid-1960s to Present

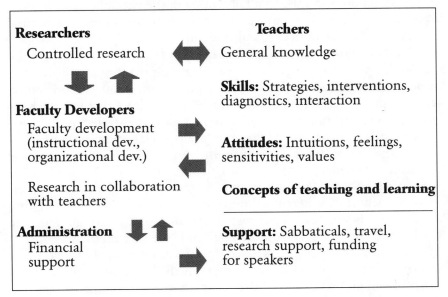

FIGURE 2.5
Teaching as the Facilitation of Learning

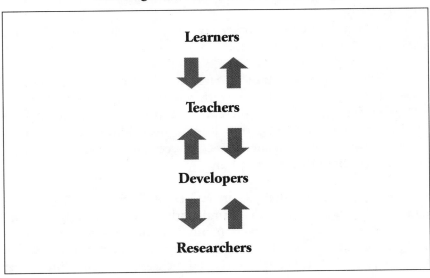

Cognitive scientists (e.g., Brown, Collins, & Duguid, 1989; Lave, 1988; Vigotsky, 1986) gave us further support for interest in teacher-student interaction. Learning that takes place in the natural setting is more likely to transfer to that setting, including the social setting, the normal interactions between teachers and students.

Constructivism, especially social constructivism, became more popular in this period. Constructivists view learning as a process of enculturation into a community of practice by means of social interaction among learners and between learners and teachers. It follows that the teacher's role lies in connecting the material to the previous knowledge and experience of the students and to the appropriate social contexts. In order to make these connections, teachers must learn about their learners—their previous experience, motivational orientation, knowledge, and skills. And, since knowledge about learners is gained through interaction, effective teaching is inherently interactive—it is a process of facilitating connections between a subject matter and an active, growing mind. The teacher became "the guide on the side," not "the sage on the stage."

My own practice was affected by constructivism. I developed a model of individualized consulting in which the consultant interprets the problem and adjusts the teacher's methods to the students' needs. I developed a procedure for improving teaching called "alliances for change." In this procedure, two teachers act as consultants for one another, each interviews the students of the other teacher and tries to help him or her understand the students better and suggest ways to be more helpful.

It is easy to find contemporary examples of teachers who view their role as one of interacting with students to facilitate learning.

> Professor Twoway (not his real name), a teacher of arts and science, engages his students with questions and games. He is knowledgeable, skilled at presenting, and interactive. The students who attended said they learned from him despite what they described as arrogance and condescension. He received no feedback about their view of him.

Finally, let's assume that you are interested in improving your teaching today. You will still be able to find workshops on teaching performances and on the skills of interaction, but you will also find some new elements. For one, you would be more likely to find help in the area that Karron Lewis (1996) called the personal dimensions of faculty life: career consulting, wellness programs, retirement planning, and stage-of-life. You might also find that developers are interested in your relationship with your students.

BELIEF SYSTEM IV: THE TEACHER-STUDENT RELATIONSHIP AS A VEHICLE FOR LEARNING

The focus on the relationship had very early roots, in the 1940s with the work of Martin Buber (1947), and is still growing today. In Buber's educational philosophy, teaching includes a conscious awareness of the teacher-student relationship as a vehicle of teaching. The teachers' responsibility included helping the learners actualize their potential through personal engagement. Ursula Franklin (1990) argued that focus on relationships is a return to the old apprenticeship system before education became alienated from its social context and became institutionalized. Douglas Robertson (1996) has argued that the need for teachers to learn how to manage the dynamics of helping relationships is particularly important in helping the learner with transformative learning, an intensely emotional kind of learning that requires trust and support.

My colleagues and I are currently providing practice for psychiatry supervisors in relationship skills. We enact a scenario that presents supervisors with a relationship problem and invite the audience to discuss methods of dealing with it. In the "watch scenario," for example, a staff person expounds on a topic at length while a resident steals a look at her watch. The staff person snaps: "Is there somewhere you'd rather be?" After that brief scenario we invite the audience to speculate as to what is happening and what to do about it.

In my teaching setting there are many examples of clinical teachers who are effective by virtue of their excellent relationships with their students. Yet some of these teachers lack expertise in some areas or the ability to explain clearly.

IMPLICATIONS FOR TEACHERS

My journey into the history of faculty development has convinced me that both teaching and our practice are guided by beliefs about the role of teachers and about the type of relationship between teachers and students. I have identified four belief systems: teacher as content expert, who serves as a resource to the learner, like a book or a picture; teacher as performer, who makes learning happen by transmitting information or shaping students; teacher as facilitator, who encourages learning through interaction with the learner; and teacher as helper, who uses personal engagement and the teacher-learner relationship as a vehicle for learning.

Since these belief systems tend to predispose teachers to particular strategies of teaching, it is tempting to ask whether some belief systems, and thus some strategies, are superior to others in promoting learning. In other words, do these four belief systems form a hierarchy of teacher development? It seems more likely that, under the right conditions, a teacher who holds any of these conceptions of teaching can be effective.

Why is this so? If we accept the assumption that any individual teacher is not the only influence on the learner but is part of a system of influences, then each teacher need only supply a necessary, not a sufficient, ingredient of learning to be considered effective (Bess, 2000). Since the basic ingredients of learning are 1) motivation of some kind, 2) deliberate practice with feedback (or knowledge of results), and 3) options or alternatives, then a successful teacher will supply one or more of these ingredients that are not supplied by other components of the system, such as other teachers, administrators, books, settings, or the learners themselves. A teacher who has the good luck to land in a situation in which he or she is providing just what the learner needs will likely be effective. A teacher who is not so fortunate can improve her or his match with student needs by changing strategies, doing something different. The problem with belief systems is that they tend to reduce flexibility by limiting teachers to particular types of strategies.

Dr. Kontent, the child psychiatry expert who preferred not to teach residents, nevertheless promoted learning because her residents needed the information that she had. The residents also needed feedback but they provided feedback for one another by identifying their own areas of confusion because they were highly motivated, self-directed learners. Residents in this situation also needed help in striking an appropriate relationship with Dr. Kontent. The residency coordinator helped with the following advice: "Observe her and ask questions but do not expect her to clarify your learning needs."

Ms. Drama, the performer, our patient-educator who delivered information about diabetes but who did not take questions or establish a relationship with her audience, had some content expertise, a highly developed performance, and little appreciation for the interactive and relational roles. Although the patients needed relevant content, Ms. Drama did not interact with the patients to ensure that her content was relevant to the patients. She did not need to. The match was already made by the coordinators of the visit who had previously surveyed and screened the learners, admitting only newly diagnosed diabetics who had a uniform knowledge level. The patients also needed answers to specific questions which Ms. Drama did not provide but the regular ward nurse told the group, prior to her visit: "Jot down any questions that you have and I'll answer them later. Ms. Drama is a great performer but what she tells you is all she knows. She can't really answer questions." The ward nurse also helped create an appropriate relationship with the group by telling the patients: "We are really fortunate to have her coming here."

Our facilitator, Professor Twoway, engaged his students with questions and games during an interactive lecture, but his extreme anxiety gave him a rigid, haughty appearance in class. In small group interaction with his TAs he established a warm, supportive relationship. The TAs, in turn, helped students to see him in a kinder light.

Our clinical mentors, who are good examples of the fourth role, build alliances—authentic, trusting relationships—with their learners. Such relationships allow mentors to refer their students to colleagues for help in the areas in which they are not expert.

The teachers in these four examples were lucky. Circumstances provided them with a good match between what they offered and what the learner needed. To put it another way, what they could not provide the learner was provided by other components of the system. In contrast, teachers who are ill matched to the learning needs of their students generally get low ratings and need help. One role of the developer may be to arrange the elements of the teaching situation so that such teachers can succeed without changing their belief system. Of course, teachers who possess the conceptual flexibility to move from one belief system to another, to radically change roles not just strategies, as the situation requires, are in a much better position to succeed. Perhaps a second service of the professional developer, then, is helping teachers broaden their conceptions of teaching and learning.

IMPLICATIONS FOR DEVELOPERS

Can a developer, who is limited to one of these four belief systems, be effective in helping teachers? Let us take the case of a developer who holds the same belief system about teaching as the client. They are likely to enjoy pleasant interaction that may result in better teaching if they are lucky. Assume that I, as developer, hold a performer model of teaching. Professor Gunnar, the ultimate performer, tells me that he had been sharpening his lecture all weekend. He has a dynamite lecture, targeted perfectly for his students that is going to slay them in the aisles. He asks me, as a teaching consultant, to evaluate his effectiveness. The professor and I can delight in sharing war stories as I reinforce his behavior and arm him with even more powerful techniques for dramatic presentation. If his performances supply what the students need from him, I will succeed in helping him improve his effectiveness.

However, Professor Gunnar's orientation toward teaching performances may cause him to overlook strategies such as listening to students or building a supportive relationship. And if the latter is the missing ingredient, then I could help him most effectively by finding out what the students think about him and helping him form an alliance with his students, rather than by improving his classroom performance. If I were unable to think beyond the performance role I would be unable to help him.

Second, let us assume that I hold a different model of teaching from that of my client. If I held the facilitator model my reaction to Gunnar might be quite different: "He wants me to do a body count! His militaristic language and the narrowness of his conception of teaching—which invites no input from the students—offend me. He violates my cherished beliefs about the interactive nature of teaching." I might judge him; focus on what he fails to do rather than what he is doing, to use Bob Kegan's (1994) analysis. Not a good beginning for a consultant-teacher relationship.

How much better if I were able to see Professor Gunnar's approach to teaching as emanating from a legitimate belief system about the role of teaching rather than from a sadistic desire to harm. As a developer, I need to keep from feeling threatened, personally violated, when my definition of teaching is challenged. To do this, I need to mentally step away from my own values and definitions (Kegan, 1994). Kegan's (1994) research indicates that only at this level of consciousness are people able stand apart from such belief systems as I have outlined here, to see them as "out there," as "objects," rather than as part of oneself. Moreover, this ability is not a discrete skill that we developers can learn at a POD workshop. It requires an evolution of consciousness, a gradual developmental process. And only about half the population has reached this level.

I am fairly certain that I have this ability to stand apart from and avoid being completely identified with any one of the four belief systems about teaching. The resulting flexibility enables me to arrange teaching contexts in which teachers can make effective contributions to learning even if their view of teaching is more limited. I confess that thinking about this evokes a warm feeling of professional competence, a rare treat for developers, as if I am living in a three-dimensional world helping flatlanders negotiate their two-dimensional spaces. But what happens when I encounter Professor Post Modern who functions at Kegan's next level of consciousness? I'll tell you. Professor P. M. heard my lecture at POD and, although she understood what I meant by these different roles, she saw them as different modes of herself manifested in different contexts. Most of the time, she said, her teaching embodies all of these roles.

How do I help Professor P. M. when my best practice consists of adjusting relatively durable elements of the system so that my client can be an effective contributor? What is my role in helping a teacher who is not a durable element? It's nuclear, as the surfers say. As I write this I feel the familiar strain that attends growth mixed with anxiety about my role as a developer in a postmodern world. At present I can see postmodernism with peripheral vision only. When I look at it directly it disappears, like a very dim light.

REFERENCES

Australian Vice Chancellors' Committee. (1963). *Teaching methods in Australian universities* (Report). Melbourne, Australia: UNSW Press.

Beard, R. M. (1970). *Teaching and learning in higher education.* Harmondsworth, England: Penguin.

Bess, J., & Associates. (2000). *Teaching alone, teaching together: Transforming the structure of teams for teaching.* San Francisco, CA: Jossey-Bass.

Bligh, D. (1972). *What's the use of lectures?* (3rd ed.). Hertfordshire, England: Penguin.

Brown, J. S., Collins, A., & Duguid, P. (1989). Situated cognition and the culture of learning. *Educational Researcher, 13,* 32-41.

Buber, M. (1947). *Between man and man.* London, England: Collins.

Buxton, C. (1956). *College teaching: A psychologist's view.* New York, NY: Harcourt Brace.

Centra, J. A. (1976). *Faculty development practices in U.S. colleges and universities.* Princeton, NJ: Educational Testing Service.

Cooper, R. (1958). *The two ends of the log: Learning and teaching in today's college.* Minneapolis, MN: University of Minnesota Press.

Falk, B., & Dow, K. L. (1971). *The assessment of university teaching.* London, England: Society for Research into Higher Education.

Fernstermacher, G. D. (1986). Philosophy of research on teaching: Three aspects. In M. C. Wittrock (Ed.), *Handbook of research on teaching* (3rd ed.) (pp. 37-49). New York, NY: Macmillan.

Fox, D. (1983). Personal theories of teaching. *Studies in Higher Education, 8* (2), 151-163.

Franklin, U. (1990). *The real world of technology.* Toronto, Canada: CBC Enterprises.

Gaff, J. G. (1975). *Toward faculty renewal: Advances in faculty, instructional, and organizational development.* San Francisco, CA: Jossey-Bass.

Gage, N. L. (Ed.). (1963). *Handbook of research on teaching.* Chicago, IL: Rand McNally.

Kegan, R. (1994). *In over our heads: The mental demands of modern life.* Cambridge, MA: Harvard University Press.

Lave, J. (1988). *Cognition and practice: Mind, mathematics and culture in everyday life.* Cambridge, MA: Cambridge University Press.

Lewis, K. G. (1996). Faculty development in the United States: A brief history. *The International Journal of Academic Development, 1* (2), 26-33.

Many, W. A., Ellis, J. R., & Abrams, P. (1969, Spring). In-service education in American senior colleges and universities: A status report. *Illinois School Research,* 46-51.

McKeachie, W. J. (1951). *Teaching tips: A guidebook for the beginning college teacher.* Lexington, MA: D. C. Heath.

McKeachie, W. J. (1969). *Teaching tips: A guidebook for the beginning college teacher* (7th ed.). Lexington, MA: D. C. Heath.

McKeachie, W. J. (1978). *Teaching tips: A guidebook for the beginning college teacher* (8th ed.). Lexington, MA: D. C. Heath.

Miles, M. B. (1959). *Learning to work in groups: A program guide for educational leaders.* New York, NY: Teachers College, Columbia University.

Orme, M. (1977). *Effective teaching techniques* (video). Toronto, Canada: Ryerson TV Studios.

Pratt, D. D., & Associates. (1998). *Five perspectives on teaching in adult and higher education.* Malabar, FL: Krieger.

Robertson, D. L. (1996). Facilitating transformative learning: Attending to the dynamics of the educational helping relationship. *Adult Education Quarterly, 47* (1), 43-53.

Schön, D. A. (1995, November/December). The new scholarship requires a new epistemology. *Change,* 27-34.

Sullivan, L. L. (1983). Faculty development: A movement on the brink. *College Board Review, 127,* 20-21, 29-31.

Tiberius, R. G. (1986). Metaphors underlying the improvement of teaching and learning. *British Journal of Educational Technology, 17* (2), 144-156.

Vigotsky, L. (1986). *Thought and language.* Cambridge, MA: MIT Press.

Contact:

Richard Tiberius
University of Toronto Faculty of Medicine
Centre For Research in Education at the University Health Network
200 Elizabeth Street, 1 ES 583
Toronto, Ontario, M5G 2C4, CANADA
(416) 340-4194
(416) 340-3792 (Fax)
Email: r.tiberius@utoronto.ca
Web: http://www.library.utoronto.ca/www/cre

or

Department of Psychiatry
University of Toronto
Centre for Addiction and Mental Health
Clarke Division, 8th floor, Room 826, 250 College Street
Toronto, Ontario, M5T 1R8, CANADA

Richard Tiberius is at the Centre for Research in Education in the Faculty of Medicine at the University of Toronto, Canada, and is Professor of Psychiatry. His main roles include collaboration with health science faculty on educational research projects, supervision of resident research, and various faculty development activities. He teaches graduate courses in research methods and educational development at the Ontario Institute for Studies in Education, University of Toronto.

3

Linking Change Initiatives: The Carnegie Academy for the Scholarship of Teaching and Learning in the Company of Other National Projects

Barbara Cambridge
American Association for Higher Education

The scholarship of teaching and learning provides an overarching framework for progress on a number of important educational issues today. The Carnegie Academy for the Scholarship of Teaching and Learning encourages connections with other national projects that deal with issues such as defining student learning outcomes, building an infrastructure of support, and establishing evidence for purposes of accountability in mutually supportive ways. Connecting such efforts honors faculty time in the midst of multiple demands and raises the likelihood of significant, lasting impact on the quality of teaching and learning.

INTRODUCTION

On many vibrant campuses, change efforts can exceed energy levels. Faculty members with real commitments to student learning are exploring a variety of approaches, taking up writing across the curriculum, learning to assess critical thinking, implementing technology in their teaching, incorporating students in their research, representing student work in program reviews, explaining to legislators the need for developmental courses, refining assignments for collaborative learning groups, and on and on. Sometimes faculty members have to say, "I can't do anything more right now. I just don't have the time."

Time is the most precious resource for faculty members. If a faculty member decides to dedicate effort to a particular project, then it is important that the results of that project be used in as many ways as possible. For example, if a faculty member adopts student portfolios as a learning and assessing tool, the time invested in development and implementation will be better spent if the portfolios contribute to assessing student progress, representing the university in accreditation, and providing a basis for curricular changes.

This call for multiple uses of initiatives, however, is not a call for easily finished tasks. For example, scholars of teaching and learning explore the intellectual problems that emerge during the process by which novices and experts learn in their disciplines. These problems are not things to be solved and done away with. They are, as Randy Bass puts it, the kind of problems at

> the heart of the investigative process.... Changing the status of the problem in teaching from terminal remediation to ongoing investigation is precisely what the movement for a scholarship of teaching is all about. (1999, p. 1)

> Ultimately, the measure of success for the scholarship of teaching movement will not be the degree to which I can—by focusing on the "many layers of practice" at the heart of teaching—discover *solutions* worth implementing, but the extent to which it is successful in discovering *problems* worth pursuing. (1999, pp. 8-9)

In other words, Bass contends that really intriguing problems in teaching and learning will necessarily and interestingly take time to investigate. During that time, faculty members will undoubtedly be engaged in other work as well, work that has potential to be consonant with this ongoing scholarly work in teaching and learning if we look for productive connections and interactions.

For the 2001 American Association for Higher Education (AAHE) National Conference on Higher Education, Pat Hutchings, Senior Scholar at the Carnegie Foundation for the Scholarship of Teaching and Learning (CASTL), and I examined a set of national projects involving learning and teaching (Hutchings & Cambridge, 2001). We looked for productive connections between the work of individual scholars, campuses, and disciplinary associations in CASTL and the work of other national initiatives. Earlier, we had noticed that many campuses had affirmed that their participation in the Campus Program, one of three activities of the higher education program at the Carnegie Foundation for the Advancement of Teaching, had given them an occasion to link across their campus multiple and disparate efforts to improve teaching and to make it more scholarly. Unlinked pockets of activity had resulted in duplicative or, at the least, nonmutually supportive efforts. Faculty members felt pulled in many directions, and administrators worried about effective uses of resources. The Campus Program offered a way to link programs promoting scholarly teaching for the purpose of setting campus conditions for supporting the scholarship of teaching and learning. Campuses that had begun to value or who valued scholarly teaching saw the opportunity to take a next step by bringing their projects together to set conditions necessary for supporting faculty who do or want to do the scholarship of teaching and learning, and for institutional approaches to change that in themselves can be scholarly work.

An array of national programs also offers productive links for work on the scholarship of teaching and learning. Three categories of programs focus on defining student learning outcomes, building an infrastructure of support, and establishing evidence for purposes of accountability. Describing these categories in this chapter, I will include a total of 15 examples, often using language with which the program defines itself and well aware that you will be able to name other projects that could be on the list. This set of projects is meant as a heuristic to prompt thinking about ways to be explicit about the multiple uses of the processes and outcomes of work in these important initiatives.

DEFINING STUDENT LEARNING OUTCOMES

Individual campuses, cohorts of campuses by institutional type or common interests, and disciplinary groups are all doing the hard work of identifying appropriate student learning outcomes for degree programs, preparation for citizenship or the work place, or preparation in majors. Five national projects illustrate the power of groups working together to accomplish these tasks.

Greater Expectations, an initiative of the Association of American Colleges and Universities (AAC&U), has convened a panel of leaders in education, government, business, and community action to develop a statement of aims and purposes for 21st-century college-level study. The panel will articulate and disseminate liberal learning outcomes that should emerge from a college education. A set of selected campuses is identifying best practices and assisting through their experience other campuses wanting to achieve these outcomes with students. (http://www.aacu-edu.org)

The League for Innovation in the Community College also has taken on an expansive task related to student learning outcomes. In the 21st-Century Skills Project, the league is defining what knowledge, skills, and abilities community college students need to be active, contributory 21st century citizens. After identifying knowledge, skills, and abilities, the project will provide new approaches for certifying learning so that students have more personal information about their learning achievements and so that standards for learning are responsive to requirements of the knowledge age and global economy. Sixteen community colleges are involved in the demonstration phase of this work. (www.league.org)

Twenty-seven other institutions are working together in the Student Learning Outcomes Initiative led by Alverno College. They are creating a framework and examples that identify and illustrate the assumptions, principles, and practices that campuses can use in making student learning the organizing principle of their work. The framework deals with clarity about student outcomes; teaching, learning, and assessing; alignment of structures and resources; and continuous improvement. Not advocating a certain set of outcomes, this project emphasizes the need for each institution to define its outcomes as a precursor to everything else it does. (Tim.Riordan@alverno.edu)

Two other projects look at disciplinary frameworks in their emphases on outcomes. The National Council on Education and the Disciplines, organized by the Woodrow Wilson National Fellowship Foundation, engages high school and college faculty through their disciplines in developing course sequences for grades 11–14, with attendant standards and assessments. They focus on four core literacies: language arts, history, math/quantitative thinking, and science. The aim is to connect the organizational and political structures that administer K–16 with the disciplinary communities that provide the intellectual content of reform. (www.woodrow.org.nced)

In the Quality in Undergraduate Education (QUE) project as well, the emphasis is on a seamless transfer environment based on what students know and can do. Faculty members from clusters of four- and two-year colleges are working to develop voluntary discipline-based student learning outcomes in the undergraduate major. Focus disciplines include biology, chemistry, English, history, mathematics, and physics. States with participating institutions include California, Georgia, Maryland, and Nevada. (www.gsu.edu/que)

Scholars of teaching and learning often ask the same questions and puzzle about the same problems as faculty members and administrators in these five projects. For example, Mills Kelly, in history at George Mason University, reflects on what doing history means for undergraduate students in beginning history courses. What do they need to know how to do in order to do history? At Miami University, Ted Wagenaar has asked the question of himself and colleagues within the American Sociological Association: "What do sociology majors need to know and be able to do?" In the field of music, Susan Conkling at Eastman School of Music has puzzled about what undergraduates need to undertake to become professional musicians.

Campus Program institutions question, too, the outcomes that they insist on for their students. Augustana College undertook general education reform by, among other activities, studying what others saw as desired outcomes for undergraduates and then determining what was important for their particular students. The University of Michigan has concentrated on investigating through interdisciplinary course development the skills and knowledge important to its students. The first campus-wide work at the University of Georgia after the establishment of its Teaching Academy focused on the first-year experience of students and the senior-year experience, asking questions about how students progress from one to the other and what outcomes they achieve by their senior year.

Faculty members and faculty developers can ask themselves about the relevance of work by faculty members, administrators, and campus groups at a single institution to these national projects. Because many campuses are working on defining, documenting, and assessing student learning outcomes, they may find intersections among projects. Subsequent linking up of people and initiatives can increase the value of the work of each.

BUILDING AN INFRASTRUCTURE OF SUPPORT

CASTL's design assumes that change occurs not only with individual effort but also with an institution's commitment to change. Although part of that commitment includes developing policies and practices that support the scholarship of teaching and learning, sustainability demands infrastructure. On the national level, five projects contribute to systemic change through attention to faculty preparation, faculty development, and the reward system.

Two projects concentrate on infrastructures that promote curricular and programmatic change to prepare university faculty who have perspective and skills to treat their teaching as a legitimate area for scholarly inquiry. Preparing Future Faculty, a joint project of the Council of Graduate Schools and the Association of American Colleges and Universities, establishes partnerships between colleges and universities to develop and sustain university-wide and departmental programs for doctoral students to cultivate a new generation of faculty members who take teaching seriously as a central part of their work. Recent collaborations between institutions that prepare and institutions that hire faculty have involved a variety of disciplines and disciplinary associations. (http://www.preparing-faculty.org/) (http://www.aacu edu.org/Initiativies/futurefaculty.html)

The Carnegie Foundation for the Advancement of Teaching is also Rethinking the Doctorate in a project with that name. This five-year program of research and collaborative efforts has three components: conceptualizing the common core and the diversity of doctoral programs, especially across disciplines and professions; empirical work with a small number of doctoral programs as they experiment with new forms of education; and treating this work as scholarship of teaching and learning by research and convenings that enable stakeholders to build on one another's work. (www.carnegiefoundation.org)

This scholarly approach of building on one another's work is a hallmark of the Flashlight Program, part of the Teaching, Learning, and Technology Group that is an affiliate of AAHE. Among an array of initiatives is Flashlight Online, which enables investigators to combine their own questions with selected, validated items chosen from the Flashlight Current Student Inventory, administer surveys on line, get analyses from Flashlight, and share studies with others. Training, an online library, and studies conducted for institutions are other initiatives that support the building of infrastructures. (http://www.tltgroup.org/programs/flashlight.html)

A center is one kind of infrastructure created to support efforts at change: The centers for teaching and learning at many institutions stand as examples. But Georgetown University has established a center that serves a national constituency. The Center for New Designs in Learning and Scholarship (CNDLES) generates work on reflective practice, learning technologies, and advanced study in teaching and learning. The latter provides resources for the scholarship of teaching and learning and a scholars-in-residence program among other services. (http://www.georgetown.edu/main/provost/candles/)

The final two examples in this series feature national infrastructures addressing the ways in which faculty members are acknowledged for their scholarly work. Establishing a Model Infrastructure to Sustain Communities for Peer Review of Teaching builds on work with course portfolios and peer review to develop a system of peer evaluation for teaching materials viewed as scholarly, intellectual work. Participants from University of Nebraska, Lincoln; Kansas State University; Indiana University, Bloomington; Texas A&M; and the University of Michigan, Ann Arbor are developing discipline-specific rubrics for assessing portfolios as well as a network of shared expertise. (www.unl.edu/peerrev)

A related project, run by the Samford Center for Problem-Based Learning, is establishing a national network to facilitate national peer review of the design, delivery, and documentation of problem-based learning courses and curricula. Examples of peer-reviewed courses and curricula will be made available in the project's web-based clearinghouse. (www.samford.edu/pbl)

Campuses must decide what kind of infrastructure best fits their own needs in supporting scholarship of teaching and learning on their campus. For example, Texas Tech University has created a Teaching Academy to undertake campus projects. Foothill College created a physical structure to house its Teaching Academy. On the other hand, Buffalo State College determined that an academy, physical or virtual, would not serve its needs as well as a networking among locations of work across the campus. Similarly, Penn State University has established a Teaching and Learning Consortium, made up of a steering committee and teams for planning and evaluation, coordinating, department heads, learning academy faculty, teaching assistants, students, learning support units, and deans. The University of Portland has convened a standing committee from all academic units on campus as well as from a variety of campus committees. At the University of Notre Dame, as on many campuses, the Center for Teaching and Learning coordinates efforts throughout the institution. The vast majority of campuses in the Campus Program have identified a sustaining and sustainable infrastructure supported by senior administration as essential to change in campus culture necessary for establishing the centrality of the scholarship of teaching and learning.

Faculty members and faculty developers can examine the infrastructure on their own campus. They can then compare practices those of faculty members and administrators in the five national projects described in this section. They may discover ways to link work in a way that facilitates systemic change.

ESTABLISHING EVIDENCE FOR PURPOSES OF ACCOUNTABILITY

Although most faculty members do scholarly work in teaching and learning to improve student learning and to add to the knowledge base in their disciplines, their work can also contribute evidence for various kinds of accountability. Both state legislatures and accrediting bodies are paying closer and closer attention to the topic with which this piece began: student learning outcomes.

The recent highly publicized *Measuring Up 2000: The State-by-State Report Card for Higher Education* (National Center for Public Policy and Higher Education, 2000) highlighted in the public eye the dearth of evidence available for grading states in one crucial area: student learning. Although data could be found to judge on the areas of preparation, participation, affordability, completion, and benefits, not one state had enough evidence to rate it on student learning. Because reports will be issued again in at least 2002 and 2004, pressure is on states to generate information that can be used by this kind of measurement.

One recent development that offers hope for legitimate data for the report card, and equally or more importantly for internal improvement, is the National Survey of Student Engagement (NSSE). This national survey of first-year and senior students focuses on their college experiences using research-based indicators of undergraduate quality. The survey provides benchmarking through national norms of educational practices and performance by institutional type, diagnosing by identifying areas where schools can enhance students' educational experiences, and monitoring through documenting institutional improvement over time. Acknowledging that student learning occurs outside as well as inside the classroom, the survey emphasizes what students do with institutional resources in moving toward learning goals. (www.indiana.edu/~nsse@indiana.edu)

A second kind of accountability, applicable to both private and public colleges and universities, is accreditation. Recognizing that student learning has been underemphasized in the past, regional accrediting bodies, as well as many specialized accreditors, are revising their processes and standards to focus much more closely on student learning outcomes. A trailblazer in this accreditation reform is the Western Association of

Schools and Colleges (WASC), whose new accreditation process focuses on educational effectiveness. Making accreditation more useful to institutions, the process enables an institution to decide in an initial proposal on a focus for accrediting visits and to generate evidence that concentrates not on inputs but on outcomes, especially those of student learning. (www.wascweb.org)

Helping institutions to generate, document, and represent the requisite kinds of evidence for this purpose is one objective of the Urban Universities Portfolio Project. Six universities are creating web-based institutional portfolios to demonstrate effectiveness to various stakeholders, experimenting with new approaches to multiple kinds of institutional evaluation. One consequence of the project for Indiana University-Purdue University Indianapolis (IUPUI) (which cosponsors the project with AAHE), California State University at Sacramento, Georgia State University, Portland State University, the University of Illinois at Chicago, and the University of Massachusetts, Boston has been greater clarity about student learning outcomes and the kinds of evidence warranted by different audiences about progress toward outcomes. (www.imir.iupui.edu/portfolio)

Institutions in the Campus Program are setting the scene for being able to supply valid and reliable evidence of student learning for purposes of accountability. When completion rates are questioned, for instance, Middlesex Community College will be able to state what the motivations of their students are for attending Middlesex and how the faculty are addressing issues of motivation, all because of the college's last two years of scholarly work as a faculty investigating motivation. Attentive to demands for critical thinking skills among graduates, Shawnee State University has created a group of initiatives centered on fostering and assessing critical thinking in the general education program, with one desired outcome being measures for multiple uses. The Center Scholars at the Center for Instructional and Professional Development at the University of Wisconsin, Milwaukee (UWM) have examined issues in teaching and learning that will enable UWM to document its commitment to the learning outcomes outlined in the Milwaukee Plan, the institution's stated mission against which it is judged both by the state and by its accrediting body.

Faculty members and faculty development staff members can identify campus projects that might intersect with these national projects addressing accountability. As a campus decides to undertake collective activities around the scholarship of teaching and learning, it can design work that links with both the purpose of improvement and that of accountability.

Faculty development on any campus necessarily has multiple emphases. As faculty development staff members approach faculty members, departments, or schools to undertake a new initiative, they can try to link that new initiative to a current one or to a goal that already has support. The current project or goal might be local, or it might even be national. The currency of being part of a national movement is many times golden.

The Carnegie Academy for the Scholarship of Teaching and Learning itself has added currency to established or emergent campus work. But it, too, benefits from finding links to, supports from, and contributions to other national projects. The line up in this chapter foregrounds a few of many initiatives that find ties to CASTL's work and to the work of campuses that honor the scholarship of teaching and learning.

Honoring the time of faculty members and the objectives of improving what we know about teaching and learning, let's provide links, build bridges, join hands, or use other such metaphors to identify the ways in which we augment and aggregate the good work around the scholarship of teaching and learning going on at both the national and local levels.

REFERENCES

Bass, R. (1999, February). The scholarship of teaching: What's the problem? *Invention: Creative thinking about learning and teaching, 1* (1), 1-10.

Hutchings, P., & Cambridge, B. (2001). The Carnegie Academy for the Scholarship of Teaching and Learning (CASTL). *Projects and initiatives that influence the environment for CASTL's work.* Paper presented at the Annual Forum on Faculty Roles and Rewards, Tampa, FL.

National Center for Public Policy and Higher Education. (2000). *Measuring up 2000: The state-by-state report card for higher education.* Washington, DC: Author.

NOTE

For more information about the Carnegie Academy for the Advancement of Teaching and Learning, see www.carnegiefoundation.org. For more information about the Campus Program, see www.aahe.org and aahe.ital. utexas.edu.

Contact:

Barbara Cambridge
Vice President for Programs
American Association for Higher Education
One Dupont Circle, Suite 360
Washington, DC 20036
(202) 293-6440, x760
Email: bcambridge@aahe.org

Barbara Cambridge is director of teaching initiatives at the American Association for Higher Education. She is on leave from Indiana University–Purdue University Indianapolis where she is Professor of English and Associate Dean of the Faculties. At AAHE, Cambridge coordinates the Campus Program, one of the three activities of the higher education program at the Carnegie Foundation for the Advancement of Teaching.

4

Could It Be That It Does Make Sense? A Program Review Process for Integrating Activities

Terrel Rhodes
Portland State University

This chapter presents a model for a comprehensive program review process that can be used on any campus. Faculty developers maintain a critical role in a campus-wide program review initiative. This model is based upon the development of institutional priorities that guide the development of goals and objectives for academic units across the campus. The program review process is based on a core of regularly produced institutional data that can be used by all units to inform decision-making. The review process is conducted on an annual or biannual basis with periodic major review coinciding with accreditation visits. The ultimate success of the model is tied to making budgetary and resource allocation decisions based on the assessment that grows out of the program review process.

INTRODUCTION

There are times when many faculty and administrators in higher education find themselves in one of those periodic places where they are ask, "Is this why I went into higher education?" Thinking back to when I entered graduate school, I was attracted to an academic career by a combination of opportunities to pursue research interests and the excitement of teaching students about my field of study. Of course, the flexible time frame for engaging in professional activities and the degree of autonomy afforded by the professorate were also appealing.

49

Many years later, the attractions haven't really changed, but the demands on faculty and administrators have. The costs of providing higher education have risen, but the resources have not kept pace. The opening of higher education to a much broader range of students has succeeded, but the corresponding preparation of faculty to teach these new students has not. The demand from tuition payers for accountability has increased, but the support and enthusiasm for generating evidence of performance has lagged behind. It would appear that the days of reading books, writing articles, and teaching students are gone, lost in an increasingly complex academic world which does not resemble the vision set forth in our doctoral programs.

However, all is not lost. It is true that faculty are being asked to do many more "administrative" activities than ever before: writing more reports, engaging in more committee work, spending more time on institutional planning, etc. On the whole, faculty members have been fairly good about assuming these new responsibilities. The serious complaints arise primarily when faculty perceive that all of their time, energy, and good thinking results in nothing being done, no changes or improvements, and recommendations that are ignored. When an institution solicits the involvement of its faculty and asks them to engage their most important resource, their minds, it is incumbent upon the institution to demonstrate how it has paid attention to the investment of its faculty.

The program review process can provide a way to organize many of the activities that faculty love to hate but need to do, and help provide meaning to a whole set of activities in which we ask faculty to be engaged. Program review is a process for knitting together an institution's mission with the various data-gathering and reporting activities required by external and internal decision-making and accreditation of programs.

PROGRAM REVIEW

Program review is designed to enhance planning within and among academic units to effectively use campus resources and advance university priorities. Program review brings together the assessment process, enrollment management, and external and professional accreditation reviews with strategic budget planning and decision-making. The overall goal of program review is to allow academic units within normal activities to articulate their goals and objectives in relation to the university's priorities through a regular process of internal and external review of qualitative and quantitative information about program activities, demonstration of progress toward achievement of goals, and the use of outcomes for program improvement.

Figure 4.1 presents a conceptual model for review of university programs. The university operates within a larger context of external entities that are connected to the university in various ways (e.g., governmental agencies that regulate processes and behaviors, employ graduates, etc.). Community groups and agencies, alumni, graduate schools, employers, and professional and regional accrediting bodies all affect the operation of the university in one form or another. Each in some way influences the program mix offered by the university, the student body that attends the institution, and the mission and priorities of the campus.

Within the institutional environment, the university engages in many activities. The inputs are composed of the people, the physical and social capital, the available resources, and the publicly enunciated mission and priorities. A whole set of processes result from the activities conducted by the input actors, resulting in an array of outputs. In the normal process of conducting activities, individuals and programs determine priorities for their attention. These priorities become the foci of any review process.

The review process itself begins with the enunciation of unit goals and objectives related to the activities of the unit. Data are collected that illuminate the purposes of the review. Funds and institutional support are required to conduct the program review. A whole set of processes is involved once the goals, objectives, and data are collected. Perhaps the most important processes involve analysis of data and reflection by members of the unit on the progress toward achieving goals and objectives, and on the appropriateness of continuing to maintain the goals and objectives or to develop new goals.

The program review process is accomplished through a recurring schedule of goal setting, data-gathering, and reporting. Each unit

- establishes its goals and objectives related to teaching, scholarship, and service for its respective programs

- provides analysis of data received and/or collected to demonstrate progress toward the stated goals and objectives

- reports on its progress toward meeting its goals and objectives within the unit's and the university's mission and priorities

The key to the entire program review process is the outcome of the review process in terms of its influence on institutional decision-making.

FIGURE 4.1
Conceptual Model for Reviews of University Programs

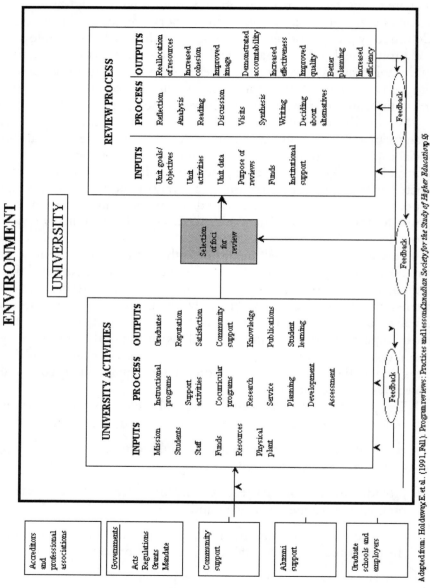

Adapted from: Holdaway, E. et al. (1991, Fall). Program reviews: Practices and lessons. *Canadian Society for the Study of Higher Education* 6.

If the outcome part of the process is ignored (e.g., if decisions are not based on review outcomes and resources are not reallocated) the process will soon become an empty exercise. Feedback occurs at all stages, influencing every other aspect of the process. This recursive process very quickly will reveal whether the program review activities result in tangible benefits, decisions, or outcomes grounded in the review findings (Holdaway, 1991).

Program Review Criteria

Decisions to allocate or reallocate resources must be based on criteria that are accepted by the actors within the institution. Typically, the criteria used to assess achievement of goals and objectives are the same criteria that are used for making many other decisions in the institution, or that are required to be gathered and reported to reflect various types of performance by individuals, units, or the campus as a whole. Figure 4.2 presents common criteria for program review derived from an examination of types of information that higher education institutions across the country regularly gather and report to a variety of agencies and for a variety of purposes.

FIGURE 4.2
Common Criteria for Program Review

Centrality to the University's Mission

How well does the program meet the university's expectations and priorities?
Indicators:

- Qualitative assessment based on interpretation of university mission
- Quantitative measures related to performance in the areas of enrollment, outreach, scholarship, research, and student learning outcomes

Quality of Faculty

How well do the faculty support the university's expectations?
Indicators:

- National rankings of schools, colleges, departments
- Publications and citations, presentations
- Offices held in national organizations
- Journal editorships, editorial boards
- Number of sponsored research and grants

- Prizes, awards, and recognition
- Visibility in campus, local, regional, national, and international communities (number of members elected, accolades)

Effectiveness of Curriculum
How well does the curriculum serve students, university, community?
Indicators:

- Student satisfaction
- Graduate's satisfaction
- Employer satisfaction
- Student attrition, retention, graduation
- Level of integration and articulation to other parts of university curriculum (coordination of course offerings with other majors, degree programs, scheduling times, etc.)
- Proportion of graduates in community-based learning courses or number of courses
- Assessment of student learning outcomes
- Student performance on professional tests
- Admissions to graduate schools
- Percentage with jobs after graduation (in field, salary)
- Student awards and recognition

Effectiveness of Program
How well does the program serve the university?
Indicators:

- Number of faculty FTE, (GAs), full-time (part-time), gender, race/ethnic
- SCH production: lower, upper, graduate
- Average class size: lower, upper, graduate
- SCH/faculty FTE
- Number of degrees awarded
- Contribution to general education, science and engineering: number of courses, scheduling, etc.
- Number/proportion of diverse students
- Number/proportion of diverse faculty
- Number of international courses and students
- Number of community partnerships

Cost Effectiveness
Relative to other university programs and compared to national norms.
Indicators:
- Proportion of budget from grants and contracts
- Proportion of budget from tuition
- Cost per SCH
- Cost per degree granted
- Cost per faculty FTE
- SCH per faculty

Level of Institutional Support
Indicators:
- Support per SCH
- Support per faculty FTE
- Faculty development (total or per FTE?)
- Facilities

The criteria and possible measures are grouped into primary categories and are linked to documents that exist in one form or another at every higher education institution.

Many of the criteria will look very familiar to any faculty member or administrator (e.g., publications, citations, and professional presentations at conferences, and student retention and graduation rates). In addition, each higher education institution will have its own criteria that reflect the mission of its institution (e.g., at Portland State University, the proportion of graduates who took community-based learning courses and number of community-based learning courses).

Six primary categories of criteria emerge from the examination of performance documents common to higher education. All other categories of criteria flow from the first category: university mission. Every accrediting agency, whether it be a professional association or a regional accrediting body, starts with the mission of the institution. The activities of the institution must flow from and be consistent with the mission. By basing program review on the mission—by asking the question, "How well does the program/unit meet the university's expectations and priorities related to the mission?"—a critical component of accreditation review is embedded across the institution's day-to-day activities.

The next three categories of criteria reflect central portions of any university's mission: the quality of faculty, the effectiveness of the curriculum in serving students, and the effectiveness of the program as a whole in serving the university. Many of the criteria listed under these categories are found in routine data-gathering and reporting by academic units for purposes of tenure, promotion, new program development, rankings, etc.

The final two categories of criteria reflect financial factors related to cost effectiveness of programs and the level of institutional support for the programs in achieving their goals and objectives in relation to other units. Since higher education increasingly has to compete for resources with many other priorities, the ability to demonstrate cost effectiveness becomes important in reviewing an institution's programs. This is not to suggest that programs that are less cost effective than others will result in decisions to eliminate or scale back programs, but it must be at least part of the review process in the overall decision-making for the university. Centrality to mission, or to the core curriculum, might easily outweigh lower performance on cost effectiveness measures. In addition, the level of institutional support for the program is an important ingredient in assessing program performance. Programs that achieve wonderful outcomes with little institutional support may be able to make a case for more institutional support to allow the program to achieve even higher performance levels, or to try development of new or innovative extensions of the program.

No single criterion or category is designed to overwhelm the others. It is the overall performance of the program on all measures that provides the broad basis for examining outcomes and decisions. It is important to remember that the program review process provides as much value to the unit itself through its analysis and reflection on program improvement as it does to the institution generally for decisions related to resource allocation.

The Annual Review
Units report in a relatively brief format on progress toward goals on an annual basis to their respective faculties and deans, then to the office of academic affairs (OAA) and the budget process (Figure 4.3). The academic unit annual report would incorporate the criteria as presented in Figure 4.2. The unit would use the report to plan for the next year(s) and to make adjustments based on the year's data collection. Anomalies and unanticipated outcomes can also be addressed and discussed by the unit.

The reflective component each year enables the unit to continuously check on effectiveness, provides an opportunity for mid-course adjustments in goals and objectives or allocation of activities and resources within the unit, and informs administrative units beyond them about progress toward agreed upon goals.

Colleges and schools, through the dean's office, then prepare a similar annual document reporting on the college/school progress toward achieving its goals and objectives. The college/school goals and objectives are not simply a compilation of the unit goals and objectives; rather, they are the priorities of the college/school that position it within the institution's overall mission. The department and program units within the college/school have built their goals and objectives from the college/school

FIGURE 4.3
Annual Review Process

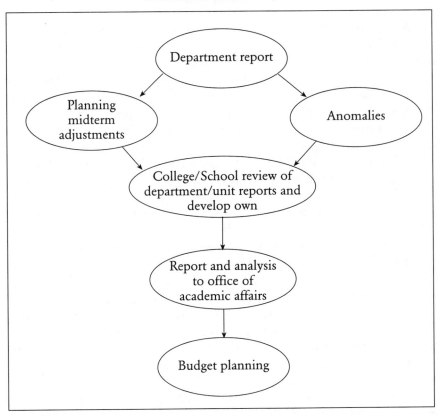

goals and objectives, so it is a fairly easy process to demonstrate college/ school progress through compiling achievements of its units. Since all levels of reporting use the same set of criteria, a common language is maintained throughout the process which facilitates ease of communication both within and across units, colleges, and schools. Colleges and schools forward their annual report to the provost along with the individual reports from the units within the college/school.

The office of academic affairs reviews the college/school reports and provides feedback through the deans on the directions and accomplishments of units across the campus. The college/school reports allow OAA to then prepare an overall set of priorities for the budget process. The annual cycle of the program review process readily reveals progress on accomplishing institutional goals and objectives, allowing the resources of the institution to be directed on an ongoing basis to where they can best be utilized to support the efforts of faculty within the units in all parts of the campus.

A large proportion of academic units already engage in regular program review in conjunction with their professional accrediting bodies, or in the case of some departments that don't have professional or external accrediting agencies, the periodic review developed by their dean. The latter is typically the case in many arts and sciences colleges and some fine arts departments. To streamline the program review process, maximize its value, and reduce its redundancy, the program review process needs to build on the existing accreditation requirements as much as possible. The accreditation schedule would serve as the major point for a periodic, summative self-study and review by the dean and the provost's office (Figure 4.4).

In the program review process presented in Figure 4.4, annual reviews that incorporate the criteria discussed earlier would allow academic units to track progress on achieving goals and objectives as well as reduce the amount of work required at the time of an accreditation visit. Through annual reviews, most of the necessary information would already be collected in a form required by the accrediting agency. In addition, the annual documentation of progress on student learning outcomes and other goals would add a necessary dimension expected by most of the professional accreditation agencies for assessing outcomes and using the assessment information to improve decision-making about the program.

In the annual review, the unit's stated goals and objectives would each be addressed through use of the information gathered in conjunc-

FIGURE 4.4
Program Review Cycle

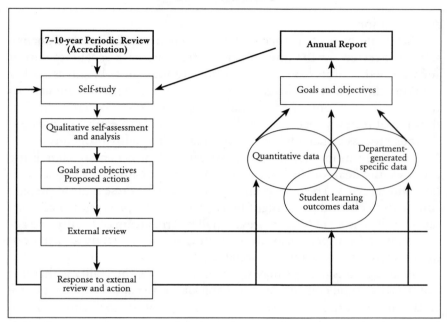

tion with the criteria identified in Figure 4.2. The combination of quantitative data (typically supplied by a campus's office of institutional research and planning), data on student learning outcomes, and any other data collected by the unit in responses to specific goals and objectives of the unit, is the foundation for documenting progress toward accomplishment of the unit's goals and objectives. The assumption is that progress will not be uniform on all goals and objectives, or that every goal and objective is designed to be achieved every year. Rather, every goal and objective is included in the annual report because it was considered important enough to be a stated goal or objective, and therefore, should remain a continuous part of the unit's collective consciousness. Indeed, many student learning outcomes may only have data collected on a periodic schedule rather than every year.

The unit analysis of the data, the use of the data to inform decision making, and the unit's reflection on the meaning of the data for action by the unit form the basis of the annual report. The annual reports over a series of years provide a continuing indication of performance for the unit in relation to goals and objectives that are linked to the priorities of the institution.

Accreditation

The schedule of visits by accreditation agencies prompts a summative self-study review for the units. Accreditation visits are usually spaced in such a way that units have time to enunciate goals and objectives, gather data on achievement of the goals and objectives, and implement actions based on the outcomes of the data analysis and reflection embedded in the annual review process. Accreditors will be able to easily see the continuous process utilized by the unit to maintain quality programs.

For those units that do not have external professional accrediting agencies, the dean of the college or school can conduct a quasi-accreditation unit review. The dean prepares a schedule for these units to prepare summative self-studies as might be requested for a professional accreditation visit. The dean then invites a small external team of faculty and administrators from peer institutions to review the self-study and to conduct a site visit just as a professional review team would conduct.

Although this process may seem cumbersome, the reality is that it is not nearly as time-consuming or complex as it first appears once it is operational. The program review process has a front-loaded time component. In other words, it takes time to develop and articulate institutional priorities. It takes time to develop and articulate college/school goals and objectives and unit goals and objectives that build from the institution's priorities. It takes time to develop appropriate measures for the achievement of the goals and objectives. This development and articulation process is most useful when it builds on data that are already collected and reported for other institutional purposes. The process can also often reveal where data are being collected that have no useful purpose. Frequently, data are still being collected and reports prepared when the purpose for doing so has passed or is no longer clear.

CONCLUSION

The organization of unit decision-making and action-taking around agreed-upon goals and objectives results in greater institutional coherence. Program review allows for the focusing of institutional resources on priorities. It also allows for every unit on a campus to determine how they want to link with institutional priorities, and to demonstrate how they contribute to the goals of the institution. The key to the process is the collection of relevant data and the use of the data to inform decisions about each unit's goals and objectives. The success of program review rests on the allocation and reallocation of resources based on progress toward achieving priority institutional goals. The engagement of the institution's many constituencies in the development of institutional priorities at the outset of the process ensures the necessary broad-based support for the over arching goals from which unit goals and objectives will flow.

Program review can be the vehicle for creating broadly understood meaning within an institution and among the many groups who comprise the extended university community. Program review can create coherence in activities and greater effectiveness in the allocation of resources. Ultimately, the program review process can help focus an institution and provide a mechanism for conducting necessary conversations about institutional mission, direction, and priorities.

REFERENCE

Holdaway, E., et al. (1991, Fall). Program reviews: Practices and lessons. *Canadian Society for the Study of Higher Education, 9*, 2-11.

Contact:

Terrel Rhodes
Vice Provost for Curriculum and Undergraduate Studies
Portland State University
Box 751
Portland, OR 97207
(503) 725-3000
Email: trhodes@pdx.edu

Terrel Rhodes is Vice Provost for Curriculum and Undergraduate Studies at Portland State University. He is the institutional liaison with the Northwest Association of Colleges and Schools. His teaching and research interests have involved policy analysis, program evaluation, and assessment. He holds an appointment as Professor of Public Administration.

Section II

Teaching and Learning Centers

5

Getting Started with Faculty Development

**Nadia Cordero de Figueroa and
Pedro A. Sandín-Fremaint**
University of Puerto Rico, Río Piedras

As a result of an academic senate decision to reconceptualize the baccalaureate, the Río Piedras Campus of the University of Puerto Rico began, in late 1994, a major transformational process that has led it to rethink itself as a community of learners. One of the principal instruments of change has been our Center for Academic Excellence, created in early 1998 as a result of the transformational process. This chapter discusses the process that led to the creation of the center, as well as its structure, activities, and vision for the future. We hope that our experience will be useful to those institutions thinking about venturing into the area of faculty development.

INTRODUCTION

Although many of our decisions turn out to be relatively inconsequential, some of them are truly fateful. Such was the case with the University of Puerto Rico's Río Piedras Campus when its academic senate made the decision, in late 1994, to reconceptualize the total curricular structure of the baccalaureate. This decision, made in response to a proposal presented by the College of General Studies—the academic unit in charge of most of the general education component on the Río Piedras Campus—that the senate examine a revision of this college's mission, has led to a rather penetrating process of reconsideration of much more than the undergraduate curricula. Among other consequences, it has led to a fresh interest in the teaching-learning processes as perhaps the very soul of curricula.

In this chapter, we would like to share with our readers the Río Piedras Campus's experience getting started with faculty development. Although there had been in the past isolated efforts to provide support for faculty in the area of the teaching-learning processes, it was only in early 1998 that this concern became a line item in the campus's budget, with the creation of our center for Academic Excellence. In what follows, we will recount some of the steps taken—and some of the lessons learned—in designing, creating, and developing our Center for Academic Excellence.

SETTING THE CONTEXT

In 1995, just months after the academic senate's decision to reconceptualize the baccalaureate, the Río Piedras Campus was accepted to participate in the American Council on Education (ACE)/Kellogg Project on Leadership and Institutional Transformation. The project committee soon decided to support the reconceptualization process by focusing on several work areas that would supplement the senate committee's work redesigning undergraduate curricula. One of these areas concerned teaching-learning processes, including research.

The task force in charge of this area soon began to conceive of institutional strategies that would promote better teaching-learning practices. Through a process of research and discussion, the task force began to envision the Río Piedras Campus as a community of learners, and this concept, in turn, triggered new visions and understandings of teaching-learning processes. As a result, the task force began to work on a policy document that would offer concrete recommendations for this area of institutional concern. The document, titled *Towards a Community of Learners: Reflections and Recommendations on the Teaching-Learning Processes at the Río Piedras Campus,* was officially adopted as policy by the chancellor and the dean for academic affairs in 1999.

One of the recommendations made in this document was precisely the creation of a center that would support faculty in developing teaching skills, incorporating modern technology into their practice, and conducting action research in their classrooms, among other activities that enhance faculty development and the teaching-learning process. By the time the document was adopted as policy, however, our Center for Academic Excellence had already been created. Taking advantage of a window of opportunity made available by the concurrence of both the chancellor and the academic dean, we requested funds from the campus's

Summer Initiatives Program and spent the summer of 1997 writing a proposal for the creation of the center.

ENVISIONING THE CENTER

Departing from several readings around the concept of a learning-centered institution (Barr & Tagg, 1995; Bonwell & Eison, 1991; Boyer, 1990; Farmer & Mech, 1992; Gabelnick, MacGregor, Matthews, & Smith, 1990; Grunert, 1997; Meyers & Jones; 1993, Silberman, 1996; Sutherland & Bonwell, 1996), we set out to explore, both virtually as well as in real time and space, how other institutions had organized in order to attend to the development needs of their faculty. Devorah Lieberman, Director of the Center for Academic Excellence at Portland State University (PSU), whom we had met in the course of our participation in the ACE/Kellogg Project, suggested that we use the Professional and Organizational Development Network in Higher Education (POD) directory as a source for contact information of people involved in faculty development. Thus, we started to write these people requesting information on the way they have organized in order to pursue their goals. Many responded with helpful information and materials while others referred us to their web pages.

Meanwhile, we accepted an invitation to visit the Center for Academic Excellence at Portland State University. This trip turned out to be extremely important for our purposes. The visit was masterfully designed to give us a live understanding of their center's operation and of the ways in which it relates to short- and long-term institutional goals. One of the most valuable aspects of this visit, as we went from one meeting to another shadowing Dr. Lieberman and other members of their staff, was to discover how people at PSU are using a common lexicon in speaking about their work and their institution. "Scholarship of teaching" was an expression that surfaced many times, along with the concept of developing a culture of evidence based on continuous assessment. This observation helped us to understand that the creation of a truly dynamic faculty development center needs to be rooted in a process of cultural change. The center, in turn, must conscientiously reflect the values of this new culture which are what ultimately give it a vision. To graft a new faculty development center onto business as usual would not have a significant impact.

Apart from Portland, we visited the then recently established center at the Mayagüez Campus of the University of Puerto Rico and the centers of two universities in Michigan: the University of Michigan, Ann Arbor and Eastern Michigan University. These last two were recommended by Dr. Lieberman as very different examples (in terms of size, budget, and structure) of successful faculty development efforts. We must confess that we were struck by the hospitality and helpfulness of each and every faculty developer that we approached both personally and through the Internet.

Dr. Lieberman also suggested that if we could only attend one professional conference per year that it be the POD conference. We have been to POD conferences for the past three years and must say they are perfect for faculty developers. As new practitioners, we attended their preconference workshop for beginners and found it to be both informative and stimulating (Brinko & Menges, 1997; Wadsworth, 1988). Attending POD's annual conferences are the best way to make sure that your new center is on the right track and on a par, at least in terms of vision and good ideas, with much more experienced ventures.

With all this input, and taking very carefully into account the peculiarities of our own institution, we sat down and developed our proposal which we presented to the task force in charge of developing the policy document on the community of learners and, eventually, to both the chancellor and the dean for academic affairs. The center we envisioned for the Río Piedras Campus was conceived in light of the values espoused by this document and in view of the anticipated curricular changes that should emerge from the academic senate's process of reconceptualizing the baccalaureate. Thus, it would develop work in the following areas: 1) teaching-learning, including technology, 2) assessment and action research, and 3) service-learning. As of this writing, due mostly to budgetary constraints, most of our work has been in the first area, although we have made some ventures into the second one.

One of our concerns was finding a way of giving the center a measure of autonomy from the administration while, at the same time, making sure that it had the administration's support. Thus, it was decided that the center would be under the sponsorship of the deanship for academic affairs, but would be overseen by an advisory board made up of well-regarded faculty from the different colleges, of which the dean for academic affairs would be a member.

Although our center was officially created in January 1998, it was not until a year later that we were assigned facilities that would enable us to move from being only a virtual endeavor. Meanwhile, there was a shift in key positions on our campus: Both the chancellor and the dean for academic affairs changed. This meant that we would need to expend much of our energy simply making sure that the new chancellor and dean would be brought into the loop. Actually, a change in such important positions would have normally entailed the end of our project. Under the ACE/Kellogg Project, however, the development of the change agenda had been entrusted basically to faculty. Thus, there was a grassroots investment in the project by members of the academic community. And this investment gave a certain weight and prestige to our initiative. Thus, in January 1999, notwithstanding yet another change in the chancellorship, the Center for Academic Excellence was officially inaugurated, ten months before the policy that recommended its creation was actually approved! Perseverance is indeed a virtue.

Our center is staffed by a part-time director, a part-time associate director, five part-time resident professors, a full-time secretary, a research assistant (assigned by the dean for graduate studies and research), and a work-study undergraduate assistant. We are housed in temporary quarters which, although small, have been furnished in a pleasing and welcoming manner. We have a reception area, two small offices, a meeting room, and a very small storage area where we keep materials, our photocopier, and an old refrigerator (essential for storage of refreshments served at meetings!). We also oversee a computer lab for faculty, whose operations are coordinated by a full-time nontenure-track professor.

WHAT WE HAVE ACCOMPLISHED

The very first type of activity we developed was a series of workshops offered on Friday mornings or afternoons, which we called Viernes Didácticos (Pedagogical Fridays). Between six and eight of these workshops are offered each term on a wide variety of subjects, most of which are suggested by participants. Although we do use many professors from the College of Education for these workshops recruiting faculty from all of the other colleges. We do not want to give the impression that one should be an expert in pedagogy in order to develop innovative and creative teaching-learning practices. Fliers are made both for the list of all workshops offered during a given term and for each individual workshop. These are also announced over the campus's radio station. The following are the titles of the Viernes Didácticos offered during the spring semester of 2001.

1) Managing Stress in the Teaching-Learning Scenario

2) Rubrics: An Instrument that Contributes Classroom Assessment and Evaluation

3) Collaborative Work

4) Conceptual Maps: An Instrument that Assists Our Teaching and Evaluation Practices

5) From the Real Classroom to the Virtual Classroom: Experiences in Distance Education

6) Constructivist Teaching Strategies

7) Intellectual Property and Copyright in Cyberspace

8) The Use of Etnography for Qualitative Analysis

Attendance in these workshops increased dramatically after we hired our secretary, who has taken care of all promotion efforts. Nonetheless, we have begun to observe a drop in attendance, which may well be a sign of fatigue. Although we have never allowed ourselves to be discouraged by relatively low attendance—after all, ten professors can represent as many as 800 students—we are currently exploring ways of responding to this drop. One possibility is to dedicate a whole semester to workshops specifically addressed to department chairs or to advisors, thus giving teaching faculty a respite from their Friday rendezvous with our center.

Another strategy deployed by the center is the appointment of resident professors in the areas of action research, technology, vernacular linguistic competencies, linguistic competencies in English, and quantitative reasoning skills. In order to make these appointments carry with them a prestige that would compensate for the low pay, we made sure to seduce widely respected faculty to serve as our first resident professors. These faculty offer the center nine hours per week or one fourth of their regular load. They schedule this time of availability in different ways so that they are able to consult with individual professors, offer workshops for specific groups or departments, and produce written materials to circulate on campus.

Through a grant from the W. K. Kellogg Foundation, we have also been able to offer several institutes: Summer Institute on Classroom Research, Fall Institute on the Development of Vernacular Linguistic Competencies Across the Curriculum, Spring Institute on the Development of Quantitative Competencies Across the Curriculum. These institutes are widely promoted and interested faculty are invited to apply, engaging themselves to pursue a specific project if their application is accepted and demonstrating departmental support. In the case of the summer institute, because it is held during a time when faculty are not required to come to campus, we offer a small stipend to participants.

As a result of our first Summer Institute on Classroom Research, the Río Piedras Campus held, on April 27, 2000, its first Classroom Research Conference in which the professors who participated in the institute, along with other invited faculty, presented their research projects.

In the area of technology, we offered our first Technology and Education Fair on May 2, 2000. For this activity, we made a call for proposals to faculty interested in presenting the ways in which they have incorporated technology into their teaching-learning practice. No use of technology was considered too small or insignificant as far as we were concerned. Should we have limited our fair to grandiose ventures into the use of technology, the results could well have been counterproductive, since many could easily have despaired of ever being able to do anything remotely similar. Two forums were held during the fair on matters related to the use of technology in the teaching-learning process. Software and hardware providers sponsored the fair through cash or in-kind donations.

Since 1990, the deanship for academic affairs has run a computer laboratory for faculty. Although efforts had been made to offer faculty up-to-date technology through this lab, the truth is that academic affairs is ill-suited to run this type of operation. Thus, we persuaded the dean to transfer jurisdiction over to the center, which is better able to oversee the lab's operations and to provide it with a clearer sense of direction and purpose. Since the transfer was made effective, we have been able to present the chancellor with a proposal for the complete renovation of the lab. As of this writing, all signs are good that we will soon be able to purchase state-of-the-art hardware and software that will turn the laboratory into a truly effective tool for promoting the use of technology in the educational process.

Sustaining these efforts financially is an ongoing challenge. Our institutional budget is about one half of what we actually need to run the activities described above. Thus, we are constantly looking into ways of raising the funds necessary for the center's work. Apart from writing proposals to foundations, we submitted a proposal to our own campus under a program known as Intramural Practice. This program allows departments and individual faculty to develop for-profit activities using institutional facilities. Our proposal has been approved and will allow us to sell both summer institutes and weekend workshops outside the Río Piedras Campus.

MOVING FORWARD

Since its inception in 1998, our Center for Academic Excellence has become a noteworthy and respected presence on campus. In a report on a visit to Río Piedras, as part of our participation in the ACE/Kellogg Project, Dr. Madeleine Green, Vice President of the American Council on Education, wrote:

> The creation of the Center for Academic Excellence . . . has been key; it is not merely a center with a bunch of programs, but also a space that gives legitimacy to the dialogue about teaching and learning as well as a real set of activities . . . Several hundred faculty members have attended workshops during the "Didactic Fridays." There is clearly a demand for the Center's services. It is now a line item in the budget, which is important recognition by the Campus administration. There is widespread positive feeling about the Center, and some readiness to push the activities down into the schools and departments. It is a good sign that UPR is almost ready for the "next generation" of the Center. (M. Green, personal communication, March 9, 2000)

What does the next generation of the center look like from our vantage point? There is much work ahead of us if we are to take the Center for Academic Excellence in the direction of the vision contained in the proposal for its creation. Very little has been accomplished in the area of assessment, although we have heeded Portland's advice to develop a culture of evidence: We try to keep track of everything we do and make sure that it is evaluated. Anyone who ventures into our offices and asks what we are about will find evidence of our work and reports of our evaluations on a table in the reception area. Nonetheless, we are committed to developing the assessment area in the direction of formal assessment of learning.

Furthermore, we have not been able to do anything in the area of service-learning, which will become crucial once the academic senate approves a new curriculum. All of the proposals before the senate include the concept of a capstone seminar preferably based on service-learning.

But the task ahead of us is more complicated than just leading the center in the direction of its original vision. Recent work by the task forces involved in the ACE/Kellogg Project suggests that the Center for Academic Excellence should grow in the direction of incorporating academic support to students. The belief is that in a truly learning-centered institution it would be ill-advised to split the teaching-learning equation. If we are to promote academic excellence around the notion of the community of learners, then the center should model a new teaching-learning paradigm, one that conceptualizes teaching and learning as distinct but inextricable pieces in a heuristic process that leads to curricular innovation and, in turn, to new ways of approaching the institution's commitment to learning. Figure 5.1 attempts to express this new vision of the center.

FIGURE 5.1
**Center for Academic Excellence
(Community of Learners)**

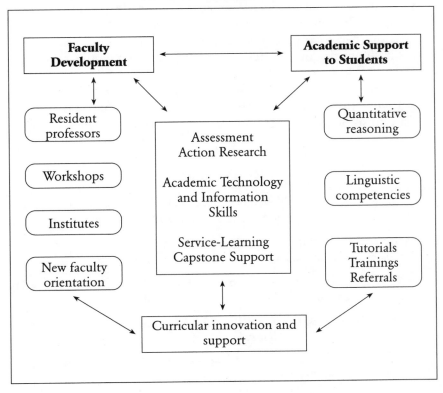

The center would have two major components: faculty development and academic support to students. Each of these components would develop its own activities addressed to its specific constituencies. The areas of assessment and action research, academic technology and information skills, and service-learning and capstone support, however, would serve both of the major components and would also develop activities and programs that bring together the teaching and learning aspects of the center's work.

We have taken our first small steps in the direction of this new vision. During the spring semester of 2000, we began to survey the campus in search of academic support initiatives. This effort allowed us to identify three types of initiatives: programs addressed to specific groups (mostly TRIO programs), centers (such as computer or writing centers), and initiatives developed by individual professors. All of the people identified were invited to attend a meeting held in January 2001, in which our plans were presented and discussed, stressing our role as supportive of the efforts already underway. A call for proposals was made for our first Academic Support Initiatives Fair, to be held on April 19, 2001. Also, we have appointed a part-time academic support coordinator and resident professors in linguistic competencies in English and in quantitative reasoning skills.

It is our hope that by the university's first centennial in 2003, our campus will already have a Center for Academic Excellence that brings faculty and students together, in new ways, around the compelling challenge of learning.

REFERENCES

Barr, R. B., & Tagg, J. (1995, November/December). From teaching to learning: A new paradigm for undergraduate education. *Change,* 13-25.

Bonwell, C. C., & Eison, J. A. (1991). *Active learning: Creating excitement in the classroom.* San Francisco, CA: Jossey-Bass.

Boyer, E. (1990). *Scholarship reconsidered: Priorities of the professoriate.* Princeton, NJ: Carnegie Foundation for the Advancement of Teaching.

Brinko, K. T., & Menges, R. J. (1997). *Practically speaking: A sourcebook for instructional consultants in higher education.*

Stillwater, OK: New Forums Press/Professional and Organizational Development Network in Higher Education.

Farmer, D. W., & Mech, T. F. (1992). Information literacy: Developing students as independent learners. *New Directions for Higher Education, No. 78.* San Francisco, CA: Jossey-Bass.

Gabelnick, F., MacGregor, J., Matthews, R., & Smith, B. L. (1990). Learning communities: Creating connections among students, faculty, and disciplines. *New Directions for Teaching and Learning, No. 41.* San Francisco, CA: Jossey-Bass.

Grunert, J. (1997). *The course syllabus: A learning-centered approach.* Bolton, MA: Anker.

Meyers, C., & Jones, T. (1993). *Promoting active learning: Strategies for the college classroom.* San Francisco, CA: Jossey-Bass.

Silberman, M. (1996). *Active learning: 101 strategies to teach any subject.* Boston, MA: Allyn and Bacon.

Sutherland, T. E., & Bonwell, C. (1996). Using active learning in college classes: A range of options for faculty. *New Directions for Teaching and Learning, No. 67.* San Francisco, CA: Jossey-Bass.

Wadsworth, E. C. (Ed.). (1988). *A handbook for new practitioners.* Stillwater, OK: New Forums Press/Professional and Organizational Development Network in Higher Education.

END NOTES

1. The Río Piedras Campus, a Doctoral II institution according to Carnegie Foundation criteria, is the oldest and largest unit (20,000 students and 1,200 faculty) of the University of Puerto Rico 11-campus system. The Río Piedras Campus will celebrate its centennial in 2003.

2. In October 1999, the academic senate's Special Committee for the Reconceptualization of the Baccalaureate rendered its final report, titled *Project: A New Baccalaureate for the Year 2000.* This report, along with an alternative proposal presented by the College of General Studies, were presented to, and discussed by, all of the colleges and other sectors of the academic community. The academic senate began to discuss the proposals during the spring semester of 2000. As of this writing, the section on the new curricular structure has been approved and most of the implementation design has been agreed upon. It is expected that the Río Piedras Campus will have approved

a new, more flexible, baccalaureate curriculum by the end of the spring semester 2001. Regardless of these decisions, however, it has become clear that the process of institutional change spurred by the academic senate's decision concerns much more than curricula: It has moved the campus in the direction of a learning-centered institution.

Contact:

Nadia Cordero de Figueroa
Center for Academic Excellence
P. O. Box 23344
San Juan, PR 00931-233444
(787) 764-0000, x2964
(787) 772-1429 (Fax)
Email: ncordero@goliath.cnnet.clu.edu

Pedro A. Sandín-Fremaint
Center for Academic Excellence
P. O. Box 23344
San Juan, PR 00931-233444
(787) 764-0000, x2964
(787) 772-1429 (Fax)
Email: psandin@coqui.net

Nadia Cordero de Figueroa is Professor of Chemistry in the College of Natural Science at the Río Piedras Campus of the University of Puerto Rico. She has been involved in teaching-learning research since the early 1970s when she developed the PSI mode of instruction for the general chemistry course. She has been Associate Dean for Academic Affairs of the College of Natural Science (six years) and Acting Dean (three years). In 1999, the Carnegie Foundation recognized Professor Cordero as Professor of the Year in Puerto Rico.

Pedro A. Sandín-Fremaint is Professor of French in the Humanities College at the Río Piedras Campus of the University of Puerto Rico, where he has served as Associate Dean for Academic Affairs. He chaired the Río Piedras' ACE/Kellogg Project on Leadership and Institutional Transformation, which supported institutional change efforts around the reconceptualization of the baccalaureate. He has been Associate Dean for Academic Affairs of the Río Piedras Campus.

Professors Figueroa and Sandín-Fremaint are cocreators and codirectors of the Río Piedras Campus's Center for Academic Excellence.

6

Research on Faculty as Teaching Mentors: Lessons Learned from a Study of Participants in UC Berkeley's Seminar for Faculty Who Teach with Graduate Student Instructors

Linda von Hoene
University of California, Berkeley

Jacqueline Mintz
Princeton University

This chapter describes the results of a research study of University of California, Berkeley's annual seminar for faculty teaching with Graduate Student Instructors (GSIs). It demonstrates that such a faculty development activity can have a significant impact not only on faculty mentoring of GSIs but also on faculty teaching, attitudes, and behaviors vis-à-vis teaching and learning in higher education. The chapter presents an overview of the seminar, a description of the format and methodology of the research project, and qualitative and quantitative outcomes.

INTRODUCTION

Since the 1980s, research universities in the United States have made a concentrated effort to improve graduate student preparation for teaching. From the first national conferences on teaching assistant (TA) training to the more recent Preparing Future Faculty programs, much progress has been made in the development of graduate students as teachers.

As evidenced by the table of contents in *The Professional Development of Graduate Teaching Assistants* (Marincovich, Prostko, & Stout, 1998), most of these efforts have focused on what centralized offices and individual departments can do to prepare the future professoriate for teaching. Considerably less attention has been given to the crucial role that front-line faculty play in this pedagogical mentorship. By "front-line" we mean those faculty members who teach lecture courses that utilize Graduate Student Instructors (GSIs). Though they may have taught for many years, these faculty members often have had no formal preparation for teaching and have not received guidance on how to be a pedagogical mentor to graduate students. The mentoring relationship fostered between graduate students and these front-line faculty members is of great importance, as it may be the only opportunity that graduate students have to learn about teaching before assuming faculty positions.

In order to address this need, the University of California, Berkeley's GSI Teaching and Resource Center introduced in 1992 an annual seminar to assist faculty in providing pedagogical mentorship and guidance to GSIs. The goal of the faculty seminar is to bring together a cross-disciplinary group of faculty who meet and work together over the course of three weeks to make their teaching with GSIs more effective and efficient.

Since 1993, the authors of this article have had the opportunity to present on this seminar nationally and internationally (Mintz, 1997; Mintz & von Hoene, 1997; Mintz, von Hoene, Duggan, & Reimer, 1995; Mintz, von Hoene, & Reimer, 1998). Participants at these sessions frequently asked what the long-term impact has been on faculty mentoring of GSIs. Based on this interest, we decided to conduct a research study of the effects of the seminar in spring 1998.

This chapter addresses the results of this research. The first section describes the seminar and its evolution. The next section discusses the instrument that was designed to gather information on the long-term impact of the seminar (Appendix 6.1) and the research employed. We then focus on one section of the research study in which participants were asked what changes took place in how they approach and carry out their mentoring responsibilities as a result of the seminar. In reporting the results of the research study, we use both quantitative and qualitative approaches.

THE FACULTY SEMINAR

The faculty seminar on teaching with GSIs is offered each spring for nine hours (three afternoons over the course of three weeks). Preparation for the faculty seminar begins in the fall. In November, the advisory committee for GSI Affairs contacts department chairs asking them to recommend faculty members who might benefit from such a seminar. The advisory committee is a subcommittee of Berkeley's academic senate and co-sponsors the seminar with the GSI Teaching and Resource Center. Once faculty names are received, we send out invitations. In order to create a working group, only those faculty who are able to attend all three meetings are accepted. In the early years, faculty participants elected to limit the seminar to 20 participants. This ensures small group discussion.

In the fall semester, GSI Teaching and Resource Center staff involved in developing the seminar brainstorm topics, speakers, and activities. We then meet with the individual faculty presenters to develop ideas for each session. In addition to key faculty members, several graduate students are invited to be on a panel at the seminar to discuss their work with faculty. Undergraduates are invited who speak about the impact of GSI teaching on their learning.

In December and January a reader of articles is compiled and a gift book purchased for the participants (e.g., Brookfield, 1995; Cross & Steadman, 1996; Hutchings, 1998; Ramsden, 1992). Though faculty will not have time to read all of this material over the course of the three weeks, the reader and gift book serve as resources for them in later semesters.

The specific topic of the seminar and the activities employed change from year to year. In the first year, for example, the seminar was geared to faculty teaching large lecture courses. In another year, the focus was on learning styles. In yet another year, pedagogical mentorship of GSIs was addressed. In order to model for the faculty participants pedagogically sound approaches that both they and their GSIs alike can utilize in their teaching, interactive methods are employed, such as case studies (e.g., to discuss a GSI/faculty conflict), fish bowls (e.g., to enable one-half of the faculty participants to observe their colleagues participating in a simulated undergraduate learning experience), think/pair/share activities (e.g., to articulate differences in learning styles), free writes (e.g., to consider what constitutes good mentoring), and faculty peer observations, among others. When appropriate, more traditional approaches such as lecture-style presentations are used (e.g., the professional development of graduate students for teaching) (Cross, 1994) and motivation theory and panel discussions with graduate students and undergraduates (Covington, 1996).

The seminar commences with a welcome from the dean of the graduate division and the chair of the advisory committee for GSI Affairs. The individual seminar sessions are facilitated by the staff of the GSI Teaching and Resource Center with carefully honed presentations and activities led by faculty, campus staff, current graduate students, former graduate students now in teaching positions, undergraduates and, on occasion, experts on teaching and learning from off campus.

The seminar is assessed twice: at the end of the third and final session and at the end of the spring semester when faculty are in a position to report how they have applied what they learned to their work with GSIs.

Since 1994, approximately 110 faculty members attended the seminar. The response to the seminar has been uniformly positive with only one person stating that she or he would not recommend the seminar to a colleague. Though responses have been positive, we also wanted to ascertain the long-term impact on the way faculty work with GSIs on their teaching. This led to a research study in spring semester 1998 to identify what changes, if any, faculty had made in mentoring GSIs.

RESOURCE FORMAT AND METHODOLOGY

The format for our study was a one-hour taped oral interview. This ensured a greater rate of return and enabled interviewers to probe responses during the interview. The questionnaire was developed by staff from the GSI Teaching and Resource Center, two humanists and two social scientists. After developing the instrument, we received input on its design from two colleagues at Berkeley, K. Patricia Cross, Professor Emerita from the Graduate School of Education, and Maresi Nerad, Director of the Graduate Division's Research Unit.

The questionnaire consists of five sections: 1) work with GSIs, 2) information on the faculty seminar and other teaching related seminars, 3) teaching preparation, 4) impact of the seminar, and 5) division of time. Section four of the questionnaire, which asks explicitly about the impact of the seminar, forms the basis of this chapter.

Three staff members from the GSI Teaching and Resource Center conducted and audiotaped the oral interviews. The interviews were coded and transcribed by a project assistant to ensure anonymity.

PARTICIPANT PROFILE

Of the 110 faculty members who had attended the faculty seminar, 31 were available to participate in our study. Of these, 22 were tenure track, with all but one already tenured. Nine participants were nontenure-track instructors. The group was split evenly between humanities and social sciences on the one hand (15) and sciences and engineering on the other (16). All seven years of the faculty seminar were represented. Twenty-four of the approximately 65 departments or programs that appoint GSIs on the Berkeley campus were represented in the study. Three-fourths of the participants had taught with GSIs for a total of one to 20 semesters, the other fourth for more than 20 semesters.

RESULTS AND ANALYSIS

In section four of the questionnaire, we asked our informants a multipart question about what changes they had made as a result of the faculty seminar. The first several categories address the impact the seminar has had on the pedagogical mentorship that faculty provide GSIs; the remaining categories ask about the impact the seminar may have had on the teaching done by faculty members and the attitudes and behaviors that characterize their relationship to teaching. We discuss our findings within these two broad categories.

IMPACT OF THE SEMINAR ON FACULTY MENTORSHIP OF GSIs

Content of the Meetings

Sixty-six percent of the participants in the study had made significant changes in the content of their weekly meetings with GSIs. Two overall changes occurred. First, respondents themselves seemed to have changed their attitudes toward the importance of the weekly meetings in preparing GSIs for teaching by indicating that they were now utilizing the weekly meetings more consciously as an opportunity for mentoring. Respondents used terms such as "more structured," "more official," "more formal," and "more focused," and that they had become "more directive" and "more explicit about expectations." The second major change was that the meetings were now devoted much more to discussing issues of teaching and learning as opposed to logistics. Several informants stated that the discussion was less about nuts and bolts and included complex issues such as teaching a diverse group of students.

When asked explicitly whether the weekly meetings now included a greater focus on pedagogy versus logistics, 66% indicated yes. One respondent described the shift in these terms: "Before it was 100% to 0 [logistics to pedagogy], now it is 80% to 20%."

Assessment of GSIs

Though all GSIs receive feedback from their students at the end of the semester at Berkeley, faculty have traditionally been less involved in GSI assessment. We found that as a result of the faculty seminar, this had indeed shifted. Approximately 50% of the participants in the study stated that they had become more involved in issues of GSI assessment. This involvement took different forms. Some had begun to observe their GSIs in the classroom. Others encouraged their GSIs to be videotaped and to participate in peer observation. Most frequently, the respondents indicated that they were discussing evaluation much more with their GSIs.

Collaboration in Course Design and Delivery

Forty-two percent of the respondents stated that they now welcome greater collaboration in course design as a result of the faculty seminar. This suggested that faculty valued graduate student input and had begun to understand the need to give graduate students more substantive opportunities in teaching that resemble what they will be expected to do as new assistant professors. The form which this collaboration took varied. Some gave GSIs the opportunity to give lectures. Others invited contributions to worksheets and homework sets. Another asked students to think not only about what they would put on a syllabus for a similar course if they were to teach it, but more importantly, why: "As a result of the seminar... I've had them [GSIs] make up a syllabus as if they were the sole instructor for the course and review its content... I ask the students if they were teaching the course what textbook they would choose and why, and then we would have a dialogue about that." One respondent stated that she or he invited graduate students to give a lecture "as a result of my greater understanding that learning how to teach is at the core of being a doctoral student."

Frequency and Length of Meetings

The goals of the faculty seminar are to make teaching with GSIs more effective and more efficient. For that reason, we were particularly interested in ascertaining whether greater focus on providing pedagogical mentorship would translate into more time required on the part of the faculty member. This research confirmed that the quality of time spent mentoring GSIs increased more than the quantity of time. Thirty-nine percent stated that the frequency of meetings had increased. No respondent indicated that this was negative. For some respondents, increased frequency of meetings enabled the introduction of a more predictable structure in which to discuss pedagogy: "Prior to the faculty seminar, meetings with GSIs were infrequent and sporadic and almost always related to administrative matters.... [Now I hold] regular meetings in which time is devoted to pedagogy and its application to that particular course as well as separate time devoted toward administrative matters." The increased frequency of meetings seemed to be an investment into making the teaching of the course and the relationship to the GSIs more satisfying. Some indicated that they now held a presemester meeting to get the GSIs prepared for teaching.

Time Spent Mentoring GSIs

Thirty-five percent had increased the amount of time mentoring GSIs while 65% had not. When comparing the data on changes made in the content of the weekly meetings (66% with greater focus on pedagogy), the increased focus on assessment of GSIs (45%), the increase in opportunities for GSIs to contribute course design (42%), and the overall increase in time spent mentoring GSIs (33%), it is apparent that the quality of pedagogical mentoring has increased far more than the time spent mentoring GSIs. These data suggest that faculty mentorship of GSIs is both more effective and more efficient.

Impact of the Faculty Seminar on Faculty Development

Though the faculty seminar has focused primarily on how faculty can work more effectively and efficiently with GSIs, there were significant secondary gains derived by faculty early on in the process. At this research university, faculty do not often seek out activities for their own pedagogical development. The rewards system at Berkeley encourages faculty to spend far more time on their research than on their teaching. Boyer (1990) asserts, however—and this concurs with our findings as well—when asked, many faculty admit wanting to devote more time than they currently do to teaching. Faculty have also stated that they run the risk of becoming stigmatized if they demonstrate too much enthusiasm for teaching. Though many faculty members attend the seminar for the express purpose of doing a better job in teaching with GSIs, our research study demonstrated clearly that faculty attitudes to teaching and learning in higher education, their philosophies of teaching and learning, and even their engagement with the literature on pedagogy were positively impacted by the seminar. These secondary gains described below are a significant outcome of the seminar.

Teaching of Undergraduate Courses

Fifty percent of our respondents indicated that as a result of the faculty seminar they had made changes in the methods they use to teach undergraduates. These changes were primarily in three areas: more interactive teaching, increased attention to assessment and ongoing feedback, and a greater attentiveness to diversity. One respondent underlined the increased degree of consciousness that she or he brings to teaching as a result of the seminar: "I am more conscious of the rationale for assignments and how they fit into course objectives."

Teaching of Graduate Level Courses

As might be expected, there was less impact of the seminar on the manner in which faculty teach graduate level courses. Nonetheless, it is remarkable that a full 33% of the respondents indicated that they had made changes to the methods they employ in teaching graduate courses as a result of the seminar. These changes were similar to those that were made in the undergraduate courses: more class involvement, less lecturing and coverage, attentiveness to differences in learning styles, and seeking out early feedback.

Level of Interest in Teaching and Learning in Higher Education

Sixty-seven percent of the respondents stated that as a result of the faculty seminar their level of interest in teaching and learning in higher education had increased. Some stated that they were more interested and more aware of pedagogical issues and resources. Others felt they had begun to understand that teaching is a complex process that involves effort.

Involvement in Teaching Related Activities

Faculty interviewed indicated a greater involvement in teaching and learning activities since the seminar. Although interest in some of these activities may have antedated the faculty seminar, 25% of the respondents indicated that they were participating in writing projects pertaining to pedagogy, and 66% stated that they were reading more in the pedagogical literature. In addition, 50% of the participants reported increased involvement in departmental, campus, and national activities pertaining to teaching and learning and preparing graduate students for teaching. Some participants began to serve as members of departmental or campus-wide committees involving preparing graduate students for teaching. One stated that she or he had begun teaching the departmental pedagogy seminar for GSIs as a result of the faculty seminar. Because of a seminar segment on the teaching portfolio, some faculty respondents stated that they had recommended the job search process in their departments be changed to include teaching portfolios.

Impact on Philosophy of Teaching and Learning in Higher Education

In addition to the more tangible results described above, 55% of the participants revealed that as a result of the faculty seminar their philosophies of teaching and learning had changed. Many of the statements made by the respondents and the changes that had occurred in their philosophies of teaching and learning reflected an integration of recent pedagogical theory that stresses collaboration, deep learning, reflective practice, and a student-centered classroom. For example, one respondent began to look at learning as a cooperative arrangement and stated: "It's not just me throwing information at them, but it is learning together. I will get the most out of my teaching if we learn cooperatively. I am teaching the students how to learn, but we all do it together. It's not just me tossing bones to the dogs." Another described the shift as follows: "Focusing on student learning and asking at every point how do we best help the students learn is really a different question than how do I best teach this material, how do I get up and explain it as clearly as I can?" Another stressed that she or he was "paying more attention to deep learning issues" and placed more value on ongoing evaluation and fostering "better communication among GSIs themselves."

Other respondents described shifts in their pedagogical thinking in affective and developmental terms. For example, one described his or her experience with the seminar as "a ripening." Another described his approach to teaching along the lines of Perry's (1970) developmental stages by stating that she or he had "become much clearer of the fact that there are no right and wrong ways" but that teaching is instead "an open process . . . in which you aren't the center." Still other respondents mentioned that the seminar had enabled them to see teaching more from the GSIs' point of view and that it had enabled them to appreciate GSI roles and capabilities. Seeing the process through the eyes of the GSIs, one respondent stated that it "made me try to make the work more worth-while." The seminar also seemed to give faculty a language for discussing teaching and learning. One put it this way: "The faculty seminar gave me a vocabulary and philosophy to discuss my teaching and learning inter-ests with GSIs." Another stated that it had enabled him/her to "think about my legacy as an educator."

CONCLUSION: THE ENLIGHTENMENT EFFECT

Though many of these affective outcomes might be viewed as intangible, they reflect a very important shift in attitude toward teaching among fac-ulty and should be viewed as a result of the faculty seminar. In the process of conducting our interviews, one of the participants in the study referred to a concept from the field of social science research to describe the nonlinear, somewhat diffuse impact the seminar had on her. She ex-plained that the seminar had an "enlightenment" effect on her teaching and her work with GSIs. Applied to the context of social science research and policymaking (Janowitz, 1970), this concept, described in an article written by Carol Weiss (1977), suggests that "the major effect of research on policy may be the gradual sedimentation of insights, theories, con-cepts, and ways of looking at the world" (p. 535). Though the participants in our study were able to attribute changes in their work with GSIs and in their own teaching to the faculty seminar, the greatest achievement has been, in our opinion, the enlightenment function of the seminar.

Through the seminar, participants took part in a process that led to major shifts in their attitudes toward teaching and preparing graduate stu-dents to teach, and enabled them to be "receptive to widened horizons and untraditional angles of vision" (Weiss, 1997, p. 545). It is our belief that graduate student mentoring, undergraduate education, and the cam-pus culture for teaching and learning are benefiting from these new atti-tudes and practices that have resulted from the seminar and its enlight-enment effect.

ACKNOWLEDGMENTS

We would like to acknowledge the contributions of Lisa Smiley and Sharon Waller to the construction of the questionnaire. We would also like to thank Sharon Waller for conducting some of the oral interviews and Debbie Russell for her assistance in transcribing the interviews.

REFERENCES

Boyer, E. (1990). *Scholarship reconsidered: Priorities of the professoriate.* Princeton, NJ: Carnegie Foundation for the Advancement of Teaching.

Brookfield, S. D. (1995). *Becoming a critically reflective teacher.* San Francisco, CA: Jossey Bass.

Covington, M. (1996). *Motivation, achievement, and self-worth.* Presentation at the 4th annual Faculty Seminar on Teaching with GSIs, University of California, Berkeley.

Cross, K. P. (1994). *How to professionally develop GSIs for today's world of higher education.* Presentation at the 2nd annual Faculty Seminar on Teaching with GSIs, University of California, Berkeley.

Cross, K. P., & Steadman, M. (1996). *Classroom research.* San Francisco, CA: Jossey Bass.

Hutchings, P. (Ed.). (1998). *The course portfolio.* Washington, DC: American Association for Higher Education.

Janowitz, M. (1970). *Political conflict: Essays in political sociology.* Chicago, IL: Quadrangle.

Marincovich, M., Prostko, J., & Stout, F. (Eds.). (1998). *The professional development of graduate teaching assistants.* Bolton, MA: Anker.

Mintz, J. (1997). *Mentoring supervisors of postgraduate students.* Presentation at the University of Strathclyde, Glasgow, Scotland.

Mintz, J., & von Hoene, L. (1997). *Mentoring for (a) change: Working with faculty to rethink the role of teaching in graduate education.* Presentation at the 5th national TA Conference, Minneapolis, MN.

Mintz, J., von Hoene, L., Duggan, J., & Reimer, J. (1995). *Teaching with teaching assistants: A cross-disciplinary dialogue with faculty.* Presentation at the 4th national TA Conference, Boulder, CO.

Mintz, J., von Hoene, L., & Reimer, J. (1998). *Pedagogical mentorship: The role of faculty in preparing graduate students to teach.* Presentation at the American Association for Higher Education Conference on Faculty Roles and Rewards, Orlando, FL.

Perry, W. (1970). *Forms of ethical and intellectual development in the college years.* New York, NY: Holt, Rinehart, and Winston.

Ramsden, P. (1992). *Learning to teach in higher education.* London, England: Routledge.

Weiss, C. H. (1977). Research for policy's sake: The enlightenment function of social research. *Policy Analysis, 3,* 531-545.

Contact:

Linda von Hoene
Campus-wide Consultant, GST program
University of California, Berkeley
301 Sproul Hall, #5900
Berkeley, CA 94720-5900
(510) 642-4456
Email: vonhoene@socrates.berkeley.edu

Jacqueline Mintz
Director, McGraw Center for Teaching and Learning
Princeton University
Firestone Library C-15
Princeton, NJ 08544
(609) 258-2575
(609) 2581433 (Fax)
Email: Jamintz@princeton.edu

Linda von Hoene is Director of the Graduate Student Instructor Teaching and Resource Center at the University of California, Berkeley. She received her PhD in German Literature and Culture from the University of California, Berkeley, with a dissertation on the topic of gender and fascism. She has published journal articles and book chapters on rethinking the teaching and learning of foreign languages through psychoanalytic, feminist, and postcolonial theory.

Jacqueline Mintz is founding Director of the McGraw Center for Teaching and Learning at Princeton University. Formerly, she was founding Director of the GSI Teaching and Resource Center at the University of California, Berkeley. A PhD in Comparative Literature from the University of California, Berkeley, she now writes on values in higher education and faculty development.

APPENDIX 6.1

FACULTY SEMINAR RESEARCH QUESTIONS

*Name: _____

*Title: _____

*Department: _____

*Year seminar was attended: _____

*Focus of Faculty Seminar that year: _____

*Interviewer: _____

*Date: _____

Part 1: Work with GSIs

1) Are you currently teaching with GSIs?

2) Are you currently working with GSIs as a faculty adviser for GSI affairs, pedagogy seminar instructor, or some other capacity?

3) In past semesters have you worked with GSIs in any of the capacities mentioned above:

Faculty adviser for GSI affairs _____ # of times _____

Pedagogy seminar instructor _____ # of times _____

Other _____

Part 2: Information on Faculty Seminar and other Teaching Related Seminars

4) Prior to the faculty seminar had you attended any workshops, conferences, or seminars that focused on teaching issues?

yes _____ no_____

** If yes, can you provide the names of the seminars/conferences and when and where they took place?

5) Since attending the faculty seminar have you attended any workshops, conferences, or seminars that focus on teaching issues?

yes _____ no_____

** If yes, can you provide the names of the seminars/conferences and when and where they took place?

Part 3: Teaching Preparation

6) While in graduate school, were you a graduate student instructor or TA?

yes _____ no _____

If yes, how many times did you teach?

7) As a TA or GSI in graduate school, did you teach with a primary instructor?

8) As a graduate student did you ever have complete responsibility for teaching a course, including designing the syllabus?

yes _____ no _____

If yes, could you please describe the circumstances?

9) Did you ever teach a stand-alone course in which you were the sole instructor but were not responsible for course design and curriculum?

yes _____ no _____

10) As a graduate student did you receive any preparation for teaching through your university such as:

Orientations for new GSIs _____

Workshops or other seminars on teaching _____

Observation and feedback _____

Individual mentoring by a faculty member _____

Other _____

If any of the above are checked, what did you take away from that experience?

11) Did you feel prepared for your teaching responsibilities when you first began to teach as a graduate student?

yes _____ no _____

Please explain.

12) Did you feel prepared for your teaching responsibilities when you began teaching as a faculty member?

yes _____ no_____

Please explain. _____

13) Did you feel prepared to teach with GSIs at Berkeley?

yes _____ no_____

Please explain.

14) How did you know what to do when you began working with GSIs?

15) What did you find to be the most rewarding aspect of working with GSIs when you first began?

Is this different now?

16) What did you find to be the most difficult aspect of working with GSIs when you first began?

Is this different now?

Part 4: Impact of the Seminar

17) What were your primary motivations for attending the faculty seminar?

18) Would you describe for me what you believe has been the overall impact of the faculty seminar on you?

19) Were there any specific aspects of the seminar that you believe were particularly beneficial?

20) As a result of attending the faculty seminar have you made any changes in regard to your work with GSIs in the following areas?

Frequency and length of meetings with GSIs

Content of meetings

Distribution of how time is spent in meetings on logistics versus pedagogy

Nature and extent of collaboration in course design and delivery

Assessment of GSIs as teachers (classroom observation, videotaping, conferencing)

The amount of time spent mentoring GSIs

Have you made changes in any other area as the result of the faculty seminar that you would like to mention?

21) As a result of attending the faculty seminar has anything changed in regard to your teaching methods or teaching style in courses with undergraduates?

yes _____ no_____

If yes, in what way(s)?

22) As a result of attending the seminar has anything changed in regard to your teaching methods or teaching style in the graduate level courses you teach?

yes _____ no_____

If yes, in what way(s)?

23) As a result of attending the faculty seminar has your level of interest changed in issues of teaching and learning in higher education?

yes _____ no_____

24) As a result of the seminar, have you done any of the following?

Read about teaching in books and journal articles _____

Written, presented, or published on teaching _____

Contributed to campus department or professional association activities on teaching _____

Contributed to campus department or professional association activities vis-à-vis GSIs _____

25) As a result of attending the faculty seminar has there been a change in your philosophy of teaching and learning in higher education?

yes _____ no_____

If yes, in what way(s)?

Part 5: Division of Time

(Give the faculty member two pieces of paper with a circle drawn on each piece.) If you were asked to make up a pie drawing representing how you currently spend your time in the following areas, how would you divide up the pie? Please indicate the percentage of the pie currently taken up by each activity.

     I. Teaching
    II. Mentoring
         Undergraduate students
         Graduate students
         GSIs
   III. Research
   IV. Service
         Departmental committees
         Campus-wide committee work
         Professional associations
    V. Work as an administrator
   VI. Other (please explain)

Please say a few words about this division of responsibilities.

Now, take the second pie. How would you like the pie to be divided? Please indicate the percentages as you would ideally like to see your time distributed.

Please say a few words about this division of responsibilities.

Part VI: Academic and Professional Background

Undergraduate degree from: _____

Graduate degree from: _____

Length of time on faculty at Berkeley: _____

Have you taught as a faculty member at other schools before Berkeley?

If so, where? _____

For how long? _____

Did you work with GSIs/TAs? _____

Is there anything else that you would like to say that you have not been specifically asked to address?

*   To be filled in by interviewer

** Can call people back on this if necessary

7

Evaluating Teaching Workshops: Beyond the Satisfaction Survey

David G. Way
Virleen M. Carlson
Susan C. Piliero
Cornell University

Workshops are a prevalent approach to fostering instructional development for both teaching assistants (TAs) and faculty. Frequently we evaluate workshops by asking participants to fill out a satisfaction-oriented survey at the end. To what degree do such surveys evaluate adequately the workshop's long-term effect on participants' learning? The authors explicate earlier investigative work on transfer of training, and present the results of a follow-up survey to two groups of TA workshop participants designed to assess the degree to which conditions theoretically conducive to the transfer of training exist at their institution.

INTRODUCTION

Teaching assistants (TAs), both native and nonnative English speakers, are frequently prepared for their university teaching duties through voluntary, and sometimes mandatory, attendance at workshops (Lambert & Tice, 1993); our university is no exception. A standard means of evaluating workshop design is through end-of-training satisfaction surveys that often ask for both qualitative and quantitative responses from participants. Rarely are the participants' learning outcomes assessed through follow-up measures of classroom data. Workshop designers and presenters might benefit more from knowing whether there is either any carryover of workshop content to actual classroom practice, or if conditions are present in the participants' home departments to encourage the classroom implementation of new ideas and teaching methods introduced in workshops. It is the second of these questions that this chapter focuses on.

We surveyed two groups of workshop participants: the first group, one month after participating in the workshop, and the second group, six months later, to determine whether conditions were present in their daily lives that would encourage transfer of the training experience to their classroom practice. We used many questions from a study conducted in 1998 (Notarianni-Girard, 1999), in which our institution was one of the 12 original colleges included in the database. We found some conditions that Notarianni-Girard's study defined as facilitating the transfer of training present on our campus.

The term "transfer of training" evolved from business and industry training literature, where it was originally expressed as "transfer of learning" (Huczynski, 1978; Huczynski & Lewis, 1980; Noe, 1986). By the mid-1980s, the notion of conditions that facilitate or inhibit the transfer of training outcomes beyond the training experience was documented in the K-12 staff development literature (Showers, Joyce, & Bennett, 1987). Notarianni-Girard defines transfer of training as "the degree to which trainees continually and effectively apply the knowledge, skills, and attitudes gained in a training context to the job" (1999, p. 120). A simpler definition states that "transfer is the degree to which behavior will be repeated in a new situation" (Detterman & Sternberg, 1993, p. 4).

STUDY BACKGROUND

Our study had its beginnings in 1996, when Deborah Notarianni-Girard, then a graduate student in the University of Connecticut's Department of Educational Leadership, asked our university, along with 11 other institutions, to participate in a study dealing with transfer of training for graduate students. Out of a total of 75 graduate students on our campus who received her survey, approximately 61 students returned it, giving her a response rate of over 80% for our campus. Notarianni-Girard's study was designed to address the following four research questions through a post-training survey.

1) To what extent are there facilitating factors present in the work environment of teaching assistants trained in a TA training program?

2) To what extent are there inhibiting factors present in the work environment of teaching assistants trained in a TA training program?

3) To what extent did/do teaching assistants perceive supervisor support before, during, and after training?

4) To what extent did/do teaching assistants perceive peer support before, during, and after training?

Her study asked graduate students to rate all training experiences, whether at the university or departmental level. In contrast, our survey was concerned solely with a university-level workshop series. The purpose of our study was to determine the degree to which conditions conducive to the transfer of TA workshop training were present at our university, and to use the results for guiding our strategic planning efforts and improve the effectiveness of the TA development program.

DESCRIPTION OF THE STUDY

In the spring of 2000, a survey was conducted of TAs who took workshops in either fall 1999 or spring 2000. Of the 198 surveys mailed, 69 were returned after an emailed follow-up reminder. Twenty-two graduate students participated in the fall 1999 workshop series, while 25 attended the spring 2000 workshops (two students did not declare which semester they participated), yielding a 34.8% return. The responders represented five colleges and 31 academic departments; 31 were male, 36 were female, and two did not declare their gender. Their previous teaching experience ranged from zero to six semesters.

The survey consisted of two parts. Part one included 17 statements paralleling Notarianni-Girard's earlier survey. The respondents were asked to rate the degree they agreed or disagreed with the statement. The statements were then grouped into the four areas representing her earlier research questions.

The first group of survey items was designed to determine the extent of facilitating factors present in the work environment of teaching assistants who attended our workshop series (see Appendix 7.1, Research Questions Group I).

The next set of statements were designed to determine to what extent inhibiting factors are present in the work environment of teaching assistants who attended our workshop series (see Appendix 7.1, Research Questions Group II).

Notarianni-Girard's third research question, "To what extent did/do teaching assistants perceive supervisor support before, during, and after training?" was addressed through the next set of survey items (see Appendix 7.1, Research Questions Group III).

The fourth research question answered in Notarianni-Girard's earlier study was addressed through the fourth group of survey items (see Appendix 7.1, Research Questions Group IV).

Part two of the survey consisted of 15 questions soliciting demographic information, suggestions for new workshop topics and formats, and other comments. Questions on demographics asked for students' gender, native language, college of enrollment, academic department, which workshop series they attended, how many semesters they had been teaching, whether their participation in the workshop was before or during their teaching assistantship, the perceived usefulness of the workshop both before and after attending, their motive for taking the workshop, whether the workshop was required or voluntary, when they started their graduate program, and when they anticipated finishing.

RESULTS

Response totals for survey questions one through three are reported in Table 7.1.

TABLE 7.1
Response Totals for Survey Questions 1–3
(Out of 69 Respondents)

Survey Questions	Yes	No	Don't Know
At the conclusion of the graduate teaching development workshops, I met with my supervisor to discuss how we would evaluate my teaching.	7	59	
TAs who receive low evaluations for their job performance are provided with supplemental teaching assistance.	11	31	14
My department provided me with information about the Graduate Teaching Development workshops.	50	17	

Questions 4 through 17 were tabulated according to their mean response on a 5-point scale, with 1 indicating strongly disagree and 5, strongly agree. Their results are reported in Figure 7.1.

FIGURE 7.1
Response Means for Survey Questions 4–17

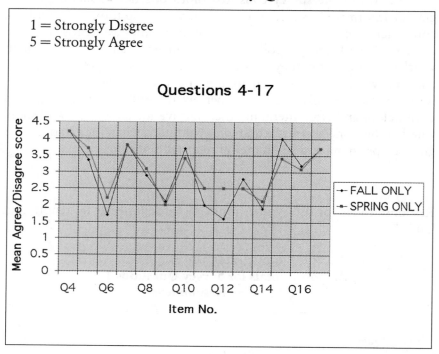

Survey items 2, 3, 4, 7, 10, and 17 had to do with the degree to which factors that facilitate transfer of training exist at our university. One obvious factor is the availability of information on training workshops. This factor is present at our university, evidenced by the percentage of respondents (50 out of 69 respondents, or 72%) who said that their department provided them with information about the workshops. Most respondents agreed (mean score 4.2 out of 5.0) that innovations or ideas they have about teaching are supported within the course they teach, and that they feel they have the freedom to conduct their teaching as they wish (3.8 out of 5.0). In addition, most respondents agreed (3.6 out of 5.0) that their TA schedule allowed them time to apply what they learned in the workshops. Finally, most agreed (3.7 out of 5.0) that their department provided sufficient resources (equipment, mentors, secretarial help) for them to be successful in carrying out their instructional responsibilities.

One item indicated an inhibiting factor in transfer training effects. Most respondents (80% of those responding to this question) reported either "no" (31 out of 56) or "don't know" (14 out of 56) when asked if TAs who receive low performance evaluations are provided with supplemental teaching assistance.

The responses to items 6, 8, and 9 have to do with the degree to which factors inhibiting the transfer of training exist at our university. Most respondents disagreed (1.9 out of 5.0) that their ideas for enhancing teaching were discouraged. Most were neutral or unsure of whether their department preferred they use familiar teaching strategies, while most disagreed (2.1 out of 5.0) that departmental rules and administrative details make it difficult for new ideas they have to receive consideration.

Items 1, 5, 11, 13, and 15 had to do with the degree to which teaching assistants receive supervisor support before, during, and after training. Most respondents (59 out of 66, or 89%) did not meet with their supervisors after training to discuss how they might have their teaching evaluated. Most respondents agreed (3.6 out of 5.0) that their supervisor was enthusiastic about their participation in the training workshops. Most did not meet with their supervisor (2.3 out of 5.0) to discuss ways to implement ideas they learned in the workshops into the classroom, nor to discuss the quality of their teaching (2.6 out of 5.0). However, most TAs perceive that their supervisor listens to their suggestions for implementing the ideas acquired during the workshops into their course (3.7 out of 5.0).

Items 12, 14, and 16 surveyed the extent to which the TAs perceived peer support before, during, and after the workshops. Most TAs did not meet regularly with other workshop TAs to discuss implementing new teaching ideas (2.0 out of 5.0), nor did they have TAs who previously attended workshops as mentors to discuss implementing new ideas (1.9 out of 5.0) A slight majority (3.2 out of 5.0) felt it was a strength having TAs from the same department attend the training with them.

SURVEY CONCLUSIONS

In general, teaching assistants agreed that factors facilitating the transfer of their workshop training to the classroom were present at our university. They were informed about the workshops beforehand, they perceived a supportive environment in their courses for innovative ideas, they felt they were free to conduct their teaching as they wished, their schedules permitted them time to apply what they learned in training to the classroom, and they felt their departments provided sufficient resources for the successful carrying out of their jobs. However, a sizable group (31 out of 69) felt that their peers who received low evaluations did not receive supplemental teaching assistance.

These results are consistent with the respondent data that Notarianni-Girard obtained from TAs at our university in her original study conducted the year before, namely that the consensus was agreement to the presence of facilitating factors existing in the TA work environment (Notarianni-Girard, 1999). Her data showed the same pattern for TAs who received poor evaluations: They apparently received no additional training.

In general, TAs agreed that conditions inhibiting the transfer of training effects were not present in their working environment. They did not feel discouraged from pursuing ideas to enhance their teaching, they were neutral or not sure if their department preferred they use familiar teaching strategies, and they felt their new ideas were considered and not hindered by department rules or administrative details. These results again were consistent with the earlier data collected from TAs at our university by Notarianni-Girard, although in her sample, most respondents felt their department preferred familiar teaching strategies.

The most serious indication for lack of transfer of training factors came from the data on supervisor support. The majority (89%) of respondents did not meet with their supervisor after training to discuss implementing the ideas they learned or the quality of their teaching, even though they felt their supervisors were enthusiastic about their involvement in training and listened to suggestions on how to implement workshop ideas. These results also echoed the data from Notarianni-Girard's study, which showed that most TAs did not meet with their supervisor to discuss implementing training or to discuss teaching quality before, during, or after training.

Questions 15 and 16 reflect a difference between males and females. Females (3.9 out of 5.0) were more likely to report that their supervisor listened to their suggestions on how to implement ideas acquired from the training workshops than their male peers (3.4 out of 5.0). Females were also more likely (3.5 out of 5.0) to find having TAs from the same department attend the training workshops with them a strength than their male peers (2.6 out of 5.0). This may reflect that females are discussing their training more with their departmental peers and supervisors than males.

Data on peer support also suggested a lack of transfer of training factors: most were not meeting with their peers to discuss implementing new ideas or being mentored by TAs who previously attended workshops. Only a slight majority agreed that having TAs from the same department attend the training with them was a strength. This trend was also prevalent in Notarianni-Girard's earlier data.

We also found a difference in the response means between the TAs who taught in English as a second language on items 14 and 16 (2.4 and 2.3, respectively) versus TAs teaching in English as a first language (1.68 and 3.5, respectively). Apparently, international TAs are more likely to meet with TAs who previously attended our workshops to discuss implementing teaching ideas than do their native English speaking counterparts. On the other hand, international TAs are less likely to consider attending training workshops with peers from their own department a strength than do native English speaking TAs. They may be grouping with compatriots from their native cultures outside their departments.

IMPLICATIONS FOR PROGRAM AND EVALUATION REFORM

From these data we are investing efforts in three areas to facilitate the transfer of training for graduate teaching assistants on our campus. First, to encourage TAs to discuss their teaching and training ideas regularly after our one-day training workshops which happen at the beginning of each semester, we will begin hosting more follow-up sessions throughout the semester. Additionally, we are developing a cohesive network of TA facilitators who assist with and coteach our university-wide workshops and college-based workshops to foster informal, departmental-based discussions of teaching and learning. The facilitators can act as liaisons with their local departments and colleges to keep us informed of evolving issues and needs.

Secondly, we are exploring ways of getting TAs to participate with their supervisors in events that support the ongoing discussion and review of teaching. We have initiated a discussion group with TAs and their supervisors who meet during the semester after the training workshops. These have been well attended by both TAs and faculty. We are developing materials that workshop participants can take back to their supervisors to support the transfer of training. These materials will help supervisors to clarify teaching goals, monitor skill development, and provide ongoing, evaluative feedback.

Finally, we are revising the ways in which we evaluate TA training programs to include more post-training data-gathering. Currently, TAs have the opportunity to have midterm student evaluations of teaching tabulated with follow-up individual consultation. Because midterm evaluation and consultation is optional, only a subset of workshop participants benefits from these. We plan to be more proactive in the future by providing workshop participants information and encouragement for follow-up evaluation after the workshops.

One outcome of our study is a revision of our working definition of transfer of training to mean that the specific skills and learning outcomes conveyed in the training will be exhibited in the appropriate situation after the training. Thus, teaching skills will be manifested in the classroom, during office hours, or in the ways that TAs interact with students. Behaviors can be directly observed by an instructional developer or supervisor or recorded on videotape.

Some training outcomes may not involve observable behaviors, but changes in the way TAs think. This may be monitored by peer TAs who participated in the workshops at the same time, experienced TAs who can mentor newer teaching assistants, or by faculty supervisors. Through discussions and meetings both before and after the workshops, specific goals and learning outcomes for teaching assistants can be identified and periodically monitored.

REFERENCES

Detterman, D. K., & Sternberg, R. J. (Eds.). (1993). *Transfer on trial: Intelligence, cognition, and instruction.* Norwood, NJ: Ablex.

Huczynski, A. A. (1978). Approaches to the problems of learning transfer. *Journal of European Industrial Training, 2* (1), 26-31.

Huczynski, A. A., & Lewis, J. W. (1980). An empirical study into the learning transfer process in management training. *Journal of Management Studies, 17,* 227-240.

Lambert, L. M., & Tice, S. L. (1993). *Preparing graduate students to teach.* Washington, DC: American Association for Higher Education.

Noe, R. A. (1986). Trainees' attributes and attitudes: Neglected influences on training effectiveness. *Academy of Management Review, 11* (4), 736-749.

Notarianni-Girard, D. (1999, Spring). Transfer of training in teaching assistant programs. *Journal of Graduate Teaching Assistant Development, 6* (3), 119-147.

Showers, B., Joyce, B., & Bennett, B. (1987). Synthesis of research in staff development: A framework for future study. *Educational Leadership, 45,* 77-87.

Contact:

David G. Way
Center for Learning and Teaching
Cornell University
420D Computing and Communications Center
Garden Avenue
Ithaca, NY 14853
(607) 255-2663
(607) 255-1562 (Fax)
Email: Dgw2@cornell.edu
Web: www.clt.cornell.edu

Virleen M. Carlson
Assistant Director for Instructional Support
Center for Learning and Teaching
Cornell University
415 Computing and Communications Center
Garden Avenue
Ithaca, NY 14853-6601
(607) 255-8425
(607) 255-1562 (Fax)
Email: vmc3@cornell.edu

Susan C. Piliero
Associate Professor of Mathematics Education
Director of the Center for Learning and Teaching
420 Computing and Communications Center
Cornell University
Ithaca, NY 14853
(607) 255-6122
(607) 255-1562 (Fax)
Email: scp4@cornell.edu

David G. Way is Director of Instructional Support within the Center for Learning and Teaching at Cornell University. His work involves teaching development programs, including seminars and workshops on teaching, individual instructional consultation, and advising college administrators on effective teaching evaluation practices for improving the university learning and teaching climate.

Virleen M. Carlson holds a PhD in Curriculum and Instruction and wrote her dissertation on TA training. She works for the Center for Learning and Teaching at Cornell University, a centralized support unit, where she serves as the Assistant Director of Instructional Support.

Susan C. Piliero is Director of Cornell's Center for Teaching and Learning, an omnibus center that includes the Office of Instructional Support for teaching assistants and faculty, the International TA Training Program, the Learning Strategies Center, and Student Disabilities Services. She is also Associate Professor of Mathematics Education, contributes to Cornell's Teacher Education program, and chairs the University's Educational Policy Committee.

APPENDIX 7.1

Research Questions Group I

Item 2. TAs who receive low evaluations for their job performance are provided with supplemental teaching assistance. (Yes/No)

Item 3. My department provided me with information about the graduate TA development workshops. (Yes/No)

Item 4. The course in which I am a TA is supportive of innovations or ideas that TAs wish to try in their teaching and/or lab assignments. (5 = strongly agree; 3 = neutral/not sure; 1 = strongly disagree)

Item 7. In the course in which I am a TA, TAs have freedom to conduct their teaching and/or lab assignments as they wish. (5 = strongly agree; 3 = neutral/not sure; 1 = strongly disagree)

Item 10. My TA schedule allows me time to apply what I learned in the TA development workshops. (5 = strongly agree; 3 = neutral/not sure; 1 = strongly disagree)

Item 17. The department in which I am a TA provides sufficient resources (e.g., equipment, secretarial help, mentors, etc.) for me to be successful in carrying out my job. (5 = strongly agree; 3 = neutral/not sure; 1 = strongly disagree)

Research Questions Group II

Item 6. When a TA suggests an idea or procedure to enhance teaching and/or lab assignments in my course, she or he is discouraged from pursuing them. (5 = strongly agree; 3 = neutral/not sure; 1 = strongly disagree)

Item 8. In the course in which I am a TA it is preferred that TAs use teaching strategies with which the department is familiar. (5 = strongly agree; 3 = neutral/not sure; 1 = strongly disagree)

Item 9. In my department, rules and administrative details make it difficult for new ideas of TAs to receive consideration. (5 = strongly agree; 3 = neutral/not sure; 1 = strongly disagree)

Research Questions Group III

Item 1. At the conclusion of the graduate teaching development workshops, I met with my supervisor to discuss how we would evaluate my teaching. (Yes/No)

Item 5. When the graduate teaching development workshops were first announced, my supervisor was enthusiastic about me becoming involved in them. (5 = strongly agree; 3 = neutral/not sure; 1 = strongly disagree)

Item 11. I meet regularly with my supervisor to discuss ways to implement ideas I learned in the graduate teaching development workshops into the classroom. (5 = strongly agree; 3 = neutral/not sure; 1 = strongly disagree)

Item 13. I meet regularly with my supervisor to discuss the quality of my teaching. (5 = strongly agree; 3 = neutral/not sure; 1 = strongly disagree)

Item 15. My supervisor listens to my suggestions on how to implement the ideas acquired during the graduate teaching development workshops into my courses. (5 = strongly agree; 3 = neutral/not sure; 1 = strongly disagree)

Research Questions Group IV

Item 12. I meet regularly with other TAs who were in the workshop with me to discuss implementation of the ideas learned in the graduate teaching development workshops. (5 = strongly agree; 3 = neutral/not sure; 1 = strongly disagree)

Item 14. I meet regularly with TAs who previously attended the graduate teaching development workshops as my mentors to discuss implementation of the TA training methods and ideas. (5 = strongly agree; 3 = neutral/not sure; 1 = strongly disagree)

Item 16. A strength of the graduate teaching development workshops was having TAs from the same department attend the training with me. (5 = strongly agree; 3 = neutral/not sure; 1 = strongly disagree)

8

Mandatory Faculty Development Works

Mona B. Kreaden
New York University

This chapter tells the story of a successful, ongoing, mandatory faculty development program. It explains the historical reasons why a business school in a large, urban Research I institution felt the need to make their program mandatory, examines how it was developed, and the university faculty development program's role in the process. The author makes the case that mandatory programs can be successful in faculty development when they are administered by an outside credible entity, are faculty driven, and guarantee confidentiality.

INTRODUCTION

It is the conventional wisdom of faculty development practitioners that requiring faculty to participate in teaching improvement efforts would be unsuccessful because of resentment and resistance on the part of those who are being forced to participate (Morrison, 1997; Sorcinelli, 1997). Faculty members guard their autonomy and would treat any mandatory program as a threat to their academic freedom and integrity.

Yet, the Stern School of Business at New York University (NYU) has been successful in implementing the Stern Teaching Effectiveness Program (STEP), a mandatory process that requires all faculty members to participate in teaching improvement efforts. Faculty unanimously accepted its guidelines in 1996, and STEP is in the middle of its third two-year cycle (January 2001).

The purpose of this chapter is to highlight how mandatory programs can be successful in faculty development when they are administered by an outside credible source, are faculty driven, and guarantee confidentiality.

THE STERN SCHOOL OF BUSINESS
FACULTY DEVELOPMENT PROGRAM

Since the early 1990s, business schools increasingly competed for stature, and students' opinions of the teaching quality became increasingly important. In order to maintain the stature and standards of the Stern School of Business, the school's dean placed more emphasis on teaching quality for tenure, promotion, and merit decisions. For instance, in tenure decisions, while outstanding research generally remains as a top priority, highly effective teaching became an important consideration. This increased attention to teaching quality created the challenge of how to provide adequate support for faculty to meet the new standards.

In fall 1995, Stern's faculty council formed the Stern School Teaching Effectiveness Committee (comprised of respected Stern faculty), and charged them with the task of establishing a program that would improve teaching throughout the school. The committee met often and worked diligently to develop a proposal that was presented at the spring semester all-faculty meeting.

The EQUAL Commission (an NYU initiative to Enhance the Quality of Undergraduate Academic Life) was created in 1993 as a faculty development program whose mission focused on improving teaching effectiveness throughout New York University. The director of EQUAL was known to several committee members and was invited to attend one of the meetings to discuss various efforts EQUAL was employing to improve teaching at NYU.

She discussed the efficacy of private one-to-one consultations (Piccinin, 1999) and close observations placing an emphasis on formative evaluation (Wilkerson, 1988), a form of feedback meant to help the instructor improve teaching separate and apart from summative evaluation for promotion and tenure purposes. She also stressed the importance of confidentiality in order to build trust between the faculty member and consultant.

The director offered a variety of observation processes: Small Group Instructional Diagnosis (S.G.I.D.) (Diamond, 1988) (see Appendix 8.1) as a way of engaging the students in the formative process; classroom observation while the instructor is videotaped; and a classroom observation without video. Each of these involves a pre-observation meeting between faculty member and consultant, along with follow up discussions about the observation. Subsequent visits are arranged as requested.

EQUAL's director stressed the importance of these processes being voluntary. In order to get the best results she emphasized the necessity of faculty having a wide choice of observation methods in order to serve different teaching styles, class size and type, and instructor comfort level during the process.

The committee expressed concern that a voluntary program would not attract those needing teaching support the most and making it remedial would disadvantage faculty who were singled out. They believed that requiring every faculty member to participate in the program would be more effective. The committee did, however, take the EQUAL director's other suggestion about giving each faculty member the choice of observation offerings. Thus, the Stern Teaching Effectiveness Program (STEP) was drafted (Stern School of Business, 1996).

In addition, Stern's Teaching Committee members realized that instituting a mandatory program for faculty, without prior consent, would not engender program success. At a school-wide faculty meeting, STEP was presented and after discussion, voted upon. Despite the unorthodoxy of launching a mandatory teaching program, the faculty-at-large agreed to pilot test STEP for two years in order to gauge its effectiveness. Because the pilot was approved by the faculty-at-large, it stood a good chance of succeeding (Stern School of Business, 1996) (see Appendix 8.1 for the approved program).

Implementation

Once the pilot testing of STEP was approved, the vice dean of faculty was required to implement it and make sure it succeeded. He met with EQUAL's director in order to find out if EQUAL would be able to support three of the four evaluative procedures in STEP. (In addition to the processes the director had suggested above, Stern faculty opted for peer observation as well, where faculty members exchange observation visits.) The director agreed to provide support for STEP, if Stern would provide the resources to hire the number of consultants required to serve approximately 200 full-time faculty members.

Logistics

To avoid the possibility of 200 people requesting consultations in one semester, Stern's vice dean and EQUAL's director devised a schedule to ensure that consultations would be spread out over the full two-year pilot program, approximately 50 per semester (Table 8.1).

An initial cohort of seven part-time consultants was recruited and trained from existing full- and part-time faculty at NYU and other institutions in the area. This number has grown to 12 part-time plus one full-time faculty development consultant as demand for consultations grew. Consultants are paid on a per-consultation basis, rather than hourly.

Over the length of the pilot, both Stern's vice dean and EQUAL's director kept close watch on the flow of consultations, and carried on an active email dialogue with each other on its progress. At all times, consultations and reports were (and continue to be) confidential.

TABLE 8.1
Breakdown of Consultations Performed by Semester and Type

	Fall 1996	Spring 1997	Fall 1997	Spring 1998
Observations	12	3	8	13
Videos	5	21	24	15
S.G.I.D.s	10	6	13	7
Peer Reviews	14	23	5	16
Totals	41	53	50	51

Consulting Requirements

Taking into consideration the culture of the business school, EQUAL's director knew that it was important to have consultants who were effective lecturers and teachers of large classes, as well as good discussion leaders. She also understood the importance that Stern faculty placed on content coverage and made sure to recruit consultants from Stern's Management Communication Department to serve those who felt that the understanding of content was important to the consultant's ability to give good feedback. After the first two years, there were very few faculty requests for consultants with content expertise.

Consultant Recruitment

The recruitment of consultants was and continues to be based on the following criteria.

- At least three years' experience teaching in a college classroom

- Highly seasoned consultants who would work with more senior faculty

- Excellent reputations as teachers

- Respected as serious academics who are invested in their teaching and experienced in different pedagogical techniques, in addition to the straight lecture method

- A teaching philosophy that is student-centered

Consultant Training

Every consultant hired is observed teaching or comes highly recommended by other faculty who understand what EQUAL is looking for. As part of the consultants' orientation, they each meet individually with the director for about one hour and a half to discuss the requirements of the consulting process. They also are encouraged to contact the director with any questions or problems they encountered throughout the process.

EQUAL's director is aware that despite unanimous approval for the STEP pilot, Stern faculty may be reluctant and possibly resentful to participate in a required program. And she understands that the consultants have to be trained in order to achieve satisfactory results. In her meetings with the consultants, she stresses that every professor who requests a consultation from EQUAL must walk away from the experience with three results.

1) A feeling that they had a positive experience in the consultation— that the process "wasn't so bad"

2) A solid teaching suggestion that they can exercise without too much difficulty in the next class meeting

3) A discussion with the consultant that focuses on the faculty member's approach toward teaching

Assigning Consultants

It was important to know if faculty attitudes toward participation are resistant to participate, eager, or acquiescent because it is required. In general, faculty express the attitude that if they are going to have do it, they "may as well get something out of it." With an eye toward making the instructor feel as relaxed and open as possible, seniority, gender, attitude, and class size are taken into consideration when assigning consultants.

Because of the large numbers of faculty involved in STEP, individual interviews with applicants are not possible. Therefore, an application form was designed describing the options faculty members can choose, and to gather enough information to assign appropriate consultants. This application also gives the assigned consultant information to open a discussion when meeting the instructor prior to the observation (see Appendix 8.2 for a sample form).

Methodology. Consultants are trained to always be positive and to approach the process in a collaborative way—as a colleague who has been invited to give feedback rather than to evaluate. They are instructed to listen carefully to what the instructor wants to talk about—to follow, rather than lead. And if there is some glaring thing that the instructor is doing unconsciously, the consultant is to use tact and diplomacy when inserting it into the dialogue—usually by asking a question rather than making a statement (e.g., "I notice that when you are doing thus and such, you.... What is the effect you intend when you do that?"). Feedback from faculty who have been observed indicates that this method is effective.

Process
In order to build trust, consultants meet with the instructor prior to the class. This allows the instructor the opportunity to meet the person entering his or her classroom and for both to discuss teaching goals and issues. At all times, the discussion is positive and supportive, and if the teacher indicates dissatisfaction with the mandatory process, the consultant expresses empathy in a collegial manner.

After the classroom observation or S.G.I.D., the consultant and faculty member meet once more to debrief. This meeting is crucial to the consultation's success. In order to create a relaxed and open environment, the consultant must be empathetic and collaborative in his or her manner. Consequently, the faculty member will be more open to suggestions and more willing to implement them. Consultants are encouraged to offer follow-up support should the instructor wish to try some new teaching techniques. However, any further collaboration must be voluntary on the instructor's part.

Follow-up
After each consultation, a feedback form is sent to the participating faculty member. This assures quality control over the consultants' work, as well as providing feedback for subsequent consultations. Frequently, instructors ask for further information on a particular pedagogy, which al-

lows for and encourages follow-up discussions. In the few instances where consultations were unsatisfactory, the director contacted the professor to determine the cause. In those cases, the dissatisfaction related to the "mandatory" nature of the process. Faculty members consistently report that the process itself has been a positive and useful learning experience (see Appendix 8.2 for typical qualitative faculty feedback about the process).

Ongoing consultant training. The consulting cohort meets at least once a semester to review their requirements and discuss their experiences working with Stern faculty. They often talk about specific consultations and the kinds of issues they are dealing with during the process of the STEP program. To honor the confidentiality of the clients, faculty names are never revealed.

These meetings serve as a continuing development process for the consultants as they discuss their experiences. They obtain ideas and advice from each other and in learning about others' experiences, they can be prepared for the unanticipated. In every case, the consultants report that this process has helped them learn about their own teaching. In addition, EQUAL supplies the faculty consultants with up-to-date reading materials related to the consultation process (see Appendix 8.4 for a current list of readings).

OUTCOMES AND CONCLUSION

At the end of the two-year pilot period (1996–1998) Stern faculty evaluated the program. They unanimously voted to make STEP a permanent part of Stern's faculty development efforts.

Based on qualitative feedback from faculty, analysis of student evaluations, and discussions with faculty participants, Stern's administration deemed the project a success. They concluded:

> Summarily, the administration and the faculty are extremely pleased with the program. The Stern Teaching Effectiveness Program continues to fulfill its initial mission by placing significant emphasis on program delivery and the highest quality education. We also are delighted to report that STEP's success is also renowned outside the Stern School of Business. In fact, it is fast becoming a model for the rest of the University, and for other schools. In our recent AACSB (American Assembly of Collegiate Schools of Business) accreditation review, the program was

praised as an innovative and distinctive feature, and should, in the words of the AACSB consultants, be replicated nationwide.

The Stern School of Business is committed to this endeavor and understands the effect on the overall curriculum as well as the importance of good communication and platform skills to instructional effectiveness, and its subsequent and lasting impact on learning. STEP will remain an integral part of the Stern School's ongoing process of skill development and enhancement. (Stern School of Business, 1999)

As EQUAL concluded the second two-year cycle of STEP, there has been a marked increase in voluntary follow-up requests for consultations in addition to the one-time required biannual "checkup." Faculty members have had the experience of being observed in a nonthreatening way, are more trusting of the consultants, and are contacting them independently as they feel the need—signs that they are more invested in their teaching. In addition, Stern faculty are talking more about teaching in formal and informal settings. In Hutchings's (2000) terms, they have begun to develop a culture of teaching.

Unexpected benefits of this program have been

- increased alumni contributions as they learned about Stern's efforts toward improving teaching effectiveness

- other schools, departments, and programs throughout the university are now encouraged by Stern's success to experiment with structured programs that suit their individual cultures

- increased revenues to EQUAL allowed for the hiring of a full-time faculty development consultant, which enhanced its credibility and visibility, and made faculty development a more respected and supported program by the central administration

The STEP program is successful for several interrelated reasons.

- It was designed by a faculty committee and agreed to by the faculty-at-large

- The school turned to a credible and respected faculty development program to administer it

- EQUAL's director made the effort to understand the Stern culture and trained the consulting cohort accordingly, with quality control and continuous reinforcement

- Confidentiality is guaranteed

Looking toward the future, a more systematic investigation needs to be designed to evaluate student learning outcomes and teaching improvement. However, client satisfaction with the mandatory process is a necessary first step.

ACKNOWLEDGMENTS

Special thanks to Stephanie Nickerson and Patrick McCreery for their assistance in preparing this essay.

REFERENCES

Diamond, N. (1988). S.G.I.D. (Small group instructional diagnosis): Tapping student perceptions of teaching. In E. C. Wadsworth (Ed.), *A handbook for new practitioners* (pp. 89-93). Stillwater, OK: New Forums Press.

Hutchings, P. (2000). Promoting a culture of teaching and learning. In D. DeZure (Ed.), *Learning from* Change: *Landmarks in teaching and learning in higher education from* Change *Magazine 1969-1999* (pp. 1-4). Sterling, VA: Stylus.

Morrison, D. (1997). Overview of instructional consultation in North America. In K. T. Brinko & R. T. Menges (Eds.), *Practically speaking: A sourcebook for instructional consultants in higher education* (pp. 121-130). Stillwater, OK: New Forums Press.

Piccinin, S. (1999). How individual consultation affects teaching. In C. Knapper & S. Piccinin (Eds.), *Using consultants to improve teaching* (pp. 71-83). New Directions for Teaching and Learning, No. 79. San Francisco, CA: Jossey-Bass.

Sorcinelli, M. D. (1997). The teaching improvement process. In K. T. Brinko & R. T. Menges (Eds.), *Practically speaking: A sourcebook for instructional consultants in higher education* (pp. 157-158). Stillwater, OK: New Forums Press.

Stern School of Business. (1996). *Stern teaching effectiveness program (STEP).* Unpublished report, New York University, Stern School Teaching Effectiveness Committee.

Stern School of Business. (1999). *Stern teaching effectiveness program activities report: Academic year 1998-99.* Unpublished report, New York University.

Wilkerson, L. (1988). Classroom observation: The observer as collaborator. In E. C. Wadsworth (Ed.), *A handbook for new practitioners* (pp. 95-98). Stillwater, OK: New Forums Press.

Contact:

Mona Kreaden
3 East 69th Street
New York, NY 10021
(212) 737-1752
(212) 794-3084 (Fax)
Email: mona.kreaden@nyu.edu
Web: www.nyu.edu/projects/teaching/resources

Mona Kreaden was founding Director of EQUAL (an NYU initiative to Enhance the Quality of Undergraduate Academic Life), New York University's campus-wide faculty development initiative, which has been transformed into the Center for Teaching Excellence. Her expertise is in program development and change management. She is currently doing international consulting on how to get started in faculty development.

APPENDIX 8.1
STERN TEACHING EFFECTIVENESS PROGRAM (STEP)

Prepared by the Stern School Teaching Effectiveness Committee
Bruce Buchanan, Eric Greenleaf, Richard Levich (Secretary),
Christine Kelly, William Silber (Chair), Richard Sylla;
Thomas Pugel, Frederick Choi (*ex-officio*)

Adopted by the Stern School Faculty, May 1996

Background

The creation of a Teaching Effectiveness Committee was proposed by the Faculty Council and ratified in the Fall 1995 faculty meeting. The committee was charged with the responsibility of "designing a formal teaching effectiveness program for the Stern School . . . including a training program to introduce new faculty to teaching at Stern, to be put in place by the beginning of the 1996–97 academic year." We were not charged with and we did not address the evaluation of teaching performance. The Teaching Effectiveness Committee met throughout the Fall 1995 semester and presents this report for consideration by the faculty.

This report reflects the discussion at an open meeting of the faculty on March 27, and additional feedback from faculty colleagues.

Introduction

Anecdotal evidence suggests that teaching at Stern is quite good. Our goal is to see that teaching at Stern becomes even better. To do this, we want to raise the level of consciousness about teaching, and make teaching an integral feature of Stern's culture. To some degree, this consciousness-raising has already begun. In hiring, promotion and tenure decisions, increasing emphasis is being placed on teaching effectiveness. Teaching statements and teaching materials are part of each faculty member's dossier. We hope to make discussions about teaching part of the culture at Stern, much as discussions about research are already a part of that culture.

The main body of our proposal focuses on *diagnostics* designed to help faculty identify how to improve teaching effectiveness. Diagnostics should encompass both the delivery and substance dimensions of teaching. The committee feels that the proposal should treat all faculty equally—whether young or old, tenured or untenured, tenure-track or clinical, proficient at teaching or not. However, we also feel that it is reasonable to place separate requirements on first-year faculty to help them adapt to the Stern teaching culture.

Pilot Program
The committee recommends that we pilot the new program (Stern Teaching Effectiveness Program, or STEP) for two years. The first-year faculty will participate in both pilot years. Other faculty will participate in either year one or two. During the second year of the pilot program, the committee will evaluate the program and make a recommendation to the full faculty for adoption. If STEP is adopted, the committee will address issues of how adjunct faculty should be treated.

Diagnostics
The committee recommends that all faculty members participate in the process to enhance teaching effectiveness. The process we propose calls for each faculty member to take a more in-depth look at his or her teaching effectiveness. The committee thinks that there are many ways to obtain feedback on teaching effectiveness, and that a faculty member should be allowed to choose from a set of alternatives.

Diagnostic Alternatives
After considering a number of alternatives, the committee proposes four specific diagnostic processes:

(i) *Videotaping.* A classroom session is videotaped and evaluated by a trained consultant. The faculty member and consultant review the tape. The consultant offers suggestions for improving teaching effectiveness.

(ii) *Audit by Communications Expert.* A classroom session is audited and evaluated by a trained consultant. The faculty member and the consultant review the consultant's evaluation. The consultant offers suggestions for improving teaching effectiveness.

(iii) *Small Group Instructional Diagnostic.* A classroom session is audited by a trained consultant. Toward the end of the class, the instructor leaves the room and the consultant takes over. Students are divided into groups of 4–8 and given about 3 minutes to discuss each of three questions: What do you like about the class, what needs improvement in the class, and what specific suggestions do you have for improving the class? The class reassembles, and the consultant invites each group to report back their answers to the three questions. Discussion develops during the reporting process. The consultant writes a report and meets with the faculty member to review the suggestions. [This aspect of the process differentiates it from a "focus group" run by a trained facilitator who might not be familiar with teaching.] The faculty member completes the process by discussing the results with the class and deciding what steps (if any) will be taken.

(iv) *Peer Review/Faculty Pairing.* A classroom session is attended by a fellow faculty member, who then provides feedback on possible ways to improve teaching effectiveness.

More About the Diagnostic Process

(i) *Confidentiality.* The committee thinks that the results of the annual diagnostic choice must be held confidential. The videotape and all copies of reports must be turned over to the faculty member at the end of the process. The purpose of the diagnostic process is to improve teaching effectiveness, not to provide an alternative measurement and/or reporting method on attained teaching performance.

(ii) *Professional and Impartial Evaluation.* The committee thinks that (except when the Peer Review/Faculty Pairing option is chosen) the diagnostic evaluation must be performed by a professionally trained consultant.

(iii) *The Small Group Instructional Diagnostic.* The committee hopes that faculty would find it in their interest to try this diagnostic procedure, which is already being offered at NYU through the EQUAL commission. A number of Stern faculty have recently tried this technique and have been happy with the results. A one-page description of the program is attached for your information.

(iv) *Peer Review/Faculty Pairing.* The faculty member undergoing review should select a faculty reviewer in consultation with his or her department Chair.

First-Year Faculty

The committee believes that first-year faculty should be required to make additional preparations to enhance their teaching effectiveness, and increase their familiarity with the teaching culture at Stern. We propose three components for first-year faculty:

(i) *Orientation: Workshop.* First-year faculty should be required to attend the orientation workshop on teaching organized by the Management Communication area.

(ii) *First Semester: Audit Stern MBA Classes.* Most first-year faculty are granted a reduced teaching load of two rather than three Stern classes. The committee proposes that during their first semester at Stern, first-year faculty be required to audit (attend) classes of experienced faculty. In many cases, it would be desirable to audit classes of the course that the new faculty member will teach in the Spring semester, but this need not be a requirement. The details of the audit could be worked out with the department chairperson. The faculty member would submit a report on these activities as part of the annual Faculty Activities Report.

(iii) *Second Semester: Diagnostic Alternatives.* In the second (Spring) semester, the first-year faculty member would select from among the four alternatives provided to other Stern faculty (videotape, expert audit, small group diagnostic, or peer review).

Faculty Responsibilities

To insure that faculty participate in the diagnostic process, we recommend that each faculty member report which diagnostic procedure he or she elected on the annual Faculty Activities Report.

Oversight of the STEP Program

Based on feedback from the open meeting, we recommend that STEP be implemented using a decentralized approach. The Dean's office will provide the resources necessary for arranging the alternative STEP diagnostics. Department Chairs will inform faculty about the scheduling and availability of alternative STEP diagnostics, and work informally to smooth the demand for STEP diagnostics throughout the pilot program. The Stern Teaching Effectiveness Committee will retain an oversight role to monitor the overall design and implementation of the STEP initiative.

Culture Building

In addition to the STEP proposal, the committee discussed other initiatives that might be implemented to enhance the culture of teaching at Stern.

(i) *Multiple Section Courses:* We suggest that in all multiple section courses (such as the core, but perhaps also in elective courses), faculty meet for discussions of teaching effectiveness and delivery as well as for content. Core-course faculty already meet regularly and could reallocate some discussion time toward teaching effectiveness issues. Faculty in multiple sections of non-core courses should develop a mechanism for meeting on these issues.

(ii) *Teaching Retreat:* The Dean's Office might arrange an ongoing series or a periodic off-campus program, where sessions on teaching practice would be given to and by faculty. Specific activities could include the following: (a) Faculty member gives a class, or a case, to colleagues which is followed by a discussion of the teaching technique and its success; (b) Faculty meet in groups to review and discuss class tapes; (c) Core course faculty meet to discuss interactions among the core courses; (d) Faculty with particularly innovative teaching ideas, such as multi-media or computer-assisted teaching, present them to other faculty.

(iii) *Teaching Resources Center:* We suggest that the Dean's Office establish a library of teaching materials, such as classroom videos, cases, examinations, and so forth to help faculty improve teaching skills on their own.

Conclusions

The objective of the STEP program is not necessarily to make everyone a teaching "superstar." Rather, the program is designed to make an already highly effective teaching faculty even better. We expect that everyone's teaching effectiveness will be enhanced by the diagnostic procedures proposed here, as well as by the increased attention paid to the teaching process.

APPENDIX 8.2

APPLICATION: STERN **STEP** PROGRAM
BACKGROUND INFORMATION

Contact Information

Name:_____

(Please circle) Full, Associate, Assistant, Adjunct, Clinical, TA,
          Ph.D. Student, Post Doc.

School: _____ Dept: _____
Phone: _____

Office Address:_____Fax: _____
Mail Code:_____

Course Name & # : _____
Grad: _____ Undergrad: _____

Class Location: _____ Day & Time: _____
# of Students: _____

Years at NYU? _____Email: _____

Service Requested:
Observation _____ **Video w/ observation** _____ **S.G.I.D.** _____
Preferred Dates: (1) _____ (2) _____ (3) _____
          (Please choose dates at least 10 business days
          after application submission)

Please answer the following questions to help us select the best consultant for you.
*If necessary, use a separate page. Upon completion, mail or fax **two copies of***
***your syllabus,** your answers and this form to the above address. If your syllabus*
is on the Web, please write the URL so we can access it easily._____

1. Describe briefly the content and structure of your course.

2. What are your course objectives?

3. What do you see as your strengths in teaching this course?

4. Do you have any specific teaching issues that you are interested in exploring?

5. What do you hope to get out of this process?

6. Why are you requesting this particular type of service?

7. Indicate your preference for faculty consultant:
   From Stern _____ Not from Stern _____

How to Take Advantage of EQUAL's Faculty Consultation Services

EQUAL consultants do not judge your performance
but rather observe and offer feedback.
All consultations are strictly CONFIDENTIAL.

Choose your method...

EQUAL provides three types of in-class service: **Observation, Observation with Video** and **Small Group Instructional Diagnosis (S.G.I.D.).**

Observation: At a mutually convenient time, an EQUAL consultant will sit in on your class and then review his or her confidential observation notes with you.

Video with Observation: Videotaping gives you information about your teaching style, and very often the picture *is* worth a thousand words. The effectiveness of an observation is often enhanced by simultaneous video taping. At the end of class, you are given the video to view privately prior to your consultation. You also receive a checklist to help focus the discussion. At a mutually convenient time, an EQUAL consultant will review his or her confidential observation notes and video with you.

Small Group Instructional Diagnosis (S.G.I.D.): S.G.I.D. is an assessment technique using small student group discussion to strengthen a course, increase student/teacher communication and improve teaching performance. An EQUAL consultant observes your class and after you leave the room, divides students into small groups to address these questions: *What do you like about this class? What do you think needs improvement? What suggestions would you make?* Results are tabulated and presented to you during a confidential one-on-one consultation. This method identifies problem areas and generates alternative solutions. Secondary benefits can include increased student interest, acceptance of course methodology and improved end of semester evaluations. The S.G.I.D. is done at **mid-semester** which allows time for course changes,

⁻ocess takes the last 20 to 30 minutes of class
)–45 minutes).

Return the application...

..ant will meet with you in advance to learn about your goals, ob-
..ves, strengths and concerns. This helps him or her to better observe
your class, analyze your video or work with your students. **When apply-
ing, make sure you answer all the questions and attach two copies of
your syllabus to help facilitate this pre-observation discussion.**

Inform your students...

Our office will take care of the logistics and send you a written confirma-
tion. Run your class as usual but inform your students that a videogra-
pher and/or consultant will be present.

Meet with your consultant...

After the observation and at a convenient time, your consultant will meet
with you to review the observation notes, video or S.G.I.D. results.
**EQUAL consultants do not judge your performance but rather observe
and offer feedback. All consultations are strictly CONFIDENTIAL.**

Tell us how we're doing...

After completing your consultation, you will be mailed an evaluative
feedback form by our office. Your suggestions and advice are important
to us!

Appendix 8.3
Typical Faculty Feedback About the Consulting Process

What Did You Like About This Process?

3/99 An Information Systems Professor: "I just want to thank you for your truly outstanding mid-semester evaluation of my new class. I just went through the notes again and I am still impressed by how many insights you manage to convey. I have no doubt that what you have taught me will be very useful far beyond this course. Thank you."

3/99 A Marketing Professor. "Specific things that I liked were that [the consultant] talked to me about my objectives before class, but left me some time to get things together beforehand. She was unobtrusive in class and able to debrief promptly. She did a great job of tracking and diagramming what happened in class—an interesting perspective for me. She had some theory to offer that gave me useful labels for some things that I do and insight into relationships between teaching and learning (but didn't do this in a heavy-handed way). She kept my objectives in mind and responded to them thoughtfully. Finally, she didn't feel a need to spend more time discussing things than I found useful."

3/99 An Award Winning Finance Professor: "Unobtrusive observation with excellent suggestions and comments. [The consultant] observed details about the classroom that I was never aware of. Excellent comments."

11/98 A Management Professor: "It was a great opportunity to have someone who has terrific pedagogical sensibilities give objective feedback on the design and delivery of a course in a subject that was new to the observer. And it was non-threatening!"

What Suggestions Would You Make?

4/98 An International Business Professor: "A series of sessions."

4/98 An Accounting Professor: "Perhaps for those of us who want it, a follow-up visit (by the same consultant) would be helpful, to see if some of his/her recommendations were effectively adopted."

12/97 A Management Professor: "Multiple observations would provide more representative data."

10/97 A Statistics Professor: "The course in teaching effectiveness probably should be extended beyond one class, i.e., three or four meetings.

Was the Consultant Responsive to Your Needs?

3/99 A Marketing Professor: "I found [the consultant] to be a total professional with an excellent understanding of feedback, classroom skill requirements, and the ability to explain her evaluation. Make sure that all consultants are as qualified, professional, sensitive and have equal communications skills."

11/98 A Management Professor: '[The consultant] displayed a high level of sensitivity and insight into the myriad of ideas, experiences and emotions that go into the development and delivery of a course. She helped me become aware of the strengths of my course design and reflected while creating a constructive context for improvement where appropriate."

2/98 An Economics Professor: "Everything was thoroughly professional! [The consultant] was unobtrusive; she did an excellent job. We met before class. I explained the 'procedure' in my approach to teaching. She blended in perfectly. Our meeting the next morning (post-observation discussion) went very well. I was amazed by how expertly she analyzed what I had tried to do. Thank you."

APPENDIX 8.4

READING LIST

Currently (January 2001), EQUAL Faculty Development Consultants have been reading excerpts, chapters, and articles from the following sources.

- Border, L., & Chism, N. V. N. (Eds.). (1992). Teaching for diversity. *New Directions for Teaching and Learning, No. 49.* San Francisco, CA: Jossey-Bass.

- Brinko, K. T., & Menges, R. J. (Eds.). (1997). *Practically speaking: A sourcebook for instructional consultants in higher education.* Stillwater, OK: New Forums Press.

- Christensen, C. R., Garvin, D. A., & Sweet, A. (1991). *Education for judgment: The artistry of discussion leadership.* Boston, MA: Harvard Business School Press.

- Marincovich, M., Prostko, J., & Stout, F. (Eds.). (1998). *The professional development of graduate teaching assistants.* Bolton, MA: Anker.

- Pratt, D. D., & Associates. (1998). *Five perspectives on teaching in adult and higher education.* Malabar, FL: Krieger.

- Sorcinelli, M. D. (1986). Guidelines for classroom observation. *Evaluation of teaching handbook.* Bloomington, IN: Dean of the Faculties Office. Reprinted in Weimer, M. (1991). *Improving college teaching.* San Francisco, CA: Jossey-Bass.

9

Operational Diversity: Saying What We Mean, Doing What We Say

Wayne Jacobson
Jim Borgford-Parnell
Katherine Frank
Michael Peck
Lois Reddick
University of Washington

Diversity issues, ranging from individual learning styles to institutional eq-uity, are central to teaching and learning, but identifying and addressing these is-sues is a formidable task. At the Center for Instructional Development and Re-search (CIDR), our staff is gaining ground on this work through the Inclusive Practices Portfolio, a collaborative forum for documenting, sharing, and support-ing our individual and organizational diversity initiatives. The process of devel-oping the center's portfolio and the portfolio itself are mechanisms for change within the center and a model for change at our institution and beyond.

INTRODUCTION

We often hear that instructors on our campus agree in principle to campus diversity policies, but many remain unsure how to trans-late these policies into more inclusive classroom practices. Our staff at the Center for Instructional Development and Research (CIDR) have faced a similar dilemma, knowing that diversity issues are central to ques-tions of teaching and learning, but uncertain how to integrate attention to diversity into our work with instructors and administrators in their ef-forts to improve teaching and learning on campus. In response to these parallel dilemmas, CIDR staff began working together to articulate our beliefs about diversity, translate these beliefs into action, and assess the outcomes of our actions. This work has been documented in CIDR's Inclusive Practices Portfolio, which provides us with a central location for integrating our ongoing individual and collaborative efforts. Our experience has demonstrated that a general commitment to diversity and inclusive practices can be transformed into identifiable actions, which in turn provides a basis for assessment, review, and planning for future growth. We also believe this experience provides a framework for others who wish to mobilize around a commitment to diversity.

CHALLENGES AND OPPORTUNITIES OF DIVERSITY AND INCLUSIVENESS

Part of the challenge of addressing diversity is the nature of the topic: Diversity spans many issues, from individual learning styles to institutional equity, each associated with a wide range of possible actions (Gay, 1994). Much of the campus conversation about diversity has been in terms of recruitment and retention, issues that are only indirectly related to our work as instructional developers. Thus, we found ourselves wondering how to best represent and respond to the complex array of issues included under the umbrella of "diversity," how we fit within the university's broader commitments, and how to prioritize among the many possible actions we could take.

Adding to these challenges is the fact that diversity is a politically charged topic. It is dismissed by some as political correctness; for others, it revolves around a single issue such as racial inequality. Our institution expresses commitment to diversity, but public reaction is mixed: Surveys of state residents show that most want graduates to be able to work effectively in culturally diverse settings, but many are opposed to affirmative action or hiring TAs with accents. Each of these perspectives potentially influences our clients in their work and, therefore, potentially influences how we work with them.

We found it fairly easy to agree about the challenges of addressing diversity, but we were not satisfied to continue leaving the challenges unmet. To paraphrase social activist and educator Myles Horton (1990), we felt we knew the basic reasons for our problems, but we wanted to get further than that. As a result, we began to take intentional steps to expand our knowledge, skills, and understanding of ourselves (Kardia, 1998; Marchesani & Adams, 1992), and also to articulate our assumptions and document our efforts so that they are subject to review and critical examination (Banks, 1998). Without a singular measure of inclusiveness as a basis for assessing our work, we began assembling our expressed beliefs, records of actions taken, assessments, and reflections into the Inclusive Practices Portfolio. Within the framework of the portfolio, our goal is to "analyze, clarify, and state [our] personal values related to cultural diversity, and to act in ways consistent with [our] beliefs" (Banks & Banks, 1995, p. 157). Most importantly, the portfolio has helped us work toward this goal both as individuals and as an organization, in order to make it possible to express CIDR's values and assess the consistency of our actions as an organization on our campus.

ORGANIZATIONAL CHANGE

Before the current work on the portfolio, CIDR already had a long history of involvement with diversity issues on our campus. CIDR produced a widely used video on the topic, *Teaching in the Diverse Classroom,* sponsored campus-wide forums and guest speakers, and collaborated with campus-wide diversity initiatives. Furthermore, in our work with individual instructors we have had numerous opportunities to raise questions related to diversity among their students and its implications for their teaching. However, in spite of this long history and shared commitment to diversity, we found that as a group we were not necessarily thinking about diversity in the same ways or systematically assessing our work in the area. As the make-up of our staff changed over time, we did not have the same experiences to provide common reference points as a basis for shared values and collaborative actions. We also discovered we were not consistent in our decisions about bringing diversity issues into consulting. CIDR's goal already focuses on better learning for all students (Banks, 1993), but should we proactively raise diversity issues, only respond to instructors' explicit questions about diversity, or speak in terms of better learning for all students even when instructors explicitly ask questions about student diversity?

Prompted by these questions, we began very simply with a conversation in a staff meeting about the implications of diversity on our work with clients. This seemingly straightforward process led us to the realization that our individual experiences and knowledge of diversity issues had provided us with a diverse range of insights on what we could do. However, this collection of interrelated ideas was difficult to encompass within a single shared vision for CIDR's role on campus. We wanted to collaboratively articulate this vision, building on the strengths of our diverse individual interests and experiences related to addressing the challenges and opportunities of diversity on our campus, but we were also wary of the exclusionary processes that often accompany group effort. Senge defines this unfortunately common group process as an organizational learning disability whereby "joint decisions are watered-down compromises reflecting what everyone can live with, or else one person's view foisted on the group" (1990, p. 24). We wanted our collective activities to be based upon a fundamental recognition of our own diversity, and as such to become the nexus for sharing, improving, and supporting our individual endeavors.

As we sought to implement this organizational change, it became very important to identify and acknowledge the organizational structure and culture of our center so that the process we had embarked upon would not only reflect and affirm that organization, but would also illuminate areas for change. This notion is congruent with much of the diversity, multicultural education, and organizational change literature, which argues for both institutions and individuals to begin their work in this arena by first examining themselves (Gay, 2000; Gillespie, 2000; Kardia, 1998; Laylock, 2000; Marchesani & Adams, 1992; Senge, 1990; Watkins & Marsick, 1993).

The underlying organizational framework of CIDR draws heavily upon a Total Quality Management (TQM) model that empowers individuals to work within and across teams to address and manage our daily activities. We are guided by five basic principles in particular that were drawn from Warren Deming's (1986) work in this area: 1) client orientation, 2) continuous improvement, 3) empowerment of our staff, 4) teamwork, and 5) professional development. In some ways this organizational identity positions us well to pursue change, but it also posed obstacles. For example, in one of our first conversations on diversity we found ourselves struggling to align the principle of client orientation, which often requires a responsive stance, with a desire to take on a more proactive role initiating change with our clients.

Our organization employs several of the structural elements and values of a TQM model, but the culture of our center more closely resembles that of a learning organization. In learning organizations, "learning takes place in individuals, teams, the organization, and even the communities with which the organization interacts.... Learning results in changes in knowledge, beliefs, and behaviors" (Watkins & Marsick, 1993, p. 8). Continuous learning on all levels serves CIDR staff and the campus community well, and is generally manifested in workshops, peer observations, and literature exchanges. However, few topics are as broad reaching, multi-layered, and personally challenging as diversity, and it remained a challenge for us to intentionally pursue organizational change over and above the learning of individuals and working groups within the organization. It was for this reason that the Inclusive Practices Portfolio was developed as an important orienting point for our efforts: providing a forum for documenting the complexity of the topic (diversity) and the task (collaborative learning to promote organizational change), and doing so within CIDR's normal practices of data collection, analysis, and reflection (Nyquist & Wulff, 1988).

SAYING WHAT WE MEAN

The cornerstone of the portfolio is a diversity statement, developed through a series of interactions with one another, the diversity literature, and other members of the campus community. This statement attempts to make explicit the implicit assumptions guiding our practices (Rando & Menges, 1991). Our drafting of the statement began with a challenge by Professor Geneva Gay of the Center for Multicultural Education at the University of Washington, to define our roles on campus with respect to diversity, and to determine the actions we were uniquely situated to take in those roles. This challenge helped us start in two ways: First, rather than trying to develop a comprehensive statement about diversity in higher education, we were encouraged to focus on the role our organization might be able to play on our campus. Second, it focused us on the actions implied by the principles we were trying to articulate.

In response to this challenge, staff members worked in groups to articulate or map out our organization's central roles on campus with respect to diversity. Groups presented their work to one another, and an editing group worked with the notes and concept maps to draft a statement which attempted to distill the work from each group into a single document. This draft was circulated among the staff for feedback and went through numerous revisions until staff agreed that it represented our organization's roles on campus.

Groups of staff members were then asked to draft a set of action statements implied by these roles. The action statements similarly went through numerous revisions and led us back to revise the diversity statement itself as we faced the challenges of putting the earlier draft into action. The process of articulating our principles and actions spanned a 12-

month period, ending with a staff consensus that it adequately represented the values and priorities of our work on campus, and also with the
understanding that the document was still open for further development.
A current draft of the statement is provided in Appendix 9.1.

Doing What We Say

After coming to a consensus on the statement of principles and actions,
we further developed the action statements using the Standard Practices
Survey. Staff members were asked to indicate for each action statement 1)
the extent to which it is part of their typical consulting practice, and 2)
the extent to which they think it should be part of their typical consulting practice. Sample items showing the format of the instrument are provided in Appendix 9.2.

Survey responses indicated that staff's consulting practices were
most consistent (that is, ratings for "is" most closely matched ratings for
"should be") for items directly related to exploring immediate classroom
contexts and teaching practices (for example, items *l* and *f*). Practices were
least consistent for items that implied working collaboratively with individuals or offices outside of CIDR (for example, items *r* and *q*). The next
least consistent practices were for items most explicitly related to diversity and inclusiveness (for example, items *a* and *b*). Figure 9.1 represents
the results of the survey for our consulting staff.

Figure 9.1

Standard Practices Survey Results
Typical Consulting Practices: "Is" versus "Should Be"

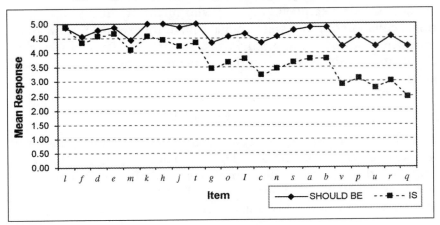

The survey results provided us with important information about our consulting practices, which we used in three ways. First, we revisited the original statement and discussed possible revisions. For example, do all staff members need to take time to stay informed about university policies and departmental changes, or is it sufficient for CIDR leadership to keep informed and pass information along as needed? Second, in our discussion of the survey results we discovered areas that we unintentionally neglected in our draft statement: 1) explicit attention to faculty diversity and identity development (in addition to diversity among students), and 2) as part of our beliefs about how change takes place, explicit attention to ongoing follow-up with clients and encouraging them to share their experiences with colleagues.

Third, and most important, we used this information to help us start examining our practices and identify areas in which we need to put our commitments into practice more effectively. Based on the survey results, staff members were asked to select a professional development activity designed with the specific goal of examining attention to diversity in our consulting practices. Examples of professional development activities included maintaining a journal of interactions with clients, taping consultation sessions, inviting colleagues to observe consultations, and presenting cases for peer review (see Appendix 9.3). Reports and reflections on these experiences were documented and added to the Inclusive Practices Portfolio for others to review.

Following these activities, staff will review the diversity statement and re-take the Standard Practices Survey. Individuals can target specific areas for continuing development by referring to colleagues' records in the Inclusive Practices Portfolio in order to see who has worked in that area previously and who might be interested in additional collaboration. We will also make plans for external review, asking others in the campus community to assess our portfolio, and asking our clients to provide feedback on their experience working with our staff on issues of diversity.

EFFECTS

As we have taken steps to articulate our goals and assess our actions, with respect to diversity on campus, we have also been mindful of the overarching question that originally prompted us to take these initiatives: As instructional developers, how can we contribute to wider campus efforts to foster a more inclusive teaching and learning community? Our efforts have helped us as a group to become more mindful of the gap between our personal and organizational values and the even larger gap between our beliefs and our actions, but how has this work affected the larger community we are a part of?

Our most direct effect to the campus is through consulting services to individuals and departments. Our work with the Inclusive Practices Portfolio has raised individual staff members' level of attention to diversity issues, and they report changes in the questions which they ask and issues which they raise as a result of our paying attention to these issues. It has also contributed to our development of materials, workshops, and Internet resources that we provide for the campus. We will continue to document staff members' reports of changes in their consulting, client feedback, and other professional development activities that allow us to examine and improve our consulting and its impact on campus. Our hope is that through these ongoing processes of documentation, reflection, and development, the portfolio will continue to evolve as a record of our collective best practices and improvement over time.

Another effect of our work has been to demonstrate the possibility of change. Since our work was reported in our university's staff newspaper and on our center's web site, we have received feedback from the campus community and have also been approached by others to assist them in the process of instituting similar changes. With a more specifically articulated statement of our own roles on campus, we are also better prepared to collaborate with other units in broader institutional initiatives. Finally, our own experience with the complexity of this process has also given us a greater appreciation of what it would take for departments to go through a similar process.

The Inclusive Practices Portfolio provides a structure for ongoing critical self-examination. Noffke (1995) describes this action research process as one in which

> Understandings and actions emerge in a constant cycle, one that highlights the ways in which educators are partially correct, yet in continual need of revision, in their thoughts and actions. The process does not end, as with traditional notions of research, with richer understandings of education for others to implement; rather, it aids in an ongoing process of identifying contradictions, which in turn, help to locate spaces for ethically defensible, politically strategic actions. (p. 4)

Like the process Noffke describes, our work with the Inclusive Practices Portfolio is not expected to reach a definitive end. Collaboratively documenting and reflecting on our practices is helping us locate spaces for our center to take action, assess outcomes of the actions we are uniquely situated to take, and position ourselves for ongoing active participation in our university's diversity initiatives.

REFERENCES

Banks, C. A. M., & Banks, J. A. (1995). Equity pedagogy: An essential component of multicultural education. *Theory into Practice, 34* (3), 152-158.

Banks, J. A. (1993). Multicultural education: Development, dimensions, and challenges. *Phi Delta Kappan, 75* (1), 22-28.

Banks, J. A. (1998). The lives and values of researchers: Implications for educating citizens in a multicultural society. *Educational Researcher, 27* (7), 4-17.

Center for Instructional Development and Research (Producer). (1991). *Teaching in the Diverse Classroom* [Video]. (Available from Anker Publishing Company, Inc., P. O. Box 249, Bolton, MA 01740-0249 or www.ankerpub.com)

Deming, W. E. (1986). *Out of the crisis.* Cambridge, MA: Massachusetts Institute of Technology.

Gay, G. (1994). *A synthesis of scholarship in multicultural education: Urban monograph series.* Oak Brook, IL: North Central Regional Educational Laboratory.

Gay, G. (2000). *Culturally responsive teaching.* New York, NY: Teachers College Press.

Gillespie, K. H. (2000). The challenge and test of our values: An essay of collective experience. In M. Kaplan & D. Lieberman (Eds.), *To improve the academy: Vol. 18. Resources for faculty, instructional, and organizational development* (pp. 27-37). Bolton, MA: Anker.

Horton, M. (1990). *The long haul.* New York, NY: Doubleday.

Kardia, D. (1998). Becoming a multicultural faculty developer: Reflections from the field. In D. DeZure & M. Kaplan (Eds.), *To improve the academy: Vol. 17. Resources for faculty, instructional, and organizational development* (pp. 15-33). Stillwater, OK: New Forums Press.

Laylock, M. (2000). QILT: An approach to faculty development and institutional self-improvement. In M. Kaplan & D. Lieberman (Eds.), *To improve the academy: Vol. 18. Resources for faculty, instructional, and organizational development* (pp. 69-82). Bolton, MA: Anker.

Marchesani, L., & Adams, M. (1992). Dynamics of diversity in the teaching-learning process. *New Directions in Teaching and Learning, No. 52.* San Francisco, CA: Jossey-Bass.

Noffke, S. (1995). Action research and democratic schooling: Problematics and potentials. In S. Noffke & R. Stevenson (Eds.), *Educational action research: Becoming practically critical* (pp. 1-10). New York, NY: Teachers College Press.

Nyquist, J., & Wulff, W. (1988). Consultation using a research perspective. In E. C. Wadsworth (Ed.), *A handbook for new practitioners* (pp. 82-88). Stillwater, OK: New Forums Press.

Rando, W., & Menges, R. (1991). How practice is shaped by personal theories. *New Directions for Teaching and Learning, No. 45.* San Francisco, CA: Jossey-Bass.

Senge, P. (1990). *The fifth discipline.* New York, NY: Currency Doubleday.

Watkins, K. E., & Marsick, V. J. (1993). *Sculpting the learning organization.* San Francisco, CA: Jossey-Bass.

Contact all authors at:

College of Education
University of Washington
12241 4th NW
Seattle, WA 98177
(206) 543-6588
(206) 685-1213 (Fax)
Email: jacobson@cidr.washington.edu
         bparnell@u.washington.edu
         kfrank@u.washington.edu
         mpeck@u.washington.edu
         redl@u.washington.edu

Wayne Jacobson is Interim Assistant Director of the Center for Instructional Development and Research (CIDR) at the University of Washington.

Jim Borgford-Parnell is a staff consultant at the Center for Instructional Development and Research (CIDR). He has a master's degree in Adult Education and has been teaching at the postsecondary level for 21 years. He is currently a PhD student in Educational Leadership and Policy Studies at the University of Washington, and also teaches education courses in the master's program at Antioch University.

Katherine Frank is a staff consultant at the Center for Instructional Development and Research (CIDR). Starting in August 2001, she will be an Assistant Professor of English and Codirector of the Writing Program at the University of Southern Colorado.

Michael Peck is a staff consultant at the Center for Instructional Development and Research (CIDR). He holds master's degrees in Social Work and in Jewish Communal Service and has clinical practice experience in family service and healthcare settings. Currently, he is completing his PhD in Social Welfare at the University of Washington School of Social Work.

Lois Reddick is a staff consultant at the Center for Instructional Development and Research (CIDR) and a graduate student in Multicultural Education at the University of Washington.

APPENDIX 9.1
CURRENT DRAFT OF THE CIDR DIVERSITY STATEMENT

Diversity and Inclusiveness in our work as Instructional Development Consultants at CIDR

In every class, there are students who differ from the instructor and from one another in ways that profoundly affect how they experience classroom activities and how they learn. Factors of identity (such as gender, race, and ethnicity) are interwoven with individual differences (such as ability and experience with the subject matter) and these work together to affect how students relate to the instructor, to one another, and to the subject matter. Our role as instructional consultants is to help instructors teach in ways that optimize learning opportunities for all their students.

Our work with diversity and inclusiveness is informed by our knowledge of faculty and student roles, relationships and interactions, by our understanding of how learning and change take place, by goals and policies of the university, and by our recognition of diversity's larger historical, political, and social contexts. In practical terms, however, this work begins with a client's request for consultation regarding his or her immediate situation.

To put this vision into practice, consultants:

- **Identify the specific contexts for teaching and learning.**

  Classroom practices are shaped by factors that are rarely visible in the classroom; for example, instructors' and students' academic and personal backgrounds, current developments in the department and in the discipline, and the history and priorities of the institution. One goal of consultation is to make these influences visible so that they become open to question, analysis, and reconsideration.

- **Encourage the successful management of the challenges related to diversity.**

  Our ultimate goal to help clients see the diversity that students bring to the classroom as a contribution to better teaching and learning, rather than as an obstacle to it. However, many clients who come to us are uncomfortable addressing issues of diversity, often due to the perceived magnitude and complexity of the task or the fear of being judged for their actions.

  Because these feelings might inhibit clients from taking action, we try to make the consulting relationship a safe, non-threatening setting for considering change. Our immediate goal is to help clients identify areas where they can begin to take action.

- **Motivate and model processes of change**.

    We try to motivate clients by helping them see how strategic choices can lead to meaningful change in their immediate situations. We do not want to disregard or minimize a client's apparent reluctance to discuss sensitive or politically charged topics, and we acknowledge the challenges they are facing.

    Change is slow, incremental, and uneven. From the beginning, we want to honor clients' concerns, experiences, and efforts they are already making to teach effectively. Utilizing a variety of information sources, we present them with opportunities to see their situations from other perspectives and with resources that provide strategies and models for change.

    In order to help clients think through and negotiate the process of change, consultants:

Ask questions about:

a) Contributions that students make to the way the course is taught, based on the different backgrounds, identities, and perspectives that they bring to it

b) Ways in which the instructor is accounting for student diversity in his or her planning and teaching; for example, varieties of learning styles, life experiences, amount of experience with the subject matter, goals for taking the course, expectations of classmates

c) Previous experiences and assumptions the client has related to student diversity (see a & b, above)

d) Challenges of the teaching situation in terms of class size, preceding and following courses, students' backgrounds and ability levels; for example, is the course required or elective, for majors or non-majors, novice or experienced learners?

e) Previous experiences the client has had in this type of teaching situation

f) What the client likes / doesn't like about this teaching situation

g) How the course is taught by, and valued by, others in the department

h) What motivates the client to request assistance or consider change at this time

i) Previous experiences the client has had with making or assessing changes in his or her teaching

j) Limitations on the changes that can be made to a course because of the shared responsibilities for change (with students, other instructors, etc.) and variables not under the client's control

Create opportunities to:

k) Help the client value and view the course from the students' perspective via student feedback, relevant research, or other data

l) Expand the client's range of options for approaches to teaching

m) Express our own experiences dealing with challenges / change

n) Provide models of ways to interact positively and productively around potentially controversial issues, in order to help clients learn to have these kinds of interactions with their students

o) Learn ourselves through means we might suggest to our clients; for example, through reflection, documentation, or peer review of our work

Keep ourselves informed about:

p) University policies regarding departmental program reviews, strategic planning, curriculum transformation, admissions, and retention

q) Departments undergoing changes related to courses offered and student opportunities

r) What other instructors, programs, or institutions, as well as our CIDR colleagues, are doing to address diversity and inclusiveness

s) Theories of learning, change, and identity development, concerning both clients and their students

Work collaboratively with:

t) Colleagues and peers within and outside CIDR (always remembering to protect client confidentiality)

u) Departmental leaders, advisors, or coordinators in positions to initiate or advocate change

v) Other units on campus; for example, the Curriculum Transformation Project, the Office of Educational Opportunity Program, Graduate Opportunities and Minority Achievement Program

Follow up with clients to:

w) Find out how designs or strategies we've developed are working

x) Request permission to share their designs or strategies with other clients

APPENDIX 9.2
CIDR STANDARD PRACTICES SURVEY

We developed this survey as the next step for building on our work with the CIDR diversity statement. The items on the survey are taken directly from the actions that are identified on the statement.

Survey Goals

The survey asks us to identify what we typically talk about when we are consulting, and also asks us to identify what we think we *should* typically talk about. The goals of the survey are to help us each find out what colleagues are doing, and to help us determine together areas in which we want to develop in our consulting.

Confidentiality

You will see that the survey gives you the option of remaining anonymous. No one will trace responses to the individual who made them, and no individual's survey responses will be singled out for presentation apart from the rest.

Feedback

There is space on the survey to comment on the survey itself and on the experience of filling it out, and there is also space to suggest additional items if you think they should be brought up for everyone to discuss. In part, we are assessing how well we are implementing the diversity statement, and in part we are assessing how well the diversity statement really captures what we think we should be doing. Please add your comments and suggestions to the survey document or email them directly to Wayne.

Real World Consultations

Finally, when you are answering the parts of the survey that address what we *should* be doing, think about the real world, rather than an ideal one. That is, ideally it would be nice to ask all these questions (and many more) so that our consulting is based on the most thorough exploration of issues possible. In the real world, however, time is limited, and so is our clients' patience to answer all the questions we might want to ask. To say that something is not a typical topic area in your consulting is not to say it's unimportant, but simply that it isn't necessary to bring it up with each and every client.

Thanks

Thanks for your participation. If you have questions about the survey or the process of filling it out, ask Wayne or Katherine.

STANDARD PRACTICES SURVEY

For each question or topic area (Part 1) and each activity (Part 2), please indicate the extent to which it is part of your consulting. Please respond to each item twice. In the shaded column indicate the extent to which that item IS your typical practice in consulting. In the other column indicate the extent to which you think the item SHOULD BE a typical practice in our consulting.

Notice that "5" does not indicate that the item is better or more important, although it does suggest that the item occurs more frequently. Use "2" and "4" for items that fall somewhere between the others.

---

1 = Not Likely–I rarely, if ever, bring this up in the course of consulting.
2
3 = It Depends–I follow this line of questioning if it seems relevant to the immediate situation.
4
5 = Typical Practice–I almost always bring this up in consulting, whether the client does or not.

Part1 Question or Topic Area	is	should be
a. Contributions that students make to the way the course is taught, based on the different backgrounds, identities, and perspectives that they bring to it		
b. Ways in which the instructor is accounting for student diversity in his or her planning and teaching; for example, varieties of learning styles, life experiences, amount of experience with the subject matter, goals for taking the course, expectations of classmates		
c. Previous experiences and assumptions the client has related to student diversity (see a & b, above)		
d. Challenges of the teaching situation in terms of class size, preceding and following courses, students' backgrounds and ability levels: for example, is the course required or elective, for majors or non-majors, novice or experienced learners?		
e. Previous experiences the client has had in this type of teaching situation		

f. What the client likes / doesn't like about this teaching situation

g. How the course is taught by, and valued by, others in the department

h. What motivates the client to request assistance or consider change at this point in time

i. Previous experiences the client has had with making or assessing changes in his or her teaching

j. Limitations on the changes that can be made to a course because of the shared responsibilities for change (with students, other instructors, etc.) and variables not under the client's control

k. Ways to help the client value and view the course from the students' perspective via student feedback, relevant research, or other data

l. Ways to expand the client's range of options for approaches to teaching

m. Ways to express our own experiences dealing with challenges / change

n. Models of ways to interact positively and productively around potentially difficult or controversial issues, in order to help clients learn to have these kinds of interactions with their students

1 = **Not Likely**—I rarely, if ever, do this.
2
3 = **It Depends**—I do this when it seems relevant.
4
5 = **Typical Practice**—I almost always do this, whether it affects a specific client or not.

	is	should be

Part 2 Activity

o. Learn ourselves through means we might suggest to our clients; for example, through reflection, documentation, or peer review of our work

p. Keep informed about university policies regarding departmental program reviews, strategic planning, curriculum transformation, admissions, and retention

q. Keep informed about departments undergoing changes related to courses offered and student opportunities

r. Keep informed about what other instructors, programs, or institutions, as well as our CIDR colleagues, are doing to address diversity and inclusiveness

s. Keep informed about theories of learning and change

t. Work together with colleagues and peers within and outside CIDR (always remembering to protect client confidentiality)

u. Work together with departmental leaders, advisors, or coordinators in positions to initiate or advocate change

v. Work together with other units on campus

Additional Items

Use this section to identify additional items that you would like to offer to the rest of the staff for discussion. As you did in the previous sections, respond to each item twice. In the shaded column indicate the extent to which that item IS your typical practice in consulting. In the other column indicate the extent to which you think the item SHOULD BE a typical practice in our consulting.

1 = **Not Likely**—I rarely, if ever, do this.
2
3 = **It Depends**—I do this when it seems relevant.
4
5 = **Typical Practice**—I almost always do this, whether it affects a specific client or not.

	should
is	be

Part 3 Additional Items

(add as many rows to the table as you need)

w.

x.

y.

z.

Comments

Do you have any additional comments on the survey items, survey construction, or the experience of filling it out? (use as much space as you need)

Name (optional): _____

Your name will not be included in any report of the compiled results. However, if you provide your name, then it will be possible to follow up with you regarding additional items that you suggested or comments that you made. You can also send your additional items and comments by email if you would like a response but you don't want to include them with this survey.

APPENDIX 9.3
CIDR STAFF DEVELOPMENT OPTIONS

The outcomes of our Standard Practices Survey suggest that as a group, we'd like to be doing more to incorporate attention to diversity into our consulting practice. In order to help us work toward this goal during fall quarter, please select an independent professional development activity, on your own or in collaboration with others. Here's a brainstormed list of possible activities:

(a) write up one or more cases with explicit attention to the role of diversity and how it was addressed in the consulting process (for example, using Michael's case presentation form)

(b) select some reading material (or a lecture, video series, etc.) which will help you improve your consulting in relation to diversity and inclusiveness

(c) select an individual to interview or interact with during the quarter (for example, someone from the Curriculum Transformation Project, GO-MAP, or Multicultural Education) in order to help you develop your consulting skills in relation to diversity and inclusiveness

(d) participate in an internet discussion list on issues of diversity, or raise diversity-related questions on another list that you typically participate in

(e) keep a consulting journal reflecting on your interactions with clients; review and reflect on how diversity was addressed (or not) in the consulting process

(f) record (on audiotape or videotape) your interactions with a client; review and reflect on how diversity was addressed (or not) in the consulting process

(g) work on a case collaboratively (co-consulting or peer observation of your consulting); meet with colleagues to discuss how diversity was addressed (or not) in the consulting process

(h) work with colleagues to role play handling particular case situations; meet with colleagues to discuss how diversity was addressed (or not) in the consulting process

(i) develop a consulting portfolio providing evidence of how your consulting practices incorporate attention to diversity and inclusiveness

These suggestions are just to get you started. Feel free to propose
something else if it will be more useful for you. Whatever you choose,
make a decision by September 15 so that it doesn't get put off until the
quarter becomes less busy in late November. I'd like to post a list of
everyone's choices so that you can have the chance to interact with people about their projects during the quarter if you like.

On our next Staff Day (January 3), be prepared to present a brief reflection on what you did and what you learned from it. The purpose is
<u>not</u> to provide a comprehensive presentation of everything you did, but
to give colleagues a sense of what they might learn by trying something
similar in the future.

10

What Do the Faculty Think? The Importance of Concerns Analysis in Introducing Technological Change

HeeKap Lee
Amy Lawson
Indiana University

Change management strategies tend to focus on the inherent characteristics of the proposed change. However, there is a personal side to change and it is reflected in what are called perceptions or personal concerns. To manage change successfully, facilitators must take measures to understand the personal concerns had by those who are required to implement the change. Moreover, this concerns analysis should be done early in the project, ideally before the change is implemented. The purposes of this chapter are to explain the importance of conducting a concerns analysis and to propose a theoretical framework for concerns analysis. The framework has been developed based on a case study of an information technology innovation project in a theological seminary. While these approaches are ideally suited for higher education settings, they are also relevant outside the academy.

Introduction

Why do some change efforts in higher education institutions succeed, and some fail? Successful changes result from a complex interplay of various factors. Some think that people will adopt a change if it has practical advantages over an existing practice. However, there are numerous examples where an advantageous change was never adopted or took a long time to be adopted. The failure to adopt a change is also due to a variety of factors, including resistance or lack of cooperation on the part of those involved in the change, and the length of time the change may require to be fully implemented (Rogers, 1995).

Besides these operational issues, what seems to play an important role in the adoption process are the set of perceptions that the people involved in a change form toward that change. This personal side to change is reflected in what can be called perceptions or personal concerns. Eggan and Kauchak (1997) define perception as the process by which people attach meaning to their experiences. This meaning that individuals attach to change plays a critical role in a change process. Similarly, Tafoya (1983) defines perception analysis as the key to understanding why people perceive needs in a specific field. In too many cases, it appears that change facilitators, or those who make plans to introduce change, base their interventions or innovations on their own needs and time lines rather than their clients' needs, concerns, and readiness to change (Hall & Hord, 1987). Recently, however, several theories have begun to address the importance of understanding how clients perceive change, and this enables the change agents to show how they adjust what they do according to their perceptions (Coffing, 1973; Hall & Hord, 1987; Tafoya, 1983). Strebel (1998) indicates that despite the best efforts of senior executives, major change initiatives in corporations often fail, and those failures have at least one common root: Executives and employees see change differently. He argues that to close this gap, managers must reconsider their employees' personal compacts—the mutual obligations and commitments that exist between employees and the company.

Ertmer (1999) identifies two categories of barriers that organizations, educational or otherwise, face during a change process: first-order barriers and second-order barriers. First-order barriers refer to those obstacles that are extrinsic to the target audience of a change, meaning the individuals who must implement the change in their daily practices. Examples of first-order barriers are lack of equipment, time, training, or support. Second-order barriers are more serious, and refer to more fundamental, intrinsic obstacles, such as the target audience's underlying beliefs or the challenging of traditional practices. She argues that traditional approaches to change have focused on helping those involved in a change to overcome first-order barriers. However, Ertmer also argues that it is a belief system, not an economic or empirical warrant, which determines the failure or success of changes. Therefore, it is necessary to understand the target audiences' motivations, frustrations, and perceptions about a change to accurately assess the needs for the change and to plan how to address these needs.

Based on this premise, this chapter will demonstrate the importance of performing a concerns analysis before a change project is conducted in an educational institution. In particular, this chapter will supply a specific framework, or model of concerns analysis, that an institution wishing to introduce a change can use to discover and address concerns their target audiences may have about the change. While the conclusions drawn here are based on the results of a specific case study (a instructional technology implementation project undertaken by a small educational institution) it is hoped that all institutions, regardless of size or educational mission, can use this framework effectively to help ensure the success of their own technological change projects.

A CASE STUDY OF INSTRUCTIONAL TECHNOLOGY CHANGE

The Context

In the mid-1990s a seminary in the midwestern United States was awarded an externally funded grant for a technology initiative, which included developing instructional computing capabilities throughout the school (Saint Meinrad School of Theology, 1995). The seminary hired two instructional interns to provide computer training to the seminary faculty and staff.

At the beginning phase of the initiative, the interns conducted a training needs analysis. The main focus of the analysis was to gather information about the kinds of training programs faculty and staff members would need. Through the analysis, however, several concerns surfaced (Saint Meinrad School of Theology, 1998). For example, faculty members did not seem to think that computer technology was a tool useful for theology education, which emphasizes personal interactions within small groups. Administrators of the initiative, however, did not pay much attention to this perceived concern. They proceeded on the assumption that faculty members always complain about new initiatives and they viewed such concerns as natural. They assumed that faculty members would eventually accept and use computers provided the faculty members received the proper training. With these assumptions in place, the administrators put effort into collecting and addressing training needs information while ignoring their concerns.

After the interns had provided in-service training for one year, they began to make informal visits to the classrooms, computer labs, library, and the faculty resource center. They found that many faculty members were not integrating computers into their teaching. According to the project implementation plan, almost all faculty members should have been using computers in their instruction after one year, since all the necessary facilities and training had been provided.

Faced with such resistance, the administration began to take the idea of concerns seriously. The administrators of the seminary learned it was not the lack of facilities or training, but concerns of the faculty that affected the success of the initiative. With this realization, they asked the interns to conduct a concerns analysis. One-on-one interviews and document analyses were used as data collection methods. All 26 teaching faculty and several administrators and staff of the seminary were interviewed.

After conducting many rounds of card sorting, the interns identified 24 categories of concerns. To analyze the concerns and to develop effective interventions for addressing the concerns, the interns designed a special framework called the "concerns matrix."

Concerns Matrix

The concerns matrix derives from the overlap of two major dimensions in the change process: the degree to which the change is compatible with the values of the target audience, and the levels of the institution where the change efforts must take place. These two dimensions are best approached as questions: 1) Is the change compatible with organizational and personal values? and 2) Are the concerns or needs addressed for both the individual faculty members and the organization as a whole?

The first dimension of the concerns matrix refers to the individual faculty member's perceptions about the compatibility of the change with personal and institutional values. In this case, values refer to those principles and beliefs considered most important and given greatest priority; in this sense, both individuals and the institutions of which they are a part hold specific, identifiable values. If the proposed change is not compatible with the value systems of individual faculty members, or with the current value system at work in the institution, then the change will be hard for the target audience to adopt. If the change is compatible with cultural or religious values then this compatibility promotes the adoption of the change (Rogers, 1995). However, the compatibility of a change with the current value system still will not guarantee its easy adoption. Even when a change is compatible with current values, the adoption of a change usually takes quite a long time because of other barriers, such as lack of organizational support or resources.

The second dimension of the concerns matrix refers to the level of the concerns. The concerns analysis of the seminary faculty revealed two distinct types of concerns: those of individual faculty members and those of the institution as a whole. Basically, these two levels of concerns originate from different contextual backgrounds. Individual concerns are based on felt needs, while institutional concerns are based on real needs. According to Monett (1977), felt needs can be identified by viewing the target audiences' personal, perceived needs, while real needs are identified by focusing on objective gaps between the current performance level and the desired performance level. Hence, a concerns analysis must incorporate both levels of concerns, individual and institutional, since the two levels of concerns have fundamentally different foundations.

Based on the overlapping interests of these two dimensions, compatibility of changes and levels of concerns, we have identified the following four areas of concern: 1) individual-compatible, 2) organizational-compatible, 3) individual-incompatible, and 4) organizational-incompatible (see Figure 10.1).

FIGURE 10.1
The Concerns Matrix: Two Dimensions of Concerns

	Compatible	*Incompatible*
Individual	Individual-Compatible	Individual-Incompatible
Organizational	Organizational-Compatible	Organizational Incompatible

In the concerns matrix above, compatibility is a matter of degree, and the extent to which the change is compatible with its context is the key issue. This is why the levels of compatibility, individual and organizational, can be separated with a dotted line in Figure 10.1. However, the two levels of concerns, individual and organizational, are separate and independent issues, separated by a solid line. This chapter will define and explore each of these areas, with a greater focus on concerns in the area of incompatibility, as these are generally more difficult concerns to overcome.

Individual-Compatible Concerns: Learning Intervention

Even when the values of a change are compatible with the target audience's values, the target audience may not accept the proposed change as planned for several reasons, including fear of the unknown and lack of information or knowledge required to implement the change.

In the initial needs analysis for the project, the interns found that the faculty's needs were diverse and the range of technology competencies was wide. Some faculty had difficulty understanding even the basic functions of technology. Several concerns were identified by the faculty members of the seminary, such as fear of technology, more work, lack of detailed information, a need for teaching and mentoring, and time conflict. Also, they expressed that they had no time to learn technology and that technology was not a priority for them.

Based on the results of the needs analysis, several learning tasks were arranged. First, each faculty member received an individual learning road map and was provided training programs to help them reach their learning goals. After participating in group-based training sessions for one year, the faculty improved their computer competencies by 0.6 points on the 5-point Likert scale (Saint Meinrad School of Theology, 1998). To address time concerns, the seminary formed a committee to reorganize teaching loads. Also, lack of time to learn was the most crucial factor in this category in the seminary. To address this concern, the seminary developed a training schedule that was flexible, meeting at different hours of the day, even evenings, so that faculty could best take advantage of the offering.

Thus, the major strategy for addressing concerns in the individual-compatible area is learning, because usually these concerns can be overcome by providing well-organized training programs, job aids, and consultation programs. Also, providing correct information in a timely manner is another useful strategy. This type of concern usually appears in the beginning stage of a change. Hence, change agents have to set up training interventions to overcome individual-compatible concerns before implementation starts.

Organizational-Compatible Concerns: Support Intervention

A change that is compatible with current organizational values is sometimes not adopted by the target audience because of a lack of organizational support (for example, a lack of organizational incentives and benefits or inadequate technical and administrative support). Concerns of this type are extrinsic to the target audience and can be addressed by the organization.

In the seminary, several concerns arose in this area, such as students' lack of involvement in the change, students' limited access to equipment and support services, general equipment and maintenance problems, and lack of organizational benefits for adopting the change. Especially, major problems for seminary faculty lay in the institution's lack of incentives or motivation for encouraging faculty members' active usage of the change. Many faculty suggested benefits and motivations both monetary and nonmonetary, such as vacations, training opportunities, and a lessened teaching burden. Instead of monetary benefits, the seminary then provided many forms of nonmonetary benefits such as training programs and visits to other technologically advanced schools. Also, a new master plan was developed which included major changes to several campus buildings over the next five years.

Ertmer (1999) explains that a support function changes as individuals in the adoption units mature. In the early stages of change, teachers tend to have a greater need for deep and reliable technical backup. Over time, however, teachers' technical dependency tends to decrease as they learn problem solving skills. Once they have gained technical competency, teachers feel an increased need for instructional and professional support as they begin exploring new ways to integrate the technology within the classroom. These concerns can be eliminated if the organization acquires resources and equipment, provides timely technical and administrative support, provides incentives or benefit systems, and maintains equipment.

Individual-Incompatible Concerns: Persuasion Intervention

People are not usually willing to spend much time on a change they do not yet value (Dormant, 1986). Ertmer (1999) called these types of concerns second-order barriers. These concerns cause more difficulties because they are less tangible, more personal, and deeply ingrained (Kirr, 1996). If the resulting resistance is not addressed well, then it can impact the target audience negatively throughout the change process.

The seminary faculty mentioned several issues in this area, such as their skepticism of technology, their comfort with current teaching methods, and their perceptions of technology as opposing personal values. They criticized technology because they perceived that it could reduce the human interaction between students and instructors. This area of concern was the most important issue in this case. The change's incompatibility with each faculty's personal values or past experiences was the critical factor in some faculty's not adopting the change. All of the faculty who were at the persuasion stage in terms of Rogers's (1995) diffusion of change framework were critically influenced by this area of concern. To them, it was very difficult to change their teaching style because it had worked well for decades.

Actually, the seminary found it difficult to address this area of concern. The administrators realized that persuasion on an individual basis was the best strategy, after noticing the faculty's resistance to the change. In fact, the seminary had not tried to persuade the faculty at the beginning of the change. For example, the change administrators did not meet the individual faculty members directly to hear their opinions regarding the change. Only in the faculty meeting did administrators try to overemphasize the positive benefits of technology. This was not an effective way to persuade individual faculty to accept the change.

In this case, the administrators were able to step back to reassess the target audience's concerns and attempt to address them. The seminary identified a core group that was very skeptical about technology even after several years had passed since the change started. To clarify their concerns, the Instructional Service Department staff conducted one-on-one interviews with faculty members to become aware of the many issues that related to this area. The department stressed that the Instructional Service staff were not attempting to change faculty's teaching styles, but to enhance their teaching styles with the use of technology. Also, the seminary established a monthly technology newsletter, both in print and on the intranet, featuring articles that addressed specific individual-incompatible concerns expressed by faculty as well as by staff and administrators. The seminary also offered faculty members the chance and means to visit other advanced technology-driven education institutions, and presented them with learning opportunities to familiarize them with the practical applicability of the technology in the seminary context. More than ten faculty members attended technology-related seminars, conferences, and workshops.

In most changes in higher education institutions, individual-incompatible concerns are critical because changes are usually introduced in an organization without considering the target audiences' values, attitudes, or interests. Hence, identifying these issues is essential at the beginning stage of a change.

Organizational-Incompatible Concerns: Collaboration Intervention
Change sometimes produces conflicts with organizational values, cultures, or climates. Organizational context and cultural incompatibility

are critical issues in a change implementation process (Ertmer, 1999; Hall & Hord, 1978). For example, Moore and Mizuba (1968) mentioned the concept of cultural incompatibility for the first time in their study, "Water Boiling in a Peruvian Town." They found the change they studied was not adopted because it was incompatible with the experience of the villagers, or the target audience. The lesson of this story has to be remembered when one is introducing change into education as well. A change's lack of compatibility with widely held cultural or religious values may well prevent the adoption of that change.

Faculty generally expressed that the change was not compatible with the seminary culture. The seminary culture focused on religious education and thus was oriented toward greater human interaction. Not only did the introduction of instructional technology seem foreign to and incompatible with the organization's mission, but faculty also expressed their isolation from the change. The change was initiated in a top-down manner, and clear goals for or directions of the change were not given to faculty, nor did they receive information in a timely fashion. Furthermore, faculty members tended to work individually rather than in teams. Every individual faculty member understood the change differently. Hence, they perceived that two incongruent change diffusion tracks existed in the seminary: tracks of the individual faculty and of the institution at large.

Collaboration is often the most useful strategy to address institutional-incompatible concerns. To address issues in this area of concern— the seminary's geographical isolation, diverse faculty disciplines, a top-down diffusion strategy—collaborative work among the seminary faculty was essential. Since the administrators had failed to share ideas from the beginning stage of the change, many faculty expressed their isolation to the change and formed unfavorable attitudes toward it. Creating a vision statement and sharing change-related experiences among the members of the target audience eventually became important tasks for the seminary.

After the interns performed the concerns analysis, the administrators were able to revise their approaches to both the innovation and the target audience. The president rector established an ad hoc faculty committee, consisting of faculty, staff, and students to address technology issues on campus. The committee's goal was to set a clear vision for technology and teaching at the seminary. They developed a vision with consensus of all faculty members and reported their findings to the faculty. To meet the mission, a set of goals was also identified in the consensus of all faculty members. Mission and goal statements made clear for all faculty members the directions of the change.

Sharing among faculty was the key activity to changing the seminary culture as the change was in process. The seminary arranged several events in which faculty members shared their ideas with other faculty members. These events included Faculty Presentation Day, Faculty Learning Day, small group interests, brown bag lunches, and learning sessions. Through the grant funds, many faculty took advantage of conference opportunities to gain more knowledge about the appropriate use of technology. Furthermore, the seminary developed external contacts to have faculty experience cultures of educational institutions where technology was compatible with, or already part of, the organizational culture at large. Eventually, the seminary was able to find and demonstrate good practices in technology for theological instruction.

CONCLUSION

The interventions described above solved many of the perceptional concerns of faculty at the seminary where this case study was performed. However, there were still concerns that could not be solved through these interventions. The concerns in the category of personal incompatibility were particularly difficult to address. The faculty members who were skeptical of technology were not persuaded to use the computers even in the five years that have passed since the initiative began in 1995. This phenomenon points to the importance of conducting a concerns analysis before a change is introduced. Some concerns in the category of organization-incompatibility were also difficult to address. The seminary tried to establish a vision statement as well as detailed action plans to address such concerns. They formed another technology committee that consisted of representatives of the faculty, students, and instructional consultants. This committee's work has just begun at the time of this article, and its impact is yet to be determined.

The concerns matrix is a framework that change facilitators, those in charge of change projects, can use to identify important concerns held by their target audience, those the facilitators expect to implement the change. The specific concerns discovered and solutions undertaken in this case study are unique to their context, an instructional technology change project initiated in a theological seminary with a relatively small faculty and student body. The concerns matrix is designed to be flexible in its applications, however. Thus, it can be used in a range of change projects by educational institutions regardless of size or mission, and may even be used in developing changes for organizations whose interests lay outside the realm of education.

REFERENCES

Coffing, R. T. (1973). *Identification of client demand for public services: Development of a methodology.* Unpublished doctoral dissertation, University of Massachusetts.

Dormant, D. (1986). *Introduction to performance technology.* Washington, DC: National Society for Performance and Instruction.

Eggan, P., & Kauchak, D. (1997). *Educational psychology: Windows on classrooms* (3rd ed.). Upper Saddle River, NJ: Prentice-Hall.

Ertmer, P. A. (1999). Addressing first and second order barriers to change: Strategies for technology integration. *Educational Technology Research & Development, 47* (4), 47-61.

Hall, G. E., & Hord, S. M. (1987). *Change in schools: Facilitating the process.* Albany, NY: State University of New York Press.

Havelock, R. G. (1995). *The change agent's guide to innovation in education.* Englewood Cliffs, NJ: Educational Technology Publications.

Kemp, J. E. (1996). School restructuring: Your school can do it. *Techtrends, 41* (1), 12-15.

Kirr, S. T. (1996). Visions of sugarplums: The future of technology, education, and the schools. In S. T. Kirr (Ed.), *Technology and the future of schooling: Ninety-fifth yearbook of the National Society for the Study of Education* (pp. 1-27). Chicago, IL: University of Chicago Press.

Monett, M. L. (1977). The concept of educational need: An analysis of selected literature. *Adult Education, 27* (2), 116-127.

Moore, S., & Mizuba, K. (1968). Innovation diffusion: A study in credibility. *The Educational Forum, 33* (1), 181-185.

Rogers, E. M. (1995). *Diffusion of innovations* (4th ed.). New York, NY: Free Press.

Saint Meinrad School of Theology. (1995). *Proposal for a campus network and technology empowerment project.* Unpublished manuscript, Saint Meinrad School of Theology, St. Meinrad, IN.

Saint Meinrad School of Theology. (1996). *Strategic plan for the Saint Meinrad development program 1996-2001.* Unpublished manuscript, Saint Meinrad School of Theology, St. Meinrad, IN.

Saint Meinrad School of Theology. (1997). *Information technology for theological teaching implementation grant.* Unpublished manuscript, Saint Meinrad School of Theology, St. Meinrad, IN.

Saint Meinrad School of Theology. (1998). *Integrating technology in instruction: Needs analysis project at Saint Meinrad School of Theology.* Unpublished manuscript, Saint Meinrad School of Theology, St. Meinrad, IN.

Strebel, P. (1998). *Harvard business review on change.* Boston, MA: Harvard Business School.

Tafoya, W. L. (1983). Needs assessment: Key to organizational change. *Journal of Police Science Administration, 11* (3), 303-310.

Contact:

HeeKap Lee
819 Campus View Apartments
Bloomington, IN 47408
(812) 857-5484
Email: heelee@indiana.edu

Amy Lawson
3000 South Walnut Street Pike
Apartment L7
Bloomington, IN 47401
(812) 323-0252
Email: amjlawso@indiana.edu

HeeKap Lee earned a doctoral degree in Instructional Systems Technology at Indiana University. He has been involved in an information technology project in Saint Meinrad School of Theology from 1998 to 2001.

Amy Lawson received her master's degree in English from Indiana University in 1999. She is now an instructor and materials developer with the Education Program of Indiana University Information Technology Services. She also trains Indiana University faculty in using web technology with their teaching.

11

Harnessing the Potential of Online Faculty Development: Challenges and Opportunities

Timothy P. Shea
University of Massachusetts, Dartmouth

Pamela D. Sherer
Providence College

Eric W. Kristensen
Orion Educational Development

This chapter explores several issues regarding the current state of online faculty development resources. First, it describes the breadth and depth of today's online teaching and learning resources. Then, it explains the benefits of designing an institutional teaching and learning center portal as a means for organizing and focusing resources. Finally, it discusses the importance of the faculty developer's role in harnessing these resources for individual and institutional advantage. The online portal provides a powerful tool for institutional change on a scale heretofore impossible for most, and puts faculty development at the center of an institution's mission.

INTRODUCTION

The recent explosion of online faculty development resources has expanded the practice of traditional faculty development. These resources have dramatically increased opportunities for faculty development in two major ways. First, they provide faculty developers many new options for supplementing and/or replacing existing faculty development activities. Second, faculty members have opportunities to use online resources to engage in faculty development activities at any time, anywhere through the Internet, and through a rapidly growing base of providers.

The number and variety of available online resources is already daunting. They are available from both academic and for-profit private concerns. Sources from academia include teaching and learning online journals, listservs, chat groups, newsletters, professional association web pages, resource exchanges, and online courses and training programs. For-profit companies offer many similar resources. Notably, we see the rapid escalation of for-profit participation in this arena. Houghton Mifflin, Harcourt Brace, WebCT, Microsoft, and eCollege comprise some of the medium- to large-size companies investing substantially in these efforts.

Two of nine trends in higher education that Arthur Levine (2000b) considers inevitable are 1) a shift from teaching to learning and 2) the addition of two new forms of higher education institutions in addition to the traditional "brick" institution—the "click" institution and the "brick-and-click" institution. The institutional teaching and learning portal, led by the faculty developer, can serve as a significant institutional bridge for moving faculty from a teaching to a learning focus and, at the same time, moving the institution from a "brick" institution toward "the more competitive and attractive...brick-and-click" institution (Levine, 2000b, p. B10).

This chapter explores several issues related to understanding current opportunities in faculty development. First, it describes the breadth and depth of today's online resources regarding teaching and learning. Then, it explains the benefits of designing an institutional teaching and learning portal as a means for organizing and focusing resources. Finally, it discusses the importance of the faculty developer's role in harnessing these resources for individual and institutional advantage.

EXAMPLES OF WEB-BASED FACULTY DEVELOPMENT RESOURCES

The latter part of the 1990s witnessed an explosion of web-based resources available to assist faculty in improving instruction. Several categories of these resources are discussed below, and examples are provided. Appendix 11.1 provides a sample of useful web resources, including the ones highlighted below.

University and College Teaching and Learning Center Web Sites
The opportunities for faculty development created through access to teaching and learning centers have created innumerable opportunities for faculty developers, faculty, and administrators. Dalhousie University's Instructional Development and Technology Sites Worldwide (www.dal.ca/~oidt/ids.html#AD) lists over 100 web sites related to higher education teaching and learning around the globe. In addition to centers for teaching and learning, their web site listings include academic departments in education and instructional technology, university and college centers for instructional technology, associations and networks promoting teaching and learning in higher education, and university centers for instructional and faculty development. For the faculty developer, as well as faculty and administrators, access to these sites not only connects centers, but also provides a library of up-to-date resources and activities on other campuses.

University and College Center Online Workshops
Several university and college faculty development centers have put workshops on the web. Some have used their institution's implementation of Blackboard or WebCT to make them available to faculty, but generally they are only available on a registration basis to faculty in their institution or system. The Adams Center for Teaching Excellence at Abilene Christian University, however, has put an Active Learning Strategies workshop on the web that is accessible to all (www.acu.edu/cte /activelearning). The web site demonstrates four strategies for classroom and online courses based on Mel Silberman's 1996 book, *Active Learning: 101 Strategies to Teach any Subject.* The workshop's introductory pages provide general information about active learning and its uses plus an overview of strategies for the classroom and for online courses. Each strategy is introduced by a general description, a comment on its instructional value, and directions for using the strategy. Printable portable document format (PDF) files containing a pre-class planning form and a post-class summary form are provided for the teacher to use in class preparation, implementation, and assessment. A series of short video demonstrations showing different stages of the strategy in a real class situation provide "touch and feel" to the online workshop. Each strategy is cross-referenced to Mel Silberman's book. This site represents the beginning of a growing number of high-quality, multimedia workshops developed and sponsored by individual centers.

Virtual Teaching and Learning Technology Centers (V)TLTC

A number of faculty developers have just recently begun experimenting with a new concept, the Virtual Teaching and Learning Technology Center (V)TLTC. An example of an innovative, well-designed, emerging center is the Appalachian College Association and its Virtual Teaching, Learning, and Technology web site. Its stated mission is "to provide a place and means for the 33 member colleges to share knowledge in order to constantly improve the education offered to its students" (www. acaweb.org/Vcenter/). The project is funded by a grant from the Mellon Foundation. The Virtual Center provides access to virtual departments (www.acaweb.org/Vcenter/virtualdepartments.htm), information technology and services, instructional design resources, Appalachian College Association libraries, workshops, training and conferences, listservs, a faculty database, and more.

The virtual component of the faculty development office is moving well past a simple, informational web site. A recent virtual conference sponsored by WebCT and hosted by Steve Gilbert of the Teaching, Learning, and Technology (TLT) Group discusses this emerging model for faculty development in some detail (Gilbert, 2000b).

Online Teaching and Learning Courses

Since 1995, there has been continued growth in online faculty professional development courses offered by college and university teaching centers, higher education professional associations, and business organizations. Due to the variety of technology and pedagogical issues involved in moving to computer-based or computer-enhanced instruction, the current trend in online faculty development seems to be an integrated series of course modules. Courses can be as short as one day or one week, and some offer a longer series of courses leading to certificates. Most courses charge a fee.

One such program is the Distance Education Certificate Program (DECP) at the University of Wisconsin, Madison. The DECP "is a professional development curriculum designed to build or enhance knowledge, skills, and leadership in distance education and training. This program offers a curriculum of core modules and electives and uses a variety of distance learning formats including modular print packages, audiotapes, videotapes, audio conference seminars, and Internet seminars to reach working professionals in their home communities" (www.wisc. edu/depd). Upon satisfactory completion of 200 curriculum hours (20 continuing education units), a Certificate of Professional Development is awarded.

Students may enroll in individual courses on a certificate or a noncertificate basis. The DECP can be completed individually as a self-paced track curriculum or as a collaborative track curriculum using a cohort learning group. Where a cohort system is used, faculty have the opportunity to become involved in learning communities outside their institutions and take advantage of expertise from other institutions and organizations. The DECP web site provides three major learning hubs which include references and resources, learner support services, and a learning center. The resources involved in developing programs such as the DECP are often beyond the reach of individual centers. Therefore, most institutions will likely be taking advantage of existing, well-developed program offerings.

Technology Product Companies
One of the major reasons for the ongoing explosion of online resources is the maturation of software tools for creating and maintaining such sites. WebCT is one of a handful of major providers for course management software, the core software for creating and delivering distance learning classes and web-assisted, traditional classes. The home page (www.webct.com) is a good demonstration of a portal (discussed later), where WebCT is providing a variety of value-added services in order to create brand loyalty in a highly competitive market. In addition to providing links for seeing a demo of the software, downloading the software for a trial period, and ordering or reordering the software, the home page contains options for

- students, including online tutoring, a career center, a scholarship database, a discussion room concerning binge drinking, an online research tool, and technical support

- instructors, that includes discipline-specific content and discussion boards, newsletters, an online course (Introduction to Multimedia), a collection of case studies of exemplary courses, online colloquia events, and technical support

One great advantage faculty developers have is that the competition in the software market will ensure regular updates and improvements to course management software.

Publishing Companies
Houghton Mifflin's Faculty Development Programs unit has provided face-to-face campus-based faculty development workshops for a number

of years. Faculty development professionals under contract have delivered these for Houghton Mifflin, which markets and supports the delivery of these workshops to campuses around the country (www.facultytraining.com). Since 1999, Houghton Mifflin Faculty Development Programs have partnered with both software companies and academic associations. Technology partnerships include WisdomTools, Inc., to use their proprietary web-based tools, and Time Revealed Scenarios, to develop online faculty development programs. Academic partners in the development of these workshops, called FacultyDirect, include The League for Innovation in the Community College, The TLT Group: The Teaching, Learning, and Technology affiliate of the American Association for Higher Education (AAHE), The Historically Black Colleges and Universities Faculty Development Network, and The National Teaching and Learning Forum.

The product consists of a suite of workshops designed for four different audiences: college and university faculty, community college faculty, teaching assistants, and those interested in the integration of technology into teaching and learning. They are available to individuals on a scheduled basis throughout the year. Enrollment is limited to 25 participants per section (a minimum enrollment of 15 is required to offer the workshop). Participants are asked to invest 20 hours for asynchronous activities and discussions during a four-week workshop. Group registration packages are also available for institutions, districts, systems, and consortia. These workshops will be scheduled according to a group's needs, and will be facilitated by Houghton Mifflin's Faculty Development Programs or they will provide training for facilitators designated by the contracting group (www.facultytraining.com/facdirect/index.html).

Associations
Good efforts are currently underway at a number of associations, though none offer comprehensive resources for teaching, learning, and technology. Three examples illustrate the range of available resources. The American Association for Higher Education's web site offers the broadest array of resources for faculty development. In particular, the Teaching Initiatives and TLT pages offer ideas and examples of faculty development activities appropriate for both individuals and institutions (http://www.aahe.org).

The Professional and Organizational Development Network in Higher Education (POD), North America's association of faculty development professionals and practitioners, is a rich source of information and publications for the development of teaching and learning in higher

education. It also sponsors a particularly effective listserv for those involved in faculty development programming (http://lamar.colostate.
edu/~ckfgill/).

The Association of American Colleges and Universities (AACU) offers a convenient group of resources in its Knowledge Network section,
which bills itself as a "resource hub for general education, teaching and
learning, civic responsibility, campus leadership and more..." (www.
aacu-edu.org).

Professional Academic Discipline Associations

Professional disciplinary associations provide a variety of member services. Most associations have interest groups or divisions focused on
teaching and are accessible online. One example is The Society for the
Teaching of Psychology (STP) (http://teachpsych.lemoyne.edu/teach-
psych/div/divindex.html), a division of the American Psychological Association (APA). STP represents the interests of psychologists in academic institutions from the secondary through the graduate level.
Among its extensive services, it publishes *Teaching of Psychology*, a quarterly journal devoted to improving teaching and learning, develops and
distributes a variety of peer-reviewed teaching and advising materials,
sponsors programs and conferences, maintains a web site *(OTRP-Online)*,
and fosters a teaching community through *PsychTeacher*™ , a moderated
electronic discussion list. In addition, it publishes a monthly electronic
newsletter, *TOPNEWS-Online*, through *Psychology Partnerships Projects*
that includes extensive links to psychology resources worldwide. STP
also provides resources through *Psych-E*, an electronic journal for undergraduates. Clearly, professional associations are major players in professional development for instructors, and increasingly, for students. Current technologies provide new and exciting learning connections and
opportunities, and instructors are encouraged to explore their professional associations' online resources.

Online Newsletters

The National Teaching and Learning Forum publishes a bimonthly
newsletter containing articles on teaching and learning in higher education. The editor aims to create a conversation on teaching and learning
on a wide variety of cross-disciplinary concerns. One or more articles
from the current issue and sample articles from previous issues are available online from the newsletter's web site. Individuals can order print

subscriptions and institutions can order site licenses for their entire faculty, making all past and current issues available online (www.ntlf.com).

Teaching and Learning Online Journals and Magazines
The development and availability of online teaching and learning journals continues to expand. Some are currently accessible in both print and online. An excellent example of an exclusively online journal is *The Technology Source*, a free, peer-reviewed, bimonthly periodical whose purpose is to provide "thoughtful, illuminating articles that will assist educators as they face the challenge of integrating information technology tools into teaching and into managing educational organizations" (http://horizon.unc.edu/TS/). The journal provides articles and resources on faculty and staff development, assessment, technology tools, case studies, commentary, etc. Because of its online format, this type of journal is readily accessible to all faculty, and like print journals, develops a community of national and international followers interested in this particular faculty development technology thrust. In addition, it is easily archived for future reference and research.

International Resources Online
The International Consortium for Educational Developers (ICED) was formed in Oxford, England, in 1993, with the goal of linking national and regional educational development networks and sharing best practices in higher education across national boundaries. It sponsors biannual conferences, the latest having taken place July 2000 in Bielefeld, Germany (www.uni-bielefeld.de/IZHD/ICED/). Its member organizations sponsor web pages with numerous resources. HERDSA (Higher Education Research and Development Society of Australasia) (www.herdsa.org.au) offers conferences, publications, and sponsors research on teaching and learning in higher education with links to many of these resources on its web page. SEDA, the Staff and Educational Development Association of the United Kingdom, offers accreditation services for faculty development professionals as well as publications, conferences, and web resources for faculty development practitioners (http://www.seda.demon.co.uk/). Particularly useful is its links page, with pointers to many resources and organizations dedicated to faculty development in the English-speaking world (http://www.seda.demon.co.uk/other.html). Links to faculty development organizations in other countries can also be found at the Society for Teaching and Learning in Higher Education/La société pour l'avancement de la

pédagogie dans l'enseignement supérieur in Canada (http://www.umani-toba.ca/academic_support/uts/ stlhe).

ADVANTAGES AND CHALLENGES

The breadth and depth of these new online resources and providers offer a wealth of teaching and learning opportunities for faculty and faculty developers. In particular, faculty developers and centers have much to gain, including

- more faculty development opportunities than ever before

- continuous provision of faculty development through anytime/anywhere delivery of resources

- easier access to information, especially at time of need

- access to providers of faculty development beyond one's institution

- increased opportunities for faculty developers to connect with and assist a greater number of faculty and for faculty to assist one another

- increased opportunities to facilitate the development of faculty learning communities inside and outside one's institution

- online opportunities for publishing teaching and learning scholarship

- expanding faculty development from an event on-campus to everywhere all the time

- opportunities to develop fresh models for faculty development

All of the above, through increased access to a larger variety and higher quality of pedagogical resources, contribute to more engaged, better informed, creative faculty with an emphasis on the role of faculty as learners. They also create a variety of new avenues for faculty to learn together and alone.

As faculty developers continue to gain experience using these new resources, they will need to be particularly mindful of how traditional faculty development practices can be utilized to maximize their benefits. In particular, faculty developers will need to focus on continuing to provide

- occasions for face-to-face faculty development events

- leadership for campus focus, direction, and coordination of all faculty development resources

- opportunities for collaboration across departments, divisions, academic/student affairs, etc.

One thing is certain: The flood of new, online resources is only the beginning. The challenge, even at this early stage, is to find a way to bring the best and most meaningful online resources to the faculty at your institution. The next section, which introduces the concept of the portal, provides a means for accomplishing that objective.

HARNESSING THE ONLINE ONSLAUGHT: THE POWER OF THE PORTAL

The previous section gives examples of currently available web resources for faculty and faculty developers. However, a number of faculty development web sites have moved past simply posting lists of web resources. This is part of a growing trend—the creation and maintenance of a cyber community. The notion of a cyber community is not a new one but neither is it an idea that has had time to mature. The most intense activity has been in the for-profit sector, often under the guise of e-business or e-commerce. Academia has jumped into the fray with vigor since 1999. For business, it is a community of customers, stockholders, suppliers, and the like. For academia, it is a community of alumni, students, faculty, administration, and prospective students. This section will summarize some of the lessons others have learned about creating successful online communities and about the important role that the portal plays.

The Portal

The portal, an increasingly common concept in today's Internet world, "is a place that draws people to it because of what it offers and what it enables" (Norman, 2000). An example of a general portal is Yahoo.com, AOL.com, or MSN.com. Each service wants you to enter the World Wide Web through them, so they try to offer the most value to the general user—an easy to use search engine, an email service, a chat room service, as well as current news, sports, and entertainment. The value they provide entices the user to continue to use their site as an entry point to the World Wide Web.

A company's home page would be another type of portal. Its purpose is to serve existing customers, prospective customers, suppliers, and stockholders. The home page would have information and services of interest to all stakeholders. Meanwhile, a very distinctive path through the site is developed for each stakeholder group so that they may pursue information and services specifically focused to their needs. Likewise, a university's campus portal will serve as a "gateway to the entire Internet and an aggregator of information on one or more areas of interest" (Pittinsky, 1999). These sites will typically have a common home page as well as different paths for current students, prospective students, alumni, and faculty. The prospective student path might include university promotion of the school, admissions, academic support, and career services. In this way, each path is "an abridged and customized version of the institutional Web presence" (Java in Administration Special Interest Group (JA-SIG) Clearinghouse, 2000), or put another way, "personalized information sources and communities of interest within a campus or university World Wide Web site" (Olsen, 2000).

The primary purpose of the portal is to provide value. Groundswell, a consulting company specializing in portal development, promotes the following characteristics for a successful, valuable portal (www.ground swell.com).

- An aggregation of products and services including

  ~ knowledge that is useful for the intended audience(s)

  ~ transactions, such as online purchasing or registering for a workshop

  ~ analytics, tools to help the user find, compare, and evaluate products

  ~ collaboration, or means to support, facilitate, and enhance personal connections;

- A people-centric, well-designed site

- A focus on developing brand loyalty, by such means as encouraging communication by email or through online registration

- An unparalleled online experience

A second, more detailed description of portal content with regard to features, information, tools, and relationships is available from David Eisler's work as provost of Weber State University (Eisler, 2000).

For the faculty developer, an institution's teaching and learning portal will be different from but linked to the campus portal or institutional web site, and also different from but linked to the various course portals that serve individual distance learning or web-enhanced classes. An institutional teaching and learning portal can provide value by offering a useful collection of resources and communication links that will attract faculty members to the site and provide incentive for them to use it again—whenever they want to be connected to a community of faculty focused on teaching and learning.

Much of the value of portals, especially an academic institution's teaching and learning portal, is fueled by two trends. First, we live in an age where faculty and students need more information than ever, and need their information refreshed and updated more frequently than ever before in order to be effective (Levine, 2000a). Secondly, due to information overload, finding the right information is often a difficult, tedious task. As teachers, faculty are being pushed

- to find new ways to improve both their productivity inside the classroom as well as enhance their role outside the classroom (Sherer & Shea, in press)

- to find ways to be more sensitive to diversity issues in the classroom

- to be more attentive to the needs of the fastest growing demographic of college students—adult learners

- to incorporate an ever-expanding array of new instructional technologies

- to successfully compete against the well-heeled, profit-making sector that is rapidly making inroads into the traditional academic marketplace

Unfortunately, there is too much information, too many attractive options, and a lot of useless information, especially on our main source of connection, the World Wide Web. Therefore, we are both overconnected and disconnected at the same time (Hallowell, 1999). This is exacerbated by the overlap of resources provided by knowledge producers and content providers, such as course management software providers, textbook publishers, PBS, and the like.

For the inundated faculty member, the faculty developer can become the architect of an institution's teaching and learning portal, providing value as a filter and as a connection point. By designing useful, well-organized, and easy-to-access content from within the campus and beyond, the faculty developer can provide access to high-quality, relevant, and coherent information. The faculty developer provides connections by identifying and providing means to communicate with both on-campus and off-campus resources. On-campus resources might include the reference librarian, media services, registrar's office, student technical assistants, sources of internal funding opportunities, and the local Teaching, Learning, and Technology Roundtable (TLTR). Off-campus links might include the national TLTR, assessment centers, professional societies, and book publishers who also provide faculty development workshops and discipline-specific online content. In doing so, the portal creates a link between faculty using the portal and the faculty development office.

While the definition of a portal is not precise, three characteristics common to most portals include: 1) a core product or service plus related, value-added products, 2) services and connections outside the site's institution, and/or 3) a clear organization of different paths through the site depending on specific interests of the end-user. The following are examples of academic web sites already described in an earlier section with some characteristics of portals.

- WebCT, a leading course management software company (http:// www.webct.com/), illustrates the idea of connecting value-added components such as discussion groups on current topics (for example, binge drinking), recent educational news, tutoring, research, and discipline-specific course content. These components are intended to get student and faculty users to come back and use the site as part of a learning community, rather than simply as a software company.

- Dalhousie University's Office of Instructional Development and Technology (http://www.dal.ca/~oidt/) lists internal resources but also maintains a list of links to instructional development and technology sites worldwide (http://www.dal.ca/~oidt/ids.html).

- Abilene Christian University's Center for Teaching Excellence (www.acu.edu/cte) focuses on internal resources but clearly defines separate, multilevel paths for first-time web visitors, information on academic computing, instructional technology available on campus, faculty interests, and policies. The site becomes an entry point and a guide to help the user get the information they desire.

A teaching and learning portal for a specific institution begins with the strategic objectives for teaching and learning within the institution. The faculty developer, as architect of the institution's teaching and learning portal, will focus on organizing the enormous variety of resources available, from on campus and throughout the web. The goal is to create a relevant, organized, and coherent site that will also integrate communication links to helpful online discussion groups, chat rooms, and the like. The next section considers the changing emphases and roles that faculty developers will want to consider in order to become a successful architect of their institution's teaching and learning portal.

EMERGING LEADERSHIP ROLES FOR FACULTY DEVELOPMENT

The emergence of online resources for faculty development, available essentially any time and anywhere, changes the possibilities for faculty developers to reach faculty and become more effective change agents on their campuses. The implementation of a significant, virtual component can provide an important lever for increasing the effectiveness of a faculty development center or program. It also creates new roles and metaphors for staff as well as programs. These changes can help move faculty development to a more central place in the everyday lives of faculty and require a greater leadership role than ever before, supporting the institution's teaching and learning mission.

One of the most important tasks to accomplish while setting up a virtual component for your faculty development program consists of making sure the aims and principles of the web site, or portal, are consistent with the mission and goals of your institution and its academic affairs office. For a fully integrated web presence on campus, faculty developers will need the full support and collaboration of those in control of the financial and staff resources needed. From there, faculty developers can begin to forge collaborations with information services, learning support services, library, printing and media services, grants, and possibly even the faculty senate and union to create a full service web site that faculty will want to use consistently.

Each campus, of course, will have many differences in what is possible and what is desirable to include in a site, but the goal is to provide a full-service faculty portal to internal and external services and programs on which faculty depend. Focus groups and surveys can provide invaluable information for the direction such a project might take.

In implementing a portal, faculty developers may need to conceive of their roles a bit differently than they have in the past. They will need technical skills and knowledge. They will need to understand how to sort and distribute information more effectively. Finally, they will need to expand their centers to encompass, at least in a virtual sense, technology, distance learning, and media services, as well as teaching. In order to accomplish this, they will need to collaborate with a number of units on campus, presumably with the support of administrators and with funding. In this way, faculty developers can become central figures in the delivery of resources to faculty.

Metaphors that capture elements of these new roles include diplomat, orchestral conductor, and outfitter. For example, to forge the collaborations necessary to implement an institutional teaching and learning portal, the skills of a diplomat would be very useful. Coordinating and managing a number of services from different offices on campus would require the skills of an orchestral conductor, to make sure the individual services work harmoniously and coherently with the whole. When thinking about the elements needed in an institutional teaching and learning portal, the skill of an expedition outfitter also comes to mind (Bulik, 2000). What will a faculty member need during a typical semester, and how can the center support it, both virtually and physically? For this, true collaboration (not just coordination) with all relevant units on campus is needed.

All of this points to a possible reordering of priorities for programs and centers. By reaching out more broadly to more people, the center's workload will undoubtedly increase. Developers will need to spend more time negotiating and developing collaborative partnerships with other units on campus. They will need to devote time to facilitating online discussions and workshops. And, they will need to continue to provide settings where they can meet with faculty members face-to-face. From the experience of faculty developers who have run online workshops, for example, it is clear that face-to-face interaction with the faculty development office dramatically increases the likelihood that online workshop participants will engage fully and complete their projects.

The metaphor of a lone outpost concerned with teaching on campus no longer serves faculty developers or their institutions well. Teaching is, in most instances, given a high place in an institution's mission, but less so in implementation. A successful faculty development program will be able, with leadership and foresight, to take the goal of supporting teaching and learning on campus from mere lip service to reality by working across departments, divisions, and administrative units such as student affairs, academic affairs, information services, and support services. This requires the ability to plan strategically with broad constituencies to create a learning community for faculty (Cox, 2001).

Useful metaphors for a virtual teaching and learning center include base camp; directory; reference desk; mentoring center; resource room; forum; and innovation, research, and/or assessment center (Gilbert,

2000b). From a faculty member's point of view, useful metaphors for a virtual teaching and learning center can include workspace, play space, studio, training center, lounge, and stress clinic. It is clear that in order to build these elements into a virtual teaching and learning center that is specifically oriented to the needs of an institution and its faculty, the faculty developer will take an active leadership role in creating true collaboration with many units on and off campus. One may see the stirrings of a learning community growing out of this collaboration. Faculty members will be able to form their own learning circles and groups to share information, communicate with colleagues about teaching and professional development, get financial support for projects through mini-grants, and register for internal or external online workshops.

Even though the priorities of institutions have moved closer to those of faculty development programs since the mid-1980s, meaningful ways to effect broad institutional change have been difficult to implement with the relatively small resources allocated to most faculty development programs. An institutional teaching and learning portal, developed collaboratively with other units on campus, appropriately funded and aligned with institutional goals, can bring to a faculty member's desktop the wealth of substantial online resources and connections with colleagues both on and off campus with a single click. This fosters an enhanced faculty learning community and allows a relatively small program to have much greater impact on teaching, learning, and professional development than would otherwise be possible. It gives faculty developers a powerful tool, a lever, for institutional change on a scale heretofore impossible for most, and gives faculty development a place at the center of an institution's mission.

REFERENCES

Bulik, R. (2000). Issues, challenges and changing metaphors: Teaching and learning in the virtual classroom. *Journal for the Art of Teaching, 7* (1), 17-34.

Cox, M. (2001). Faculty learning communities: Change agents for transforming institutions into learning organizations. In D. Lieberman & C. Wehlburg (Eds.), *To improve the academy: Vol. 19. Resources for faculty, instructional, and organizational development* (pp. 69-93). Bolton, MA: Anker.

Eisler, D. (2000). *Dave's web page* (Online). Available: http://weber.edu/deisler/portal_content.htm

Gilbert, S. (2000a). *Realizing the vision: Scaling online education from the classroom to the institution.* Presentation at the Blackboard Summit 2000, Washington, DC.

Gilbert, S. (2000b). *Virtual teaching, learning, and technology centers: Meeting the rising expectations for information technology* (Online). Available: http://webct.com/ecolloquia/viewpage?name=ecolloquia_event_10

Groundswell. (2000). *Groundswell Hawaii surf company* (Online). Available: http://www.groundswell.com

Hallowell, E. (1999). *Connect.* New York, NY: Pantheon.

Java in Administration Special Interest Group (JA-SIG) Clearinghouse. (2000). *Portal framework project* (Online). Available: http://www.mis2.udel.edu/ja-sig/portal.html

Levine, A. (2000a). *The remaking of the American university.* Presentation at the Blackboard Summit 2000, Washington, DC.

Levine, A. (2000b, October 27). The future of colleges: Nine inevitable changes. *The Chronicle of Higher Education,* p. B10.

Norman, M. (2000). Portal technology: In the looking glass. *Converge* (Online). Available: http://www.convergemag.com/SpecialPubs/Portal/portal.shtm

Olsen, F. (2000). Institutions collaborate on development of free portal software. *The Chronicle of Higher Education* (Online). Available: www.chronicle.com/free/2000/05/200005050lt.htm

Pittinsky, M. (1999). Campus and course portals in 2015. *Converge* (Online). Available: http://www.convergemag.com/Publications/CNVGOct 99/Possibilities/Possibilities.shtm

Sherer, P., & Shea, T. (in press). Designing courses outside the classroom: New opportunities with the electronic delivery toolkit. *College Teaching.*

Silberman, M. (1996). *Active learning: 101 strategies to teach any subject.* Boston, MA: Allyn and Bacon.

Contact:

Timothy P. Shea
Department of Marketing/B.I.S.
University of Massachusetts, Darmouth
North Dartmouth, MA 02747
(508) 999-8445
Email: tshea@umassd.edu

Pamela D. Sherer
Department of Management
Providence College
Providence, RI 02918
(401) 865-2036
Email: psherer@providence.edu

Eric W. Kristensen
Orion Educational Development
87 Woodward Ave.
West Gloucester, MA 01930-2450
(978) 283-9089
Email: Orion@post.harvard.edu

Timothy P. Shea is Associate Professor for the Marketing/Business Information Systems (BIS) Department at the University of Massachusetts, Dartmouth. He has primarily taught in the area of systems development, database, and total quality management. Previously, at Fitchburg State College, he served as Co-coordinator of Distance Learning. His research interests include technology diffusion in academia, e-commerce in the retail food industry, and distance learning.

Pamela D. Sherer is Assistant Professor of Management at Providence College, where she teaches courses in organizational change and development, organizational behavior, human resource management, and managing workplace diversity. She was the founding Director of Providence College's Center for Teaching Excellence and chaired its Faculty Development Committee for six years. Her research interests include faculty development practices, pedagogy and diversity issues, and collaborative learning.

Eric W. Kristensen is currently a consultant for Orion Educational Development. He began working in faculty development in 1979 at Harvard's Danforth (now Bok) Center for Teaching and Learning. In 1990, he founded and directed the Office for Faculty and Instructional Development at Berklee College of Music in Boston. Since 1999, he has been consulting with faculty development programs in the United States and the United Kingdom. He has served as President of the Professional and Organizational Development Network in Higher Education (POD) and has served as its representative to the International Consortium for Educational (ICED) Council.

APPENDIX 11.1
ONLINE SOURCES AND PROVIDERS OF FACULTY DEVELOPMENT

University and College Teaching and Learning Center Web Sites
Dalhousie University's Instructional Development and Technology Sites Worldwide
    http://www.dal.ca/~oidt/ids.html#AD
University of Kansas Listing of Worldwide Teaching and Learning Centers
    http://eagle.cc.ukans.edu/~cte/index.html

University and College Center Online Workshops
The Adams Center for Teaching Excellence at Abilene Christian
    http://www.acu.edu/cte/activelearning/

Virtual Teaching and Learning Technology Centers (V)TLTC
The Appalachian College Association and Virtual Teaching, Learning, and Technology
    http://www.acaweb.org
Center for New Designs in Learning and Scholarship (CNDLS)
    http://www.georgetown.edu/main/provost/candles/

Online Teaching and Learning Courses
Distance Education Certificate Program University of Wisconsin, Madison
    http://www.wisc.edu/depd
LERN: A one-week course (Teaching Online)
    http://www.lern.org/TeachingOnline/
UCLA: Online Teaching Program (OTP)
    http://www.onlinelearning.net/CourseCatalog/index.html
Florida State University: Five-module online professional development program
    http://www.fsu.edu/~pie/

Technology Product Companies
WebCT
    http://www.webct.com
Blackboard
    http://www.blackboard.com/
eCollege
    http://www.ecollege.com/

JonesKnowledge.com
http://www.jonesknowledge.com/

Publishing Companies
Houghton-Mifflin's Faculty Development Programs
http://www.facultytraining.com
Harcourt Brace
http://www.harcourtelearning.com/
Southwestern Thompson Learning (E-learning)
http://www.swcollege.com/front.html

Associations (resources, listservs, chat groups, archives)
American Association for Higher Education (AAHE)
http://www.aahe.org
Association of American Colleges and Universities (AACU)
http://www.aacu-edu.org
DeLiberations
http://www.lgu.ac.uk/deliberations/
Epiphany Project for Teachers of Writing
http://www.has.vcu.edu/epiphany/
Professional and Organizational Development Network in Higher Education (POD)
http://www.podnetwork.org
Tomorrow's Professor Listserv (Originates at Stanford University's Learning Laboratory)
http://sll-6.stanford.edu/projects/tomprof/

Online Newsletters
Infobits
http://www.unc.edu/cit/infobits/infobits.html
Teachdaedalus: Moderated discussion lists
http://daedalus.pearsoned.com/
National Teaching and Learning Forum (NTLF)
http://www.ntlf.com
eCollege Newsletter
http://www.ecollege.com/
Chronicle Report on Teaching (from *The Chronicle of Higher Education*)
http://www.chronicle-teaching@chronicle.com
TLT Group Flashlight Newsletter
http://www.tltgroup.org/resources/F-LIGHT/f-light_Aug2000.html

Teaching and Learning Online Journals and Magazines
The Educational Development Resource Center Online Journals in Education
   http://158.132.100.221/INET_EDU.folder/OnlineJrnls.html
The Technology Source
   http://horizon.unc.edu/TS/

International Resources Online
International Consortium for Educational Developers (ICED)
   http://www.uni-bielefeld.de/IZHD/ICED/
Higher Education Research and Development Society of Australasia (HERDSA)
   http://www.herdsa.org.au
Society for Teaching and Learning in Higher Education/La société pour l'avancement de la pédagogie dans l'enseignement supérieur (STLHE/SAPES) in Canada
   http://www.umanitoba.ca/academic_support/uts/stlhe
The Staff and Educational Development Association of the United Kingdom (SEDA)
   http://www.seda.demon.co.uk
UK Learning and Teaching Support Network
   http://www.ltsn.ac.uk

Section III

The Learner, the Professor, and the Learning Environment

12

The Millennial Learner: Challenges and Opportunities

Saundra Y. McGuire
Louisiana State University

Dennis A. Williams
Georgetown University

Students enrolled in college today are, in many respects, quite different from students enrolled a few decades ago. Learners today seem more focused on being credentialed, and less concerned with obtaining a broad-based, liberal arts education. Today's faculty may find it challenging to provide engaging learning activities for this generation of students. Millennial educators must instill in students a desire to think critically and provide them with strategies that will make them more efficient learners. Campus learning centers and faculty development centers can work together to foster an academic climate that helps all students to realize their full academic potential.

INTRODUCTION

The term "millennial learner" can take on a wide variety of meanings. For the purposes of this chapter, however, a millennial learner is defined as 1) a student of traditional college age (17–24) and 2) a student who is attending college in the year 2001 or beyond.

In discussing the challenges and opportunities presented by the millennial learner, this chapter focuses on three characteristics which are contrasted with corresponding characteristics of learners in the 1970s. These comparisons are offered as generalizations; neither group is monolithic. However, the majority of learners in each group are associated with the dominant characteristics assigned to the group. The three contrasting characteristics are their attitudes about acquiring a degree, their access to and utilization of computers, and their tolerance for nonengaging pedagogical techniques (Braxton, Milem, & Sullivan, 2000).

Table 12.1 is based on the authors' combined 60 years of experience teaching college students and assisting them in developing learning strategies. The term "producer mentality" refers to the general expectation that the student must produce a quality product before a satisfactory grade can be assigned for work performed. The term "consumer mentality" refers to the expectation that if tuition and fees are paid, a degree will be granted. Additionally, the students (consumers) must be kept satisfied during the process.

The ubiquitous presence of computers on today's campuses is unparalleled. In the 1970s, it was unlikely that any students other than computer science majors would have free access to computers on a regular basis. Today, however, if the residence halls on campus are not wired for 24 hour Internet access, many students and parents are likely to look elsewhere for college enrollment. Furthermore, it is the authors' experience that students today are more likely to require active learning strategies to keep them focused on educational pursuits than were the students in the 1970s.

TABLE 12.1
Characteristics of 1970s Learners and Millennial Learners

1970s Learners	*Millennial Learners*
Producer mentality	Consumer mentality
Very limited computer access	Ubiquitous computer access
Tolerant of nonengaging pedagogical techniques	Intolerant of nonengaging pedagogical techniques

For purposes of comparison, a contrast is also made between three characteristics of the typical millennial faculty member and the typical faculty member of the 1970s (Table 12.2) (Sax, Astin, Korn, & Gilmartin, 1999).

TABLE 12.2
Characteristics of 1970s Faculty and Millennial Faculty

1970s Faculty	*Millennial Faculty*
App. 25 years older than students	App. 30 years older than students
Uses primarily lecture format	Uses primarily lecture format
Knows little about learning mechanisms and strategies	Knows little about learning mechanisms and strategies

It is apparent that the millennial learners typically are quite different from their 1970s counterpart, but the millennial faculty members are very similar, at least with respect to the three characteristics listed.

Student and Faculty Gaps
The characteristics of the millennial learner provide special challenges for educators, but also special opportunities. There is currently a very large gap between faculty expectations of student behavior and actual student behavior. Students entering their first-year of college at Miami University reported that they had studied about an hour a day outside of class during high school (Schilling & Schilling, 1999). These same students, however, expected to spend 30–40 hours a week in academic pursuits in college, including class attendance. College faculty members expected students to spend two to three hours outside of class for every hour spent in class. This represents a significant gap between professors' expectations of the requirements for student success and the students' expectations for their own success. Even more dramatic was that the time students actually spent studying was significantly less than their own expectations. Many students actually spent 20 or fewer hours per week on academic work, including class attendance.

In addition to the expectation gap, there is a communication gap between millennial students and faculty. This gap is in large part due to the age difference between the two groups. According to the Office of Budget and Planning at Louisiana State University (LSU), the average age of full-time instructional faculty is 47.2 years, and the average age of LSU undergraduate students is 21.6 years. Faculty members are likely to have begun their teaching careers in the 1970s or early 1980s, and have expectations set by their experiences in those decades. However, today's faculty members are increasingly forced to deal with such situations as cell phones and pagers ringing in the middle of a lecture, or students IMing (instant messaging) each other during a computer class.

This communication gap also extends to the communication of learning tasks. If a faculty member assigns a paper with the expectation that much of the content will involve analysis, but the student thinks that descriptive information is all that is needed, both will be disappointed with the results. The professor is disappointed with the quality of the papers received, and the student is disappointed in the grade assigned. The student goes to the campus learning center to complain that the grade was unfair, and the professor goes to the faculty development center to complain that the students are not performing well. In a sense, both assertions are correct because the expectations for student performance were not clearly communicated to the student. Today's students must be explicitly taught the difference between activities such as description, analysis, synthesis, and evaluation in the hierarchy of learning tasks. Without explicit instruction and clearly defined expectations, they will not be able to perform at the desired level.

The Millennial Learner

In the early to mid-1990s when institutions of higher education began to transform themselves from teacher-centered to learner-centered institutions, the focus shifted from the quality of the teaching to the quality of the learning that was occurring (Barr & Tagg, 1995). When the emphasis shifted to the learner, the concept of the student as consumer began to emerge, and this, too, had significant implications for higher education.

The movie *Field of Dreams* has a well-known phrase: "If you build it, they will come." We now have in place what surely would have been considered a field of dreams by some educators—the nonelitist ones—a half century ago. We have built a vast system of higher education, and they are indeed coming—in record numbers (Baldwin, 2000). And students are not coming just for the love of learning. They are coming because they were promised something. This process has essentially created a carnival of credentialism. Students want to get their tickets punched. They want a certificate, a diploma, a degree, a title, something specific that will be their platinum card to the good life. An indication of this phenomenon is the decline in the percentage of students pursuing degrees in the liberal arts, including the sciences, and the increase in the percentage of students pursuing degrees in a pre-professional or technical field (Baldwin, 2000).

The financial rewards associated with attending college are indeed significant. According to Census Bureau figures (Reich, 2000), the average income in 1998 of families headed by someone with only a high school education was $48,434. That family income rose to $65,524 when the bread winner had an associate's degree; jumped to $85,423 with a bachelor's degree; and $101,670 with a master's degree. A professional degree raised the family to an average income of $147,170.

With so much at stake, and so many people hustling for a piece of the pie, students may not perceive themselves as having time for learning for the sake of knowledge, or for the thrill of discovery. The millennial learner is a bottom-line learner.

This was demonstrated in a recent conversation one of the authors had with a student who had been the valedictorian of her high school graduating class. The student had encountered sufficient problems with her university level science classes that she had decided to abandon her pre-med major—at least temporarily. She had decided to major in psychology, but wondered if she could hedge her bets by double majoring in a field not offered by this university. She would take those classes in another university across town, which had the appropriate department—but whose diploma carried, she thought, less luster. She was advised that taking some outside courses in a field of interest was a good idea, but that she might not be able to successfully pursue a double major at different institutions. Then, inevitably, she got to the bottom line: Would she ever find a job with just a psychology degree? Only when she was introduced to an actual psychology major with an actual job did she feel confident that her college degree in psychology would allow her to become gainfully employed.

Although students in the 1970s were plenty ambitious about what job they would get, there appeared to be considerably less anxiety about the very prospect of making a living. Certainly, a liberal arts degree from a selective college was thought to guarantee employment. But then such a degree did not cost upwards of $120,000, as can be the case today (Gose, 2000). Loans were not as universal as home mortgages and credit card balances—and, significantly, there were fewer first-generation college students, people for whom even the financing necessary for a local public college is a risky bet (Farrell, 1999). Of course students are anxious. Having so much to gain can be even more frightening than having little to lose.

So this creates a dilemma for the millennial educator. There is an old adage: Give a man a fish and he eats for a day; teach him to fish and he eats every day. Teachers believe that. When a grade school teacher encourages a child to sound out a word instead of immediately identifying it for him, she's teaching him to fish—by reading. Educators who want to facilitate student learning are handing out fishing rod kits. However, many students are looking for prepared seafood dinners to go. They might stand still for some microwaving instructions, but they have no interest in knowing how to catch it, clean it, or cook it.

In the Center for Minority Educational Affairs at Georgetown University, course tutors are assigned free of charge to students by request. First, however, a student must meet with an academic advisor, who will try to help him or her understand something about his or her own learning style, will inquire about the professor's teaching style, and will ask if the student has explored other resources, including attending professor's office hours and teaching assistants. Students will routinely listen to all the questions, nod, and ask: "Okay, can I have a tutor now?"

Students in higher education often view themselves as paying for the product, not the process. For some students, the goal is not the knowledge that results from learning but the rewards conveyed by demonstrating a temporary mastery of that knowledge.

It is, therefore, essential for educators to articulate the importance of learning as a process of self-discovery and growth. Because students may have so little knowledge and imagination about the connection between some traditional academic fields and jobs, and because both spheres are changing so fast, the skills of learning take on even greater significance.

Technology

We, in academe, must explicitly demonstrate the connection between what we do and what happens in the outside world. We do what we do because we love it. The vast majority of students we encounter will not follow in our footsteps. However, we must find a way to convey our passion to them so that they will develop the capacity to love what they do professionally. They must be taught that knowing or discovering how and why are much more important than simply knowing what (Handy, 1998). We owe them that. We owe it to ourselves.

Offering ourselves as examples of learners obviously becomes much more difficult with an increasing dependence on technology. On the one hand, the explosion of distance learning in all its forms may confound efforts to personalize the learning process. Such an environment demands an even more conscientious articulation of student learning goals. On the other hand, some students' dependence on technology—in particular on the Internet—liberates them from the presence of instructors—the older adults with whom they may wish to avoid contact as much as possible. But there are other factors to consider.

Unlike the Internet, the campus library occupies a specific physical location (or locations). Students should see the library as a resource that can never be replaced by electronic information resources. One advantage of such a place is simply the discipline involved, on a residential campus, in physically going to the library, so that one can concentrate in a dedicated study environment with fewer distractions.

In this environment, organization is imposed by the physical restrictions of space. In a library, there is a place for everything, and everything is in its place. It is possible to walk into the library and immediately find the reference desk; in close proximity are the black leather encyclopedias and green paperbacked Reader's Guide to Periodical Literature. Current newspapers are laid out on racks, older newspapers are stacked on shelves, and still older editions on microfilm. Bound volumes of magazine are in the stacks, with the older issues on microfiche or, now, on CD-ROM. In the stacks are rows and rows of books on a single subject—philosophy, Russian history, child psychology. Once you get there, you can just browse, three-dimensionally. You can hold the books, open them, flip through them, compare them. It could present a whole new learning style for anyone who might not ingest information so easily on a computer monitor.

In that physical world one can, in fact, judge a book by its cover. Scholarly abstracts look different from self-help books. It is impossible to mistake *People* magazine for the *New England Journal of Medicine,* or a small-press literary magazine for an undergraduate newspaper. An example of this occurred recently in a class one of the authors teaches. Some students completed a writing assignment in which they explored the realm of undergraduate fashion. The instructor's objective was for them to do a sociological literature search on the broad topic, and perhaps research some marketing theory. Instead, several students cited the same article from the Syracuse University student newspaper, an interview with an Abercrombie & Fitch spokesperson who was on campus.

The very freedom granted by the Internet poses its greatest challenge, especially for the impatient millennial learner. On the Internet, it's all out there, all within reach. There are no boundaries and few distinctions. Everything about the Internet conspires to obscure the fact that all sources are not created equal. One can tailor a search to more authoritative databases and journals, of course. Yet when it was suggested to these students that they consult a reference librarian before they do their Internet search, their reaction was one of utter bewilderment. Why on earth would they want to do that when they could Yahoo their way to three or four reasonable-looking sites (and cites) in 20 minutes in their rooms at their convenience—in the middle of the night if necessary.

These habits require faculty to be familiar with such research techniques, even with the most common sites a given assignment is likely to lead to. For some, however, the Internet learning curve may prove too steep. Talk of online interactive syllabi, electronic discussion groups, chat rooms, or even email is sometimes stressful for faculty and causes some professors to mentally tune out the discussion and hope that all of this will eventually disappear (Sax, Astin, Korn, & Gilmartin, 1999).

Still, this is a tremendous opportunity to teach explicitly what in the past was often taken for granted. That is, what difference does it make? Why is some information privileged over other information? Why is some more reliable, more authoritative? Why does the whole construction of human knowledge depend on a careful system of verification and accountability? Why is plagiarism considered such a heinous crime—not just copying (or downloading) someone else's work, but also sloppy citation, which is more likely when sources are floating in cyberspace with no context.

In other words, it is necessary to convince these skeptical students of what faculty know quite well and what has guided their professions: that learning is a dynamic, interactive, hands-on process. The key, really, has always been engagement.

Learning Centers

The challenge for faculty is developing instructional methodologies that will keep students mentally engaged in their own learning because students today seem to have a lower tolerance for less engaging pedagogical techniques. In recent years, teacher-centered lecturing has given way to collaborative learning, service-learning, problem-based learning, learning communities, residential colleges, and a number of other innovative techniques designed to engage the learner in the learning process (Tinto, Love, & Russo, 1993). Faculty members are beginning to take seriously the mandate to move from the "sage on the stage" to become the "guide on the side." There are several reasons that the millennial learner is less tolerant of passive learning techniques.

First, more millennial learners are formally diagnosed as ADD or ADHD, and there are many more distractions in their environment. Students in earlier decades were not being called to simultaneously talk on the cell phone, read their email, and study for a test, because the technology was not widely available.

Secondly, there is a significant increase in the amount of binge drinking occurring on college campuses. Wechsler, Lee, Kuo, and Lee (2000) reported that two of five university students (44%), in a sample of 14,000 students at 119 four-year colleges, were binge drinkers in 1999. As might be expected, missing class and falling behind in schoolwork were significant problems experienced by binge drinkers. Tinto, Love, and Russo (1993) report that engaging pedagogies, such as learning communities, service-learning, and residential colleges, can significantly decrease the incidence of high-risk behaviors, such as binge drinking, on college campuses.

Finally, students lack basic study skills. The suggested reasons for the apparent decline of general study skills have been numerous. One example is the increasing use of high-stakes testing in 4th, 8th, and 12th, grades. McNeil (2000) writes about the effects of the Texas Assessment of Academic Skills (TAAS) test on the quality of learning in Texas schools.

> When students' learning is represented by the narrow indicators of a test like the TAAS, teachers lose the capacity to bring into the discussion their knowledge of what students are learning. Test scores generated by centralized testing systems and the test-prep materials aimed at generating higher scores, are not reliable indicators of learning. (McNeil, 2000, p. 731)

Teachers have reported that the test preparation may actually hamper students' ability to read for meaning. They indicate that spending months on reading short passages and answering multiple-choice questions on these passages undermines their students' ability to read sustained passages of several pages. And because the material is meant to be forgotten soon after the questions have been answered, it is no wonder that the millennial student has difficulty with comprehension and retention of reading material in courses. Furthermore, the subjects that are not yet covered on high-stakes tests (science, arts, and social studies) are also affected because teachers in low-performing schools are required to drop instruction in those subjects and spend more time teaching for the math and reading tests. After all, it is the performance on these tests that will determine whether students are allowed to progress from one grade to the next, the rating of the school among its peers, and in some cases, even raises for administrators and teachers. It is no wonder that the millennial students will arrive on campus with a paucity of learning skills.

And that's where learning centers come in. These centers provide services and offer programs that teach students how to learn. Three techniques that have been employed at Louisiana State University with significant success are providing supplemental instruction (SI) in historically difficult courses, teaching the continuous process of learning (CPL) and intense study sessions, and the offering of the Absent Professor Program to faculty who must be away for a planned absence.

The SI program, conducted in universities throughout the United States and in several foreign countries, utilizes peer conducted collaborative learning sessions to help students in historically difficult classes (D, F, W rates of 30% or higher). The sessions help students master course content while they develop and integrate effective learning and study strategies.

The continuous process of learning (CPL) and intense study sessions are learning tools that provide students with concrete strategies for improving their study skills. CPL teaches students a four-step process for success.

1) Pre-read or read material before class

2) Go to class and actively participate in the lecture

3) Review and process class notes as soon after each class as possible

4) Utilize intense study sessions to combat procrastination

The intense study sessions are 60-minute sessions consisting of the following segments:

1) 2–5 minutes: Set goals for the next 40 minutes

2) 35–38 minutes: Accomplish the goals

3) 10 minutes: Review what was studied

4) 10 minutes: Take a break

The absent professor program, conducted jointly with the LSU Career Center, provides speakers for classes whose instructors must miss class for reasons such as professional travel, family emergencies, etc. A member of the Learning Center faculty, or a member of the Career Center staff, conducts a workshop on the topic of the faculty member's choosing. Popular topics have included résumé preparation, interviewing skills, test preparation, and techniques for mastery learning in chemistry.

CONCLUSION

It is important that learning strategies be taught by all faculty members, not just learning center faculty. Instructional development centers can play an important role in teaching faculty and teaching assistants how to do that. Liaisons between the campus learning center and the faculty development center can conduct joint workshops for faculty on effective strategies for teaching students how to learn. In this new millennium, that is the sort of effort that will inevitably lead to better education for all students.

REFERENCES

Barr, R. B., & Tagg, J. (1995, November/December). From teaching to learning: A new paradigm for undergraduate education. *Change, 13-25.*

Baldwin, J. (2000). Why we still need liberal arts learning in the new millennium. *Education Digest, 66* (4), 4-9.

Braxton, J. M., Milem, J. F., & Sullivan, A. S. (2000). The influence of active learning on the college student departure process: Toward a revision of Tinto's theory. *Journal of Higher Education, 71,* 569-590.

Farrell, C. (1999). Loans for college don't have to crush grads. *Business Week, 3637,* 147.

Gose, B. (2000). Measuring the value of an ivy degree. *Chronicle of Higher Education, 46* (19), A52-A53.

Handy, C. (1998). A proper education. *Change, 30* (5), 13-19.

McNeil, L. M. (2000). Creating new inequalities: Contradictions of reform. *Phi Delta Kappan, 80,* 728-734.

Reich, R. B. (2000). How selective colleges heighten inequality. *Chronicle of Higher Education, 47* (3), B7-B10.

Sax, L. J., Astin, A. W., Korn, W. S., & Gilmartin, S. K. (1999). *The American college teacher: National norms for the 1998-99 HERI faculty survey.* Los Angeles, CA: University of California, Los Angeles, Higher Education Research Institute.

Schilling, K. M., & Schilling, K. L. (1999). Increasing expectations for student effort. *About Campus, 4* (2), 4-10.

Tinto, V., Love, A. G., & Russo, P. (1993). Building community. *Liberal Education, 79,* 16-21.

Wechsler, H., Lee, J., Kuo, M., & Lee, H. (2000). College binge drinking in the 1990s: A continuing problem. *Journal of American College Health, 48* (10), 219-226.

Contact:

Saundra Y. McGuire
Louisiana State University
B-31 Coates Hall
Baton Rouge, LA 70803
(225) 578-6749
Email: smcgui1@lsu.edu

Dennis A. Williams
Georgetown University
Box 571087
Leavey Center
Washington, DC 20057-1003
(202) 687-4054
(202) 687-7731 (Fax)
Email: daw6@gunet.georgetown.edu

Saundra Y. McGuire is Director of the Center for Academic Success at Louisiana State University and former Director of the Learning Strategies Center at Cornell University. She is also Associate Dean of University College and Adjunct Professor of Chemistry at Louisiana State University. McGuire writes ancillary materials for general chemistry textbooks and presents workshops for university students and faculty. Her interests include improving learning strategies used by university students and reform of science teaching methods.

Dennis A. Williams is Director of the Center for Minority Educational Affairs (CMEA) and a professorial lecturer in English at Georgetown University. CMEA is the only provider of comprehensive academic support at the university. Previously he directed the Learning Skills Center at Cornell University and was a senior lecturer in the John S. Knight Writing Program there. Holder of the MFA degree from the University of Massachusetts, Williams is also a novelist, essayist, and journalist.

13

The Evolution of a Teacher-Professor: Applying Behavior Change Theory to Faculty Development

Fred Hebert and Marty Loy
University of Wisconsin-Stevens Point

This chapter introduces the sage, the thinker, the builder, and the master as four evolutionary archetypes to use as identifiable characters in the process of teaching development. Once defined, behavior change theory is applied, and stage-specific strategies are used to aid these archetypes in their evolutionary process.

INTRODUCTION

It has been said that teachers undergo a metamorphosis of sorts, and that over time, they evolve through a process of change, from novice, inexperienced teachers into expert/master teachers (Bain, 1998; Perry, 1992). Many studies have confirmed this process, defining the typical learning curve for faculty, pinpointing critical events in that development, and suggesting strategies (usually in the form of faculty development programs) to enhance or even initiate such development (Bain,1998; Perry, 1992; Shulman, 1993). As a result, most universities are creating teaching-learning centers, initiating teaching enhancement activities, and sending faculty to teaching conferences to facilitate the learning of new teaching pedagogy and improvement of teaching methods (Hargreaves & Dawe, 1989). There is no question that these faculty development programs work (Angelo, 1991; Cerbin, 1992; Hutchings, 1996). The question is: Can they work better?

One answer to this question may lie in the work of health psychologist James Prochaska. Prochaska, DiClemente, and Norcross (1992) developed a stage-of-change theory which has helped to clarify how shifts in behavior occur, enabling the design of stage-specific strategies to move people more efficiently through the change process. When applied to the evolutionary process master teachers go through, this staging theory can help determine when to employ effective strategies to facilitate teacher growth.

This chapter will introduce the *sage,* the *thinker,* the *builder,* and the *master* as four evolutionary archetypes to use as identifiable characters in the process of teaching development. Once a teacher's archetype is identified, he or she will be aided in the process of change through Prochaska's six stages. The best strategies for growth on the evolutionary continuum are determined and offered to the teacher.

BEHAVIOR CHANGE THEORY

Prochaska's behavior change theory includes six stages ordered along a continuum of motivational readiness to change. Pre-contemplation is considered the first stage of change in this continuum, as it precludes all other stages. Contemplation, preparation, action, maintenance, and finally, termination, follow.

The Pre-Contemplation Stage

Teachers in the pre-contemplation stage have no intention of changing their teaching behavior. They often feel change is hopeless, and use denial and defensiveness to justify their classroom behavior. Pre-contemplative teachers might justify their lack of development by insisting that a teacher's role is to deliver content and not entertain students. Poor teacher evaluations are often discounted because of the rigor of their class or their lack of popularity. Teachers in this stage feel safe teaching in a way they are familiar and comfortable with.

The Contemplation Stage

Teachers in the contemplation stage begin to think seriously about changing, recognizing they can improve their approach to teaching. Change could be subtle (merely refining current practices) or dramatic (considering a move from a teacher-centered to student-centered approach). Contemplating teachers begin to critically reflect on their teaching. However, because they are often uncertain of their ability to change, and because they may not know where to begin, they may view change as threatening to their professional security and comfort. Teachers in this stage may be waiting for the right moment, or even believe change will simply occur with the passing of time.

The Preparation Stage
In the preparation stage, teachers begin to establish a plan for action, focus on the future more than the past, and are excited about perceived growth in their teaching. Preparing for change might be illustrated through continued contemplation, syllabus reconstruction, creating a file of new teaching ideas, reconstructing classroom activities, and talking with colleagues about anticipated changes. Once teachers enter the preparation stage, they typically feel good about plans and are energized by the growth possibilities associated with change.

The Action Stage
Action is the overt modification of teaching practice, considered the busiest and most difficult stage of change. Action is most visible to others, and because of the private nature of teaching, the most frightening. Confidence and motivation toward lofty goals are necessary in this stage, since action is challenging and difficult. Furthermore, initial attempts at new teaching methods may fail, making familiar methods easy to fall back upon. Teachers' motives for change, therefore, must be clarified and reaffirmed. Reaffirmation is often expressed in statements such as, "I want to support student learning" or "my goal is to improve students' appreciation for learning."

The Maintenance Stage
The maintenance stage involves making the change a permanent part of teaching, and therefore presents many additional challenges to faculty implementing classroom changes. The illusion of easy change, or failure to acknowledge the long, ongoing process of change, can prevent these transformations from becoming permanent. Repeated failures, in addition, may force a teacher back into old behaviors. Three common challenges to moving beyond the action stage into maintenance are overconfidence, suggested in statements such as, "this is easy" or "this will make all the difference"; temptation to fall back into old patterns, reflected in statements such as, "it was easier back when I just lectured" and "I had

more control before I began discussions"; and self-blame, characterized by self-deflating remarks such as, "teaching in this way simply does not work for me" or even worse, "I don't have what it takes to be that kind (learner-centered) of teacher."

The Termination Stage

Termination is a stage often considered fictitious, as it indicates no further need to change and grow. There are no setbacks, only successes. Teachers in this stage are in all likelihood back in pre-contemplation.

THE FOUR EVOLUTIONARY ARCHETYPES: THE SAGE, THE THINKER, THE BUILDER, AND THE MASTER

The sage, the thinker, the builder, and the master are four evolutionary archetypes developed through our research, conversations, and experiences. The attributes of these characters help define the process of teacher development. Once these characters are defined, we apply strategies from Prochaska's six stages of change to suggest best strategies for facilitating growth on the evolutionary continuum.

While we believe there are teachers who are improving progress through these stages, we do not believe all teachers move through all stages. In fact, a large number of teaching professors are unable to evolve beyond the first stage, the sage. There may be many reasons for this, including fear of change, comfort, perceived success as a lecturer, lack of support for change, and not knowing other ways of teaching. After all, the lecture-dominated method of college teaching has been preferred for centuries and change will occur slowly, if at all. Movement through these stages is a dynamic process, often spiraling up and down on the evolutionary continuum. Teachers may find themselves straddling two stages or moving between stages at any given time during their evolutionary journey.

The Sage

The sage walks into the class, proceeds to the front of the room, finds a comfortable position, and begins to disseminate information. This teacher employs the long-dominant lecture mode and is truly the "sage on the stage." This mode of teaching is easy and nonthreatening. Generally accomplished as lecturers, sages may be capable of gaining and maintaining the attention of their audience. Regardless of one's skill, reflection is based on the teacher's efforts, not on the learning experience of the students. The sage may employ an occasional visual, overhead, or PowerPoint presentation, but the discourse remains teacher-centered. Professors who are sages know more about their subject matter than any student, and only provide students with the information required to gain credit in the course. Sages tend to enjoy the power and importance they gain through this approach. Meanwhile, students are passive recipients, taking dutiful notes, sleeping, or skipping class because they know the lectures mirror the textbook. Education is "being done" to these students, rather than provided to them, with a sense of ownership in the educational process. In this heavily teacher-centered approach, the learner is not given much consideration.

This is not to suggest lectures are ineffective or educationally unsound. In fact, in the evolutionary process, lectures serve a definite purpose. When most people begin teaching in higher education, they have a great deal of knowledge requiring organization in order for others to benefit. Quite often, the process of preparing lectures helps organize thoughts, builds confidence, and actually facilitates teacher growth. Most PhD programs do not train their graduates to be teachers; therefore, new teachers will primarily teach as they were taught, via lecture. Most teachers in higher education want to teach well and try hard to be the best teachers possible. Those who begin their teaching careers as sages are in Prochaska's pre-contemplation stage, and will benefit most from consciousness-raising activities.

Consciousness-raising activities allow pre-contemplators to see themselves as others do. Typical strategies involve formative classroom observations by a trusted mentor who provides honest feedback, suggests alternative teaching possibilities, and engages in conversations about innovative approaches to teaching. Sages need opportunities to view good teaching in nonthreatening environments in order to generate the necessary interest to motivate them into moving into the next stage. Additionally, attendance at teaching-learning conferences may provide a forum for further consideration of personal growth.

The Thinker

The thinker experiences enough cognitive dissonance with the dominant lecture mode to begin to consider different approaches to teaching. This is not to intimate that faculty members employing the lecture mode of teaching are nonthinkers; rather, it implies they are failing to think of the learning experience from the students' point of view. Thinkers have received information or feedback causing them to reflect on methods of teaching in their classrooms. They have begun to consider the impact of their efforts on student learning.

A teacher-thinker begins to question the merits of lecture, becomes aware of the issues related to student learning, and realizes the classroom can become more student-centered. Thoughts of moving toward a student-centered approach are intimidating, as lecturing is comfortable, enjoyable, and a means of disseminating large amounts of content in a short period of time. Especially if they are good at delivering lectures, thinkers may wonder, "Why change a comfortable, longstanding, time-tested way of disseminating information?" Thinkers may ask this question over and over, eventually moving forward, or remaining in the thinker stage.

At first, the thinker must move through the contemplation stage, reflecting on old teaching strategies and considering new approaches. Because contemplating teachers are curious about what change might mean to their teaching, strategies for working with those in the contemplation stage include continued consciousness-raising activities. As stated earlier, thinkers may not be completely convinced their approach to teaching is in need of change or that they possess the ability to change. Vigorous consciousness-raising, such as involvement in discussions highlighting pitfalls of poor teaching in nonthreatening ways, or encouraging collaboration with master teachers, invite contemplators to act on their curiosity and to commit to change. Reassurance and support are essential ingredients to moving contemplators into preparing for action.

After considering all options, thinkers move into Prochaska's third stage of change: preparation. Strategies for working with thinkers at this stage include encouraging critical reflection and committing ideas to a plan. Preparing for change, creating detailed plans, making intentions public, and seeking encouragement from master teachers are helpful approaches in preparing to take action. It is important to provide continued encouragement and support. Supportive strategies include encouraging attendance at teaching-learning workshops, providing appropriate books, making information available on successful teaching strategies, and establishing freedom from summative evaluation for the purpose of tenure. In this stage, it is important to shape expectations, as it is often detrimental to undertake large, wholesale changes in teaching philosophy or classroom behavior. Suggesting smaller, incremental, and manageable changes might be far more productive to someone contemplating action. Mentoring thinkers requires a "cheerleading" approach, involving a commitment of time, encouragement, and support.

The Builder

When thinkers decide to undertake new approaches, they typically move toward the creation of student-centered classrooms. This step moves them out of the thinker stage and places them in the builder stage. Builders leave the personal comfort of the sage and the constant discomfort of the thinker, and move into the domain of the third archetypical character, which could best be described as "controlled chaos." Builders accept that their approach to teaching will become more student-centered, which may lead to less personal control. Teachers who are builders find moving from passive learning to active learning both frightening and exciting. It is frightening to give up classroom control, engaging in spontaneous classroom interactions that could challenge the teacher's position as an expert. Because the teacher becomes a guide as well as a learner, it also becomes exciting to create a student-centered classroom (McKeachie, 1999).

Parker Palmer (1997) refers to a person engaged in student-centered teaching as becoming aware of one's inwardness. For better or worse, students are allowed to witness the conditions of builders' souls as well as gain subject knowledge. Teaching in this way embraces Palmer's belief that we teach who we are and that teaching is essentially a mirror to one's soul. Builders may have similar traits and qualities, and in many cases, may be very different from each other. Some may still employ a great deal of lecture, while others speak very little; some may stay close to their material, and others let loose their imaginations. Some teach with a sense of motivation, while others use intimidation. The common thread connecting them with other builders is their consideration of student learning in their teaching. In other words, they have embraced both subject matter and students. Connecting the two requires courage and openness on the part of the teacher and students. Banner and Cannon (1997) believe these qualities are found in everyone, inherent in all of us. One need not study these qualities so much as become aware of and employ them. They can and must be summoned from within both students and teacher in order for the builder to become the best teacher possible.

The concept of the builder as one who creates experiential opportunities and guided classroom interactions is hardly new to the world of education. John Dewey (1902) recognized the value of interaction and placed the student in the center of the learning experience. Paulo Freire (1971), a noted educational reformer known for giving recognition to prior knowledge and experience to all learners, supported the idea that everyone is capable of learning and capable of contributing to the learning experience of others. Active or interactive learning involves "sense-making" and social interaction, leading to generative knowledge that is usable because it is the consequence of complex thinking.

An effective and appropriate technique for one teacher may be completely ineffective and awkward in the hands of another; therefore, teaching in this fashion cannot be reduced to technique. Generally, builders choose from a wide variety of student-centered strategies, including cooperative learning, collaborative learning, problem-based learning, employment of case studies, experiential learning, and/or integrating interactive technology. Students and teachers involve themselves in analysis, evaluation, synthesis, integration, perspective taking, internal dialogue, debate, connection making, and question posing. The variety of perspectives and opinions found within a classroom of individuals (all respected for what they bring to the learning environment) encourages the intellectual discourse necessary for each to grow.

Two stages of change accompany builder growth: action and maintenance. As builders take action, implementing strategies to create student-centered classrooms, they are faced with many challenges, such as failure, student resistance to change, and lack of support from colleagues. Strategies for facilitating builders in the action stage are directed toward providing further resources, encouragement, and support. Builders who are in the process of implementing new teaching strategies should be afforded opportunities to share successes and failures, while building supportive relationships which provide consistent motivation.

In the action stage, this can be accomplished in a number of ways. Pairing people in mentoring relationships or creating cadres of experienced teachers who understand the multiple challenges involved in maintaining change can encourage a builder to overcome classroom failures. Public recognition, a letter of commendation, or a simple acknowledgement of effort may provide reward and encouragement. Reinforcement is the main goal of mentoring a colleague in the action stage. Builders committed to action require mentors who understand the pitfalls involved in trying something new. Mentors must be equally committed to the principles motivating the builder in the action stage, as well as empathetic listeners with frequent contact to provide encouragement.

Once a change effort becomes permanent, the builder enters the maintenance stage. Faculty development in maintenance requires similar strategies to those found in the action stage; however, the maintenance stage presents additional challenges of overconfidence, temptation to return to old patterns, or lack of confidence. Builders in the maintenance stage are often forgotten because of the misconception that they are "over the hump." In fact, maintaining change demands continued attention. Builders who are making their change efforts permanent need peer and administrative support in the form of continued encouragement, frequent reminders, and greater challenges. At this stage, ongoing, less frequent peer support, such as teaching circles, provide collaborative opportunities and venues to consider other new areas of change. Encouraging work on the scholarship of teaching is another viable strategy to help faculty gain comfort with classroom change.

The Master

To reach the master level is a goal for anyone progressing through the evolutionary process; but, like many goals, is difficult to attain. Striving for mastery is potentially frightening and exciting. Whether builders are trying new techniques or employing tried and true methods, they will have days where everything clicks, and other days where nothing goes as planned. On the days where everything clicks, there is an almost magical feeling present in students and teachers, which remains for a lifetime; these are moments of true mastery. However, for every magical day there are many days that, for a variety of reasons, may not go as well. Teachers may not be as organized as they should be, may be preoccupied, or perhaps not comfortable with the strategy or technique being utilized. Students may be unprepared, disengaged, disinterested, preoccupied, or simply absent. In teaching, hitting one's stride and experiencing mastery in the learning exchange takes time.

It is our belief that the master archetype is attainable, but not sustainable. In fact, teachers who believe they are masters are in all likelihood delusional, retired, or both. This notion fits with termination, the final behavior change stage, a stage Prochaska believes may be nonexistent. If you think you have arrived at this stage, it is a sure indication you have not proceeded back to step one; you are still in pre-contemplation.

CONCLUSION

Thinking about teaching is as much an evolutionary process as teaching itself. This framework is grounded in research and faculty development practice, but more so in the professional growth experiences of the authors.

This chapter represents an initial effort to understand how faculty development and behavior change theory are related and suggests the importance of providing well-placed strategies to help teaching professors evolve. The four archetypes combined with stages of change provide a framework of markers to identify faculty in the evolutionary process. Once identified, strategies can be targeted to benefit faculty at different points in their evolution. Finally, this framework makes a case for the assessment of faculty growth and change from an incremental, rather than an all or nothing perspective.

REFERENCES

Angelo, T. A. (1991). Ten easy pieces: Assessing higher learning in four dimensions. *New Directions for Teaching and Learning, No. 46.* San Francisco, CA: Jossey-Bass.

Bain, K. (1998). *What do the best teachers do?* Evanston, IL: Northwestern University, Searle Center for Teaching Excellence.

Banner, J. M., & Cannon, H. C. (1997). The personal qualities of teaching: What teachers do cannot be distinguished from who they are. *Change, 29*, 40-43.

Cerbin, W. (1992). How to improve teaching with learner centered evaluation. *National Teaching and Learning Forum, 1* (6), 6-8.

Dewey, J. (1902). *The child and the curriculum: The school and society.* Chicago, IL: University of Chicago Press.

Freire, P. (1971). *Pedagogy of the oppressed.* New York, NY: Herder & Herder.

Hargreaves, A., & Dawe, R. (1989). Paths of professional development: Contrived collegiality, collaborative culture, and the case of peer coaching. *Teaching and Teacher Education, 6* (3), 227-241.

Hutchings, P. (1996). The peer review of teaching: Progress, issues and prospects. *Innovative Higher Education, 20* (4), 221-234.

McKeachie, W. (1999). *Teaching tips: A guidebook for the beginning college teacher* (10th ed.). Boston, MA: Houghton Mifflin.

Palmer, P. J. (1997). The heart of a teacher: Identity and integrity in teaching. *Change, 29*, 15-21.

Perry, R. P. (1992). Teaching in higher education. *Teaching and Teacher Education, 8* (3), 311-317.

Prochaska, J. O., DiClemente, C. C., & Norcross, J. C. (1992). In search of how people change. *American Psychologist, 47,* 1102-1114.

Shulman, L. S. (1993). Teaching as community property. *Change, 25*, 6-7.

Contact:

Fred Hebert
University of Wisconsin-Stevens Point
123 Health Enhancement Center
Stevens Point, WI 54481
(715) 346-4413 or (715) 346-2720
Email: fhebert@uwsp.edu

Marty Loy
University of Wisconsin-Stevens Point
242A College of Professional Studies
Stevens Point, WI 54481
(715) 246-2686 or (715) 346-2720
Email: mloy@uwsp.edu

Fred Hebert is Chair of the School of Health, Exercise Science, and Athletics at the University of Wisconsin-Stevens Point. He teaches courses in health education and teacher preparation and has conducted research on teaching excellence in higher education.

Marty Loy is Program Coordinator of Health Promotion in the School of Health Promotion and Human Development at the University of Wisconsin–Stevens Point. He coordinates the College of Professional Studies faculty development efforts and heads the college Teaching Partners program.

14

Overcoming Cultural Obstacles to New Ways of Teaching: The Lilly Freshman Learning Project at Indiana University

Joan Middendorf and David Pace
Indiana University, Bloomington

Evidence has been accumulating for over a decade that approaches such as collaborative and active learning have potential for creating real increases in student learning. Yet on many campuses these ideas are having little impact on what is actually happening in classes and in the formation of institutional practices. What are the cultural obstacles that are preventing the exploration of new ways of teaching and how can these be overcome? In this chapter we will describe cultural obstacles that prevent the adoption of new ways of teaching. After presenting a few opportunities created by the current sense of crisis in the university classroom that can help offset these obstacles, the Lilly Freshman Learning Project (FLP) is outlined. The main portion of the chapter details the multiple strategies we used to overcome cultural obstacles. The chapter concludes by presenting eight strategic principles for getting new ways of teaching to take hold.

INTRODUCTION

Evidence has been accumulating for over a decade that a series of approaches, including collaborative and active learning, have the potential for creating real increases in student learning (Chickering & Gamson, 1987; Smith, 1996; Sorcinelli, 1991). Yet on many campuses these ideas are having little impact on what is actually happening in classes and in the formation of institutional practices (Angelo, 2001). What are the cultural obstacles that are preventing the exploration of new ways of teaching and how can these be overcome?

In this chapter we will briefly describe a set of cultural obstacles we found at Indiana University that prevent the adoption of new ways of teaching: 1) the dominance of research over teaching, 2) the academic departments' monopoly of occasions for interaction among faculty, 3) student-bashing, and 4) traditions of faculty independence. After presenting a few opportunities created by the current sense of crisis in the university classroom that can help offset these obstacles, the Lilly Freshman Learning Project (FLP) will be outlined. The main portion of the chapter details the multiple strategies we used to overcome these cultural obstacles. Throughout, our goal was to use the culture itself to change the culture, rather than butting heads to try to force reform. What we did was a response to the particular cultural ecology on our campus, but many of the strategies are relevant or adaptable to various higher education contexts.

CULTURAL OBSTACLES

Obstacle 1: The Dominance of Research over Teaching

On our campus, research is often so dominant that it overshadows other aspects of the university. Faculty on our campus, as probably on all campuses, are very, very busy with their research. This is particularly true in the sciences, where an interruption of ongoing research is perceived as a threat to continued participation in a research community—a perception that is probably correct in many cases. In this context, it is hard to focus faculty attention on teaching issues. Pedagogical innovators are often isolated, and, in some departments, faculty who focus on teaching are actually viewed as eccentrics (Rogers, 1995).

Obstacle 2: The Monopoly of Occasions
for Interaction by Departments

The primacy of research is given social form in the departments. As Cuban (1999) has demonstrated in his study of educational reform at Stanford, it is research that brings faculty together as colleagues, and it is research that defines their interactions. Since a great deal of the social, intellectual, and administrative life of the university flows through the department, concerns with teaching have no natural arena for expression.

Moreover, many departments also share the attributes of dysfunctional families. Faculty know what their colleagues are going to say before they say it, and they often share a common jargon that creates the illusion, rather than the reality, of communication. Colleagues will converse in a kind of shorthand without ever having to define terms or justify assumptions. These habits of communication sometimes lead to conflict and an atmosphere of mistrust that makes the department a poor site for discussions of issues as potentially threatening as teaching and learning. In such an environment, teaching is rarely part of the normal cultural exchange. It remains a personal experience, a dirty secret that is excluded from the social space shared with one's colleagues. Thus, there are few occasions in which serious discussions of teaching and learning occur.

Obstacle 3: Student-Bashing
Within the research-dominated environment of the departments, the most common conversation about teaching and learning revolves around attacks on the intellectual and moral deficiencies of students. It is repeatedly alleged, without a perceived need for proof or the examination of assumptions, that the university students lack the preparation for college level work and/or the willingness to do the work necessary for success. It is implied that faculty having this conversation would be wonderful teachers, if they only had better students.

Such perceptions are not entirely without foundation, but, since a transplant of the entire student body is not practical, they provide little assistance in responding to the real pedagogical challenges of a large public institution. And they have a very negative effect on discussions of teaching and learning. In the midst of such conversations about the supposedly inferior nature of the student body, even dedicated teachers may find it difficult to stay focused on potentially valuable explorations of pedagogy, or may even succumb to student-bashing themselves.

Obstacle 4: Traditions of Faculty Independence
Quite appropriately, independence has a high value in faculty culture. The ability to pursue lines of inquiry without seeking society's approval is a crucial element in the modern university. But in the world of research, the disciplines have practices that keep isolated scholars or scientists in touch with what their colleagues are doing and provide regular critiques of their approaches. In contrast, in the world of teaching there are no parallel channels for faculty to learn from each other's successes and

failures or to generate successful strategies for approaching common problems of teaching and learning.

CULTURAL OPPORTUNITIES

Opportunity 1: A Widespread Sense of a Crisis in the Classroom

Counterbalancing the cultural obstacles to educational reform at our university are several opportunities created by the same academic culture. First, there is a perception that something is very wrong with teaching and learning. The ubiquity of student-bashing is in itself a tacit acknowledgment that current strategies are not working. If we can redirect some of the energy being directed at criticizing the student body into a more productive exploration of strategies for increasing learning, real change might be possible.

Opportunity 2: The Lack of Community Among Faculty

The absence of social interactions outside the often-stifling framework of departments offers a second possibility for mobilizing energy behind educational reform. By offering faculty a supportive community organized around teaching, the fulfillment of social needs can be linked with exploring pedagogy, and a nonjudgmental environment can be constructed in which both successes and failures in the classroom can be shared and risks taken.

Opportunity 3: Administrative and Institutional Support

The very power of departmental culture means that administrators who are committed to improving the quality of learning are often frustrated when reforms instituted through normal channels fail to yield real results. Thus, independent programs that promise to bypass the departments and directly affect the culture of teaching are often quite attractive to administrators.

Moreover, on our campus the Teaching Resource Center, Instructional Support Services, and the Teaching and Learning Technology Lab had already created the foundation for our effort. The process of identifying appropriate faculty for our program would have been much more difficult, if not impossible, if these institutions had not already devoted thousands of hours to assisting faculty interested in improving their teaching.

The Lilly Freshman Learning Project: An Overview
Within this particular constellation of cultural obstacles and opportunities, the Lilly Freshman Learning Project (FLP) (www.indiana.edu/~flp) seeks to counter existing norms and to create a space in which a culture that supports new approaches to teaching and learning can be fostered. As Kotter (1995) and others have argued, transforming organizations is a complicated endeavor that requires systematic attention to the process of change, including developing strategies for achieving a vision. The purpose of this chapter is to detail our strategies for overcoming cultural obstacles, but a brief description of the program is necessary to place these in context (Table 14.1 outlines the Lilly FLP activities). For the sake of brevity, this description will present the program's current incarnation and not trace the steps by which we reached this point.

TABLE 14.1
Lilly Freshman Learning Project Activities

I. Spring

1) Structured individual interview: Fellows specify, as precisely as possible, what students must be able to do to succeed at various learning tasks in their courses

2) Initial meeting/team building: Fellows share a time they were very successful in helping students learn

3) Second meeting/team building: Fellows share "bottlenecks" in their courses where students find it difficult to learn

II. Two-week summer seminar

1) Fellows complete daily readings and written assignments

2) Fellows observe a class in a discipline different from their own

3) Fellows interview an undergraduate student panel

4) Fellows develop/present an innovative lesson modeling new techniques they learned

III. Follow-up and subsequent years

1) Fellows continue to meet to support each other

2) Fellows take steps to spread the ideas they learned about teaching

---

Each year the Lilly FLP develops a cohort of eight to 12 faculty leaders committed to student learning from across disciplines. Unlike programs at Miami University of Ohio (Cox, 2001) and the University of Wisconsin, Madison (Sanders et al., 1997), we did not choose to open the competition to volunteers because we sought to bring new faculty into the campus dialogue on teaching and learning, and we feared that if admission to the program was based on a competition, we would end up with the "usual suspects," that is, those faculty who are already deeply involved in issues of teaching and learning. And unlike programs at the University of Massachusetts, Amherst (Aitken & Sorcinelli, 1994), we chose not to work through department structures. Instead, an advisory board recruited Fellows using criteria that identified faculty who 1) teach large, introductory first-year level courses, 2) are tenured, 3) are open to new ideas about teaching, and 4) are opinion leaders.

The role of research on our campus made the selection process for Fellows particularly important. We sought opinion leaders who were committed to teaching but who also were respected scholars. In many cases we passed over innovators who were far more knowledgeable than their colleagues regarding teaching, but whose contributions unfortunately earned them no respect from their colleagues because their scholarship is not respected. Choosing opinion leaders was a key part of our strategy because when they return to their departments they are more likely to "spread the virus" of the new teaching approaches they learn in Lilly FLP (for more details on our selection process see Middendorf, 2000).

Annual activities commence with FLP staff leading each Fellow through an exploratory interview in which Fellows specify as precisely as possible what students must be able to do to succeed at various learning tasks in their courses. This is followed by two sessions: one dedicated to team building and the other to an informal assessment of roadblocks to learning. In a two-week summer seminar organized around daily questions (Table 14.2), faculty study the literature on student learning and contemporary approaches to teaching, participate in a class in a discipline different from their own, engage in a focus group with undergraduates on what fosters learning, and design innovative lessons that they present to the group. After the summer seminar, Fellows meet occasionally to discuss the innovations they are introducing into their classes, and they work to actively spread ideas from the seminar to other faculty.

TABLE 14.2
Two-Week Summer Seminar: Daily Questions

Day 1: What steps in thinking do my students have to do to succeed in my course?

Day 2: How does the variety of disciplinary cultures affect student learning?

Day 3: Why aren't other disciplines normal?

Day 4: Not a *tabula rasa*: How does what students already know impede learning?

Day 5: What can be done?

Day 6: What are some active learning tactics?

Day 7: Can collaborative learning increase student learning?

Day 8: Can structured problem solving contribute to student learning?

Day 9: How can assessment improve learning?

Day 10: How can we share what we learned?

The program began with a three-year grant from the president of Indiana University with additional funding for years three and four from the Dean of Faculties Office, the College of Arts and Sciences, and the Lilly Retention Initiative. This provided a stipend for each Fellow and administrative salaries. Unlike many other programs, in which faculty are simply window dressing for a staff run program or in which support staff do the bidding of faculty, the Lilly FLP, since its inception in 1996, has been a true and equal collaboration between faculty and staff. The authors of this chapter have served as co-directors of the program since its inception and were joined in the third year by the director of the Teaching and Learning Technology Lab. The assistant chancellor of academic affairs has also played a crucial role in planning the program and acquiring funds. An earlier article details our collaborations with key administrators (Middendorf, 2001).

OVERCOMING THE OBSTACLES

Overcoming Obstacle 1: The Dominance of Research over Teaching

Perhaps the most important of the cultural obstacles that the Lilly Freshman Learning Project seeks to counter is the dominance of research over teaching. On a campus like ours, just getting people to stop and pay attention to teaching, as well as research, is possibly our biggest challenge. To garner their time and attention, we asked them to set aside a two-week block of time during the summer. While the summer seminar was intellectually demanding, we sought to turn it into a positive community event through food and fellowship, and participants have consistently reported being energized by the experience. Even this relatively small commitment of time represented a departure from the normal patterns of the University, since few of the Fellows had ever taken two full weeks to collectively explore new ideas about teaching. In the context of a university in which research is rewarded financially, the fact that we were able to offer Fellows a stipend marked this program as significant. In other contexts, financial support for Fellows might not be necessary, and lack of funds certainly should not prevent the implementation of many ideas in this chapter. Once again, our program was a response to the obstacles and opportunities present on our campus. We encourage others not to let the lack of funds block the development of parallel strategies.

Overcoming Obstacle 2: The Monopoly of Occasions for Interaction by Departments

Many faculty development initiatives focus at the level of departmental chairpersons, and we recognize that this can be a very effective strategy on many campuses (DeZure, 1996; Wright & O'Neil, 1995). These projects, however, assume that department chairs recognize and foster the importance of teaching or that these leaders can be relatively easily recruited for pedagogical reform. This may be true at other universities, but is not generally the case at our campus. Not only are chairpersons generally recruited on the basis of their preeminence as researchers, but they function in the midst of a convergence of institutional pressures that give issues other than teaching and learning priority in selection and reward of faculty for special projects. In addition, in most departments on the Bloomington campus, faculty meetings are not venues that lend themselves to sophisticated and collaborative explorations of innovative teaching.

Therefore, we created the Lilly Freshman Learning Project completely outside departmental structures. In particular, we avoided asking departmental chairs to nominate Fellows. Chairs are generally under a variety of political pressures and their criteria are not necessarily those of our program. In order to avoid intradepartmental conflicts and miscommunication, we have generally avoided having two Fellows from the same department in the same year. The Fellows themselves reinforced this policy by commenting on how freeing it was to hear fresh ideas from fresh people in an environment in which they did not always have to worry about the political consequences of what they said. As we shall see later, this interdisciplinarity became an important part of the discussion.

As an alternative to the departmental structure, we worked hard to nurture an extra-departmental community. At the beginning, process was more important to us than specific ideas about teaching and learning. Within the first five minutes of the initial meeting, Fellows were talking in pairs. In the first several days of the summer seminar, we used exercises that required Fellows to move around and to interact. For example, teams of Fellows created and performed the worst lecture they could imagine. And throughout, sharing meals was a major element in-group bonding.

Overcoming Obstacle 3: Student-Bashing

Blaming students for the problems faced by higher education is so ubiquitous on our campus that it often becomes a black hole that devours all consideration of the real challenges faced by higher education. To move from seeing the problems students have in mastering material as a sign of their inadequacies to conceptualizing the same difficulties as an intellectual problem to be solved, faculty must recognize the difficulties that their subjects pose for novice learners. Therefore, in designing the Lilly FLP, we created structures within which the Fellows' own disciplines were defamiliarized. Typically, college instructors have been living within the confines of their disciplinary culture for so long that they no longer remember what makes their subject difficult to novices (Brown, Collins, & Duguid, 1989). If they can be induced to view what they teach from the perspective of someone who has no knowledge of the conventions and assumptions of their discipline, faculty can become excited about finding ways to help undergraduates through this transition.

The first step in the process is to lead new Lilly FLP Fellows through a systematic exploration of some of the most basic elements of their courses from a student's point of view. In the months before our summer seminar, Fellows participate in an exploratory interview in which we ask them to explain in detail what students have to do to complete some of the most basic tasks in one of their introductory courses. If, for example, a geologist tells us that students have to apply the concept of elasticity to rocks, we ask, "What kind of thinking must a student do to conceptualize the elasticity of a rock?" When we are told that students have to visualize the crystalline structures as they bend, we ask, "How do students do that?" As we continue to probe deeper and deeper, the faculty members eventually reach a level at which they find it difficult to articulate what they as professionals do quite automatically when dealing with problems in their disciplines. After an hour and a half of such probing, faculty generally emerge with a clearer idea of what kinds of thinking they need to model for their students, a greater appreciation for the challenges posed by their field, and a new excitement about the adventure that students set out upon every time they begin a course in a new discipline.

We sought to reinforce this process during the summer seminar by creating situations in which the differences in disciplines were highlighted. In a response to an article by Arons (1979), the Fellows individually generated lists of basic operations that students had to master to succeed in their courses. We then moved the sessions to an open area with a grid floor pattern and had the Fellows become data points on a human graph. Signs representing different operations (e.g., visualizing the movement of objects in space versus presenting clear arguments) were placed on two walls, which became X and Y axes. The Fellows then placed themselves on the graph at the point that reflected the kinds of thinking that students had to do in their courses. As the operations were changed, Fellows discussed the role of these operations in their courses, both with those standing nearby and with those who required a very different set of skills. This exercise not only helped bond the group and provided an implicit model of nontraditional ways to teach a class, but it also made them more aware that the kinds of thinking that they expect in their classes are very different than those that their students have to master in other disciplines.

Drawing upon a technique developed by Tobias (1992), we further distanced the Fellows from the forms of learning in their disciplines by sending them to classes in fields very different than their own. Upon their return, they compared their experiences and explored the differences in learning required in the various contexts. The quantitative group, for example, was very impressed with the quality of instruction in a class on the philosophy of art, but they remained puzzled by the failure of the professor to bring everything together in a clear package at the end. The humanists, by contrast, felt that they had to grab onto every word in a genetics course, fearing that if they ever lost the thread, they would never find their way through the labyrinth. To complete this identification with the challenges faced by undergraduates, we had them take part in small focus groups in which undergraduates described their difficulties in moving from one subject to another and the strategies they developed to master new material.

This process of seeing the challenges of their discipline from the perspective of their students culminated in an exercise that served multiple purposes. We had originally planned for the Fellows to model a lesson using active learning techniques in order to increase the likelihood that they would apply what they were learning in Lilly FLP to their classes. We later realized that this format provided another opportunity for the Fellows to experience learning in another discipline. When the humanists tried to solve a problem in accounting or the scientists sought to identify the phrasing in a Beatles song, they were repeating the daily experience of students as they move from department to department.

Exercises such as these turned the difficulty students have in mastering a discipline into the kind of challenging intellectual problem that faculty are accustomed to solving in the context of their own research. One Fellow described the summer seminar as "the most intellectually stimulating two weeks of my 15-year career at Indiana University." In such an environment there was little energy devoted to student-bashing, and a path was opened for new and highly creative examinations of ways to respond to the challenges of our classrooms.

Overcoming Obstacle 4: Traditions of Faculty Independence

Faculty tend to be independent individuals, self-starters who engage in opposition discourse on a regular basis. This kind of independence is valuable, but it means that special strategies are needed to create a community and explore new approaches to teaching. The first several times we ran the seminar, we unnecessarily created resistance to the program by assigning readings about the ineffectiveness of lecturing. We seemed to be telling the Fellows that some of their teaching methods were bad, and they quite naturally defended the status quo. We learned that rather than criticizing lecturing and other traditional techniques or even seeming to champion active learning, we should simply present a variety of techniques and leave it for the Fellows to decide which serve their purposes.

In our experience, faculty only begin to think creatively about pedagogy when their vision of teaching is no longer limited to the traditional professor standing at the lectern. Therefore, we sought to put new movies of classroom interactions into the participants' heads. Fellows from previous years demonstrated innovative lessons, and other invited guests introduced ideas about the complexity of student learning, while modeling a variety of teaching tactics.

We found that the program worked most effectively when we did not buck the culture. It is natural for most faculty members to enjoy standing up for their own viewpoints. When we initially gave the Fellows the chance to do this in the discussion of a reading assignment, they often spent half the morning critiquing the work. Instead of trying to limit the discussion, we learned to divert the energy that was going into verbal arguments into written exercises. Each day we asked them to write one to two hundred words in response to a specific question based on the reading. They spent the first 15 minutes each day reading one another's brief, but articulate, commentaries. This not only saved time but also built upon an activity that was natural in an academic context.

None of this would work unless we succeeded in creating strong social bonds among participants. We paid particular attention to icebreakers, exercises that had them move around, work together in different combinations, and perhaps most importantly, share meals. Within the first five minutes of the initial meeting, we had them talking in pairs about successful teaching experiences they had had, and on many occasions, we made a point of leaving the room so the faculty will focus on one another and not us.

Throughout, we encouraged them to make the program their own. We carefully structured the seminar in advance, but we readily adapted our plans to their needs. For instance, when the schedule called for the creation of two subgroups to view the model lessons, we rearranged our plan to accommodate their request to keep the group together. Guided by the tai chi principle of serving the other's intention, we had to repeatedly remind ourselves that our purpose was not to impose a set of preexisting practices on the Fellows, but rather to do what we could to further their goals. In each of the four years there has been a crucial moment when the participants "revolted" against the structure we had created, and each time we privately welcomed this as a sign that they were making the program their own.

ASSESSMENT

At the fourth year of the Lilly FLP, we are in the midst of an assessment, but there are already multiple indicators that the program has been successful. Faculty reactions have been uniformly positive. One fellow wrote that:

The FLP has empowered me to take risks in the classroom, to experiment with new ways of learning—and to feel that it is "all right" if sometimes I fall flat on my face. I have learned a great deal about the freshmen who sit in my large lecture classes— things that I did not know even as a sociologist with 25 years of experience. In particular, I have committed myself to avoiding the "easy bargain" that is all too common at universities like IU: Professors and students agree together to do less, to be less ambitious, to burden each other with fewer obligations. Looks like a win-win situation, until you realize that students are simply "learning" less and that they become resentful when they do end up in a course that really challenges them.

An accounting professor wrote:

> Some student changes over time are bad. However, some student changes over time are not necessarily bad, they're just changes. Maybe I could capitalize on those changes by changing my teaching and maybe some unfavorable student characteristics would be eliminated in the process.

Such comments are typical following participation in the Lilly FLP.

A different measure of efficacy of the program may be seen in the varied ways faculty are sharing with colleagues what they have learned in the program. A Fellow from religious studies invited the authors to lead an FLP-like session for his department about explicitly teaching the skills students need to do well on exams. A mathematics Fellow allowed five colleagues to copy and use the web-based warm-up exercises he developed as a result of Lilly FLP. A chemistry professor presented a seminar on computer-aided learning as part of a medical science colloquium. An economics Fellow presented her model lesson at new faculty orientation. Other Fellows have gone on to play an important role in key university committees dealing with teaching related activities, such as the design of new classrooms.

CONCLUSION

Our experiences in working with the Lilly Freshman Learning Project have convinced us that if instructional support personnel, faculty, and administrators want new ways of teaching to really take hold on their campuses, they must pay close attention to faculty culture and work within that culture even as they subvert it from within. As we operated within the particular social configuration at our university, a set of strategic principles emerged.

1) Defining the cultural obstacles to educational reform

2) Inviting well-respected mainstream faculty into a dialogue about teaching and learning

3) Creating a cultural space for exploring teaching outside the departments

4) Framing obstacles to student learning as an intellectual challenge to faculty

5) Structuring activities that bring out the most constructive aspects of faculty inquiry and minimize tendencies toward being overly critical

6) Placing faculty in the role of novice learners in their disciplines

7) Using the events of the program themselves as occasions to model a variety of new ways of teaching without always making that explicit

8) Giving great attention to the nurturing of a faculty community constituted around teaching and learning

9) Respecting the integrity of faculty goals and values, while serving the evolving needs of faculty rather than seeking to impose change on them

Such an approach requires strong administrative support and the devotion of great time and energy. It requires carefully developing strategies, identifying appropriate faculty to work with, and creatively planning activities. Perhaps most of all, it requires a faith in the willingness and the ability of faculty to respond to the challenges of the classroom when given a real opportunity.

ACKNOWLEDGMENTS

The authors wish to recognize the Indiana Summer Leadership Institute that served as the incubator of the Lilly FLP. Funding was provided by the President's Strategic Directions Initiative, the Dean of Faculties Office, the College of Arts and Sciences, and by special grants from university President Myles Brand and Chancellor Ken Gros Louis. Ray Smith, the Assistant Vice Chancellor of Academic Affairs, has been a constant advocate of the program, and he and Robert Orsi, then Associate Dean in the College of Arts and Sciences, shaped the initial program along with the authors. In the third year, David Goodrum also served as co-director.

REFERENCES

Aitken N., & Sorcinelli, M. D. (1994). Academic leaders and faculty developers: Creating an institutional culture that values teaching. In C. Wadsworth (Ed.), *To improve the academy: Vol. 13. Resources for faculty, instructional, and organizational development* (pp. 63-78). Stillwater, OK: New Forums Press.

Angelo, T. A. (2001). Doing faculty development as if we value learning most: Transformative guidelines from research to practice. In D. Lieberman & C. Wehlburg (Eds.), *To improve the academy: Vol. 19. Resources for faculty, instructional, and organizational development* (pp. 97-112). Bolton, MA: Anker.

Arons, A. B. (1979). Some thoughts on reasoning capacities implicitly expected on College Students. In J. Lockhead & J. Clement (Eds.), *Cognitive process instruction: Research on teaching thinking skills* (pp. 209-215). Philadelphia, PA: Franklin Institute Press.

Brown, J. S., Collins, A., & Duguid, P. (1989). Situated cognition and the culture of learning. *Educational Researcher, 13,* 32-41.

Chickering, A., & Gamson, Z. (1987). Seven principles for good practice. *AAHE Bulletin, 39,* 3-7.

Cox, M. D. (2001). Faculty learning communities: Change agents for transforming institutions into learning organizations. In D. Lieberman & C. Wehlburg (Eds.), *To improve the academy: Vol. 19. Resources for faculty, instructional, and organizational development* (pp. 69-93). Bolton, MA: Anker.

Cuban, L. (1999). *How scholars trumped teachers: Change without reform in university curriculum, teaching, and research, 1890-1990.* New York, NY: Teacher's College Press.

DeZure, D. (1996). Closer to the disciplines: A model for improving teaching within departments. *AAHE Bulletin, 48* (6), 9-12.

Kotter, J. (1995, March/April). Leading change: Why transformation efforts fail. *Harvard Business Review,* 59-67.

Middendorf, J. (2000). Finding key faculty to influence change. In M. Kaplan & D. Lieberman (Eds.), *To improve the academy: Vol. 18. Resources for faculty, instructional, and organizational development* (pp. 83-93). Bolton, MA: Anker.

Middendorf, J. (2001). Getting administrative support for your project. In D. Lieberman & C. Wehlburg (Eds.), *To improve the academy: Vol. 19. Resources for faculty, instructional, and organizational development* (pp. 346-359). Bolton, MA: Anker.

Rogers, E. M. (1995). *Diffusion of innovation* (4th ed.). New York, NY: Free Press.

Sanders, K., Carlson-Dakes, C., Dettinger, K., Hajnal, C., Laedtke, M., & Squire, L. (1997). A new starting point for faculty development in higher education: Creating a collaborative learning environment. In D. DeZure (Ed.), *To improve the academy: Vol. 16. Resources for faculty, instructional, and organizational development* (pp. 117-150). Stillwater, OK: New Forums Press.

Smith, K. (1996). Cooperative learning: Making "groupwork" work. *New Directions for Teaching and Learning, No. 67.* San Francisco, CA: Jossey-Bass.

Sorcinelli, M. D. (1991). Research findings on the seven principles. *New Directions for Teaching and Learning, No. 47.* San Francisco, CA: Jossey-Bass.

Tobias, S. (1992). Disciplinary cultures and general education: What can we learn from our learners? *Teaching Excellence, 4* (6).

Wright, W. A., & O'Neil, M. C. (1995). Teaching improvement practices: International perspectives. In W. A. Wright (Ed.), *Teaching improvement practices: Successful strategies for higher education* (pp. 1-57). Bolton, MA: Anker.

Contact:

Joan Middendorf, Director
Teaching Resource Center
Ballantine Hall 132
Indiana University
Bloomington, IN 47405
(812) 855-2635
(812) 855-6410 (Fax)
Email: Middendo@indiana.edu
Web: http://www.indiana.edu/~teaching/index.html

David Pace
History Department
Indiana University
Bloomington, IN 47405
(812) 332-0968
Email: dpace@indiana.edu
Web: http://www.indiana.edu/~pb20s/pacehome.htm

Joan Middendorf is Director of the Teaching Resources Center for the College of Arts and Sciences at Indiana University, Bloomington. She collaborates with faculty, instructors, and administrators to diffuse pedagogical innovations and co-directs the Freshman Learning Project. Designer of the Change Mapping Workshop, she has presented on leading change at more than 20 corporations. In addition, she publishes on college teaching and change in higher education. As an exercise in learning and for relations, she studies tai chi.

David Pace is Associate Professor of history at Indiana University, Bloomington and the Co-director of the Lilly Freshman Learning Project. He is also a Fellow in the Carnegie Academy for the Scholarship of Teaching and Learning.

15

Instructional Development: Relationships to Teaching and Learning in Higher Education

Kathleen McKinney
Illinois State University

The purpose of this chapter is to review recent literature on instructional development in higher education. More specifically, it defines and illustrates instructional development as a major component of faculty development. Next, it reviews research on how development activities are associated with teaching and learning. Finally, it argues there is a critical need for additional research and offers suggestions for accomplishing that research agenda.

INTRODUCTION AND LIMITATIONS

The focus of this review is to present key concepts, research findings, resources, and suggestions for future research related to instructional development and the role it plays in teaching and learning in higher education. Due to the volume of research and changes in the field, this review concentrates on material published primarily since 1995. In addition, though it can be argued that reward structures are part of faculty and instructional development, research on this topic is not included here. Finally, though there is literature on development efforts designed specifically for new faculty, nontenure-track faculty, and teaching assistants, the focus is on development efforts for tenured or tenure-track faculty or that for all instructors.

WHAT IS INSTRUCTIONAL DEVELOPMENT?

For the purposes of this review, instructional development is one component (a large one) of more general faculty development and refers to a wide range of activities at a variety of levels that aim to improve teaching and, thus, to enhance student learning. These activities can be at the individual (e.g., an instructor keeps a private teaching journal and reflects on it), dyad (e.g., an instructor works with a peer or a consultant), group (e.g., faculty members join a teaching circle to discuss their teaching), or organizational levels (e.g., department, college, or university-wide activities such as teaching workshops; national teaching conferences). The structure of such activities ranges from very informal and decentralized (such as faculty who are teaching the same course meeting over coffee to discuss teaching issues) to more formal and centralized (as in institutes offered by university teaching centers), and from short-term (e.g., a one-hour panel on teaching) to long-term (e.g., a year-long peer mentoring relationship).

Many types of instructional development activities or services are noted in the literature. These include, but are not limited to, the following: efforts to obtain formative feedback such as classroom assessment or research, peer observation or review, teaching circles, newsletters, web sites, handbooks, resource rooms, workshops, institutes, symposia, videotaping and microteaching, mentoring, small grants, team teaching, student group instructional diagnosis, one-on-one consultations, awards, and technology support (Chism & Szabo, 1996; Paulsen & Feldman, 1995; Seldin, 1995; Weimer, 1990; Wright, 1995; Wright, 2000).

Several writers have discussed models of, or the processes involved in, faculty or instructional development (Caffarella & Zinn, 1999; Emery, 1997; Licklider, Schnelker, & Fulton, 1997; Middendorf, 1998; Paulsen & Feldman, 1995; Robertson, 1999; Smith & Geis, 1996; Weimer, 1990). In one of the earliest of these, the authors describe a five-step process focusing on individual instructors: 1) developing instructional awareness, 2) gathering information, 3) making choices about changes, 4) implementing the alterations, and 5) assessing the alterations. In a more recent and somewhat complex model, Caffarella and Zinn (1999) discuss many personal (e.g., health, life transitions, personal values, self confidence), interpersonal (e.g., mentoring, level of support from department chairperson, collaboration), and institutional (e.g., resources, policy statements, competitive or cooperative climate, time for professional development) factors that enable or impede the professional development of faculty.

The Relationship between Instructional Development and Teaching/Learning?

In discussions of the characteristics of institutions that strongly support teaching and learning, one characteristic often included is the existence of faculty or instructional development efforts (Feldman & Paulsen, 1999; Paulsen & Feldman, 1995; Patrick & Fletcher, 1998; Smith, 1998; Woods, 1999; Wright, 1996). For example, Paulsen and Feldman (1995) note the following empirically based characteristics of institutional cultures that support teaching and teaching improvement.

- Support from key administrators

- Faculty shared values and ownership

- A broad definition of scholarship

- A teaching demonstration as part of the faculty hiring process

- A strong faculty community

- Supportive department chairpersons

- A strong connection between valid evaluation of teaching and personnel decisions

- A faculty development program or campus teaching center

Much of the research on the relationship between instructional development and teaching and learning is program evaluation research. The impact or effectiveness of instructional development efforts may be defined and measured in a variety of ways, including assessing the level of use of instructional development activities, general perceptions of developers, satisfaction of participants, cost effectiveness, impact on teacher attitudes or behaviors, and impact on student perceptions, behaviors, or learning. According to Chism and Szabo (1997), the most common types of information actually obtained are data on use and satisfaction.

Methods used to gather the various types of assessment data include anecdotal observations, counting numbers (e.g., attendance at a workshop), self-evaluation by staff or participants, questionnaire studies of staff or participants, interviews of participants, satisfaction scales or indexes for specific events or programs, reviews of a program by outside experts, quasi-experiments, and follow-up studies (e.g., observations or interviews) of participants after services (see also Chism & Szabo, 1997; Weimer, 1990). Recent examples of some of this work follow.

Using reviews of the writing of others, anecdotal evidence, observations, and personal expertise, some authors have proposed key characteristics or features of successful faculty or instructional development programs (Menges, 1997; Paulsen & Feldman, 1995; Seldin, 1995; Weimer, 1990; Wright, 1995). Successful programs are often implicitly defined as development opportunities that are actually used by faculty, appreciated by faculty, and both fit and are supported by the institution. Paulsen and Feldman (1995) suggest that effective services involve collaboration, consultation, feedback, and targeting new and junior faculty. Seldin (1995) lists several strategies for successful development programs: fit the program to the institution's culture, focus on long-term impact, obtain visible support from top-level administrators, use advisory boards, start small, take a positive and inclusive approach, involve faculty in as many ways as possible, obtain feedback, and recognize and reward excellence in teaching.

Another topic of study in this area is the view of faculty developers and faculty members about the role and impact of instructional development. Researchers have conducted interview and questionnaire studies on faculty needs, use of instructional improvement, satisfaction with services, perceptions of effective opportunities, and similar issues (Chism & Szabo, 1996; Eleser & Chauvin, 1998; Sandy, Meyer, Goodnough, & Rogers, 2000; Stanley, 2000; Woods, 1999; Wright & O'Neil, 1995).

For example, Wright and O'Neil (1995) report a survey of instructional developers in four countries (Canada, United States, United Kingdom, and Australia). They found that more than 60% of the institutions represented have centers or units devoted to the improvement of teaching. In addition, they report the practices these developers believe are most likely to improve the quality of teaching at their school. A few of the top-rated activities are recognition of teaching in tenure and promotion decisions, deans/heads who foster importance of teaching responsibilities, centers to promote effective instruction, mentoring programs and support for new faculty, and grants to faculty to devise new approaches to teaching.

Another example of this type of research is a study of faculty in 13 institutions in New Hampshire (Sandy, Meyer, Goodnough, & Rogers, 2000). The researchers found that 40% of faculty were satisfied with the quantity and quality of development activities offered at their schools. Faculty reported the following as positively impacting their satisfaction: the presentation of relevant and interesting topics, support for the unit by the institution, supportive colleagues, and the dedication of monetary resources. In addition, they found that faculty at institutions with instructional development units rated the importance of the quality of teaching to campus administrators higher than did faculty at institutions without such units.

Analyzing survey data from approximately 100 teaching centers, Chism and Szabo report that "... the average program reaches 82 percent of its client base with publications, 47 percent through events, 11 percent through consultation, and 8 percent through mentoring programs" (1996, p. 125). In a study of faculty development resources and services at Research I and II institutions, Wright (2000) asked respondents what new services or opportunities they planned to offer or increase in the next five years. The initiatives noted were development opportunities related to instructional technology (21%), graduate student programs (21%), assessment services (9%), peer review (9%), and preparing future faculty (9%).

Stanley (2000) offers a different approach to looking at faculty perceptions and impact on faculty. She interviewed ten faculty members who had made repeated use, over time, of consultations and other center services. She found that faculty experiment with new teaching strategies and ideas, and that they are often motivated by personal reflection and/or a situation in the classroom. These faculty members often worked alone on teaching but recognized the value of faculty development. They felt their consultations with faculty developers were helpful, and that they could speak freely and obtain resources through the faculty development unit.

Finally, there are research studies and reviews on the nature and outcomes of specific forms of instructional development programs or activities. Generally this research describes the program/activity and attempts to evaluate the program or activity using one or more methods. For example, Eison and Stevens (1995) discuss workshops and institutes. Several authors look at various mentoring or peer collaboration/review programs (Anderson & Carta-Falsa, 1996; Bernstein, Jonson, & Smith, 2000; Goodwin, Stevens, Goodwin, & Hagood, 2000; Scott & Weeks, 1996; Sweidel, 1996; Wildman, Hable, Preston, & Magliaro, 2000). Stanley, Porter, and Szabo (1997) surveyed instructional development clients about the outcomes of a consultation. Others discuss and assess the use of formative student input through classroom assessment or small group instructional diagnosis (Black, 1998; Farmer, 1999). Recent work reviews development activities in support of the use of instructional technology (Kitano, Dodge, Harrison, & Lewis, 1998; Lieberman & Reuter, 1996; Taber, 1999). Some of the literature includes reports on specific programs that incorporate a mix of several different development activities (Fulton & Licklider, 1998; Middendorf, 1998; Paulsen & Feldman, 1995; Rauton, 1996; Seldin, 1995; Wright, 1995).

What do these studies show? For much of this evaluation research of instructional development, a variety of beneficial outcomes are reported. An increased sense of collaboration and community about teaching and high levels of participant satisfaction are outcomes reported in most of the studies. A third fairly common finding is that instructors' attitudes about teaching change. For example, instructors become more self-confident, more positive, and more concerned with students. In a few of these studies, changes in teaching behaviors are reported. These include, for example, trying one or more new teaching techniques, creating a more positive classroom environment, increased use of instructional technology, and taking more time to reflect on teaching (e.g., Bernstein, Jonson, & Smith, 2000; Eison & Stevens, 1995; Farmer, 1999; Fulton & Licklider, 1998; Kitano, Dodge, Harrison, & Lewis, 1998; Stanley, Porter, & Szabo, 1997; Sweidel, 1996; Wildman, Hable, Preston, & Magliaro, 2000). Rarely are student perceptions or outcomes measured, but there are exceptions. For example, Lieberman and Reuter (1996) and Kitano, Dodge, Harrison, and Lewis (1998) look at student reactions to the use of instructional technology (after faculty attended technology institutes or other forms of training) and report mixed and positive student reactions, respectively. In addition, Bernstein, Jonson, and Smith (2000) report a detailed, longitudinal, multimeasure study of the impact of peer review on faculty attitudes and behaviors as well as student attitudes and learning. They found "uneven" affects of peer review on teaching practices and student learning.

Thus, much research on instructional development, and its relationship to teaching and learning outcomes, exists. Most of the work, however, is descriptive or correlational in nature, and focuses on instructor use of services, instructor satisfaction with services, changes in instructors' attitudes, and instructor perceptions of behavior changes.

WHERE DO WE GO FROM HERE?
SUGGESTIONS FOR FUTURE RESEARCH

Over a decade ago, Weimer (1990) identified limitations of, and suggestions for, research on the effectiveness of faculty development. Based on the recent literature reviewed here, it appears many of her conclusions hold today. We, as faculty and/or developers, understand these limitations. Designing reliable and valid research on this topic is difficult. For instance, concepts such as learning are complex and context specific, making operationalization a challenge. There are many practical and ethical constraints to conducting experimental research and drawing causal conclusions. In addition, much of this research is program evaluation conducted by development staff. Staff members report the following difficulties in evaluating their own programs: "lack of time, lack of resources, problems in designing studies, difficulties in getting the cooperation of the program users, and lack of appreciation or requirements for performing program evaluation" (Chism & Szabo, 1997, p. 60).

Thus, in many ways, it is not surprising that much of the writing in this area is still descriptive ("how to" and "best practice" suggestions, anecdotal evidence, detailed case studies) or correlational (cross-sectional, questionnaire studies of developers or faculty clients). It is also not surprising that dependent variables tend to be attitudinal and/or about faculty, rather than behavioral and/or about student learning. Data and analysis of the type already obtained are essential, but other research is desperately needed.

Despite all this useful research, we really know very little about the impact of instructional development on teaching practices and student learning. As someone with the responsibility for such development, I want to know, I need to know, much more. I want to know if, how, when, and for whom such services contribute to changes in teacher behaviors (e.g., trying a new way to present material, changing evaluation techniques, adjusting the amount of content or pace of the course, using formative assessment techniques, etc.). I want to know if, how, when, and for whom changes in teacher behaviors are related to changes in student learning and development. I want to know which instructional development practices will have the greatest impact on teacher behavior and student learning under what circumstances and at what cost.

So, where do we go from here? We need more studies attempting to measure the impacts of instructional development on teacher behaviors and on student learning. We need more longitudinal research of both a qualitative and quantitative nature following programs, instructors, and students over time. For example, we might follow a group of instructors over a period of at least two years, measuring, at regular intervals, their involvement in all types of instructional development activities, assessing key teaching attitudes and practices via interview, questionnaire, observation, or content analysis of syllabi. We could look at class or program evaluation and assessment data for these instructors' students over time as well.

More frequent use of well-designed quasi-experiments would add to the knowledge base. For example, two of my colleagues have instituted a change in their courses and are conducting their own quasi-experimental classroom research to assess the impact of graded versus ungraded homework on student participation and learning. Perhaps we could select two groups of faculty, attempting to match the groups on as many potentially relevant variables (discipline, class level and size, teaching experience, etc.) as possible. As a pre-test, we compare these two groups on a range of teaching attitudes and practices and on measures of their students' learning. We encourage, through a variety of means (and measure), high levels of use of instructional development in one group over an academic year. Finally, we compare the groups again on a post-test.

We should conduct additional research on development efforts that are any of the following: cooperative, interdisciplinary, interinstitutional, and in support of instructional technology. Furthermore, studies that link specific features of development activities to specific types of outcomes and impact are needed. For example, we need more work comparing the impact of workshops versus consultations versus small grants on changes in instructor attitudes and teaching behaviors. Thus, we need more studies that follow instructors who have participated in a particular type of development over time, observing classes, analyzing materials, and interviewing faculty and students to assess the relationship of the development activity to teacher behaviors and student outcomes. Finally, we must continue to assess what services are needed by, and are effective for, specific groups or types of instructors (e.g., by discipline or by years of instruction).

Assessing how and why instructional development works in different types of institutions is essential. What features of the institutional structure and culture interact in what ways with instructional development to change teaching and learning on campus? For example, more research is needed on the role of the academic department and department chairperson in instructional development as well as on various reward structures as a form of instructional support. We might compare, via interviews and analysis of documents, the climate in similar or related departments (e.g., Are faculty encouraged to use development services? Are development activities rewarded in annual review? To what extent is teaching and learning discussed in faculty meetings or teaching brown bags?). These departments could then be compared on instructor teaching attitudes and behaviors and student measures such as engagement or faculty contact.

How can we accomplish this, admittedly, very difficult work? We can do some of this research as part of an effort to support the scholarship of teaching and learning (SoTL) on our campuses and cooperatively with other campuses or groups (e.g., The Carnegie Foundation for the Advancement of Teaching or the Professional and Organizational Development Network (POD) or disciplinary associations). We need to draw upon the research expertise of faculty colleagues in departments such as education, psychology, and sociology. Offices and staff in instructional development can reach out to staff in college or university grant and research offices on their campus looking for ways (grants, joint projects, cosponsored workshops or internal grant opportunities) to work together on SoTL and program evaluation. For some campuses, partnerships with institutional research or assessment staff could yield useful research. Given external (e.g., parents, legislators, board members) and internal pressures to improve instruction, as well as increasing institutional and personal investments (e.g., staff, equipment, space, funds, participants' time) in instructional development, we (faculty developers, faculty, and administrators) must find the time, resources, and strategies to encourage and support this research as well as to conduct more of it ourselves.

ACKNOWLEDGMENTS AND NOTES

A different version of this paper was written for the American Sociological Association's summer workshop on the Scholarship of Teaching and Learning, August 2000. Thanks to Nancy Bragg, K. Patricia Cross, and Nancy A. Diamond for comments on earlier drafts of this paper.

References

Anderson, L. E., & Carta-Falsa, J. S. (1996). Reshaping faculty interaction: Peer mentoring groups. *Journal of Staff, Program, and Organization Development, 14,* 71-75.

Bernstein, D. J., Jonson, J., & Smith, K. (2000). An examination of the implementation of peer review of teaching. *New Directions for Teaching and Learning, No. 83.* San Francisco, CA: Jossey-Bass.

Black, B. (1998). Using the SGID method for a variety of purposes. In D. DeZure & M. Kaplan (Eds.), *To improve the academy: Vol. 17. Resources for faculty, instructional, and organizational development* (pp. 245-262). Stillwater, OK: New Forums Press.

Caffarella, R. S., & Zinn, L. F. (1999). Professional development for faculty: A conceptual framework of barriers and supports. *Innovative Higher Education, 23,* 241-254.

Chism, N. V. N., & Szabo, B. (1996). Who uses faculty development services? In L. Richlin & D. DeZure (Eds.), *To improve the academy: Vol. 15. Resources for faculty, instructional, and organizational development* (pp. 115-128). Stillwater, OK: New Forums Press.

Chism, N. V. N., & Szabo, B. (1997). How faculty development programs evaluate their services. *Journal of Staff, Program, and Organization Development, 15,* 55-62.

Eison, J., & Stevens, E. (1995). Faculty development workshops and institutes. In W. Alan Wright (Ed.), *Teaching improvement practices: Successful strategies for higher education* (pp. 206-227). Bolton, MA: Anker.

Eleser, C. B., & Chauvin, S. W. (1998). Professional development how to's: Strategies for surveying faculty preferences. *Innovative Higher Education, 22,* 181-201.

Emery, L. J. (1997). Interest in teaching improvement: Differences for junior faculty. *The Journal of Staff, Program, and Organization Development, 15,* 29-34.

Farmer, D. (1999). Course-embedded assessment: A catalyst for realizing the paradigm shift from teaching to learning. *Journal of Staff, Program, and Organization Development, 16,* 199-211.

Feldman, K. A., & Paulsen, M. B. (1999). Faculty motivation: The role of a supportive teaching culture. *New Directions for Teaching and Learning, No. 78.* San Francisco, CA: Jossey-Bass.

Fulton, C., & Licklider, B. L. (1998). Supporting faculty development in an era of change. In D. DeZure & M. Kaplan (Eds.), *To improve the academy: Vol. 17. Resources for faculty, instructional, and organizational development* (pp. 51-66). Stillwater, OK: New Forums Press.

Goodwin, L. D., Stevens, E. A., Goodwin, W. L., & Hagood, E. A. (2000). The meaning of faculty mentoring. *Journal of Staff, Program, and Organization Development, 17,* 17-30.

Kitano, M. K., Dodge, B. J., Harrison, P. J., & Lewis, R. B. (1998). Faculty development in technology applications to university instruction: An evaluation. In D. DeZure & M. Kaplan (Eds.), *To improve the academy: Vol. 17. Resources for faculty, instructional, and organizational development* (pp. 263-290). Stillwater, OK: New Forums Press.

Licklider, B. L., Schnelker, D. L., & Fulton, C. (1997). Revisioning faculty development for changing times: The foundation and framework. *Journal of Staff, Program, and Organization Development, 15,* 121-133.

Lieberman, D. A., & Rueter, J. (1996). Designing, implementing and assessing a university technology-pedagogy institute. In L. Richlin & D. DeZure (Eds.), *To improve the academy: Vol. 15. Resources for faculty, instructional, and organizational development* (pp. 231-249). Stillwater, OK: New Forums Press.

Menges, R. J. (1997). Fostering faculty motivation to teach: Approaches to faculty development. In J. L. Bess (Ed.), *Teaching well and liking it* (pp. 407-423). Baltimore, MD: Johns Hopkins University.

Middendorf, J. K. (1998). A case study in getting faculty to change. In D. DeZure & M. Kaplan (Eds.), *To improve the academy: Vol. 17. Resources for faculty, instructional, and organizational development* (pp. 203-224). Stillwater, OK: New Forums Press.

Patrick, S. K., & Fletcher, J. J. (1998). Faculty developers and change agents: Transforming colleges and universities into learning organizations In D. DeZure & M. Kaplan (Eds.), *To improve the academy: Vol. 17. Resources for faculty, instructional, and organizational development* (pp. 155-170). Stillwater, OK: New Forums Press.

Paulsen, M. B., & Feldman, K. A. (1995). Taking teaching seriously: Meeting the challenge of instructional improvement. *ASHE-ERIC Educational Report No. 2.* Washington, DC: The George Washington School of Education and Human Development.

Rauton, J. T. (1996). A home-grown faculty development program. *Journal of Staff, Program, and Organization Development, 14,* 5-9.

Robertson, D. L. (1999). Professors' perspectives on their teaching: A new construct and developmental model. *Innovative Higher Education, 23,* 271-294.

Sandy, L. R., Meyer, S., Goodnough, G. E., & Rogers, A. T. (2000). Faculty perceptions of the importance of pedagogy as faculty development. *Journal of Staff, Program, and Organization Development, 17,* 39-50.

Scott, D. C., & Weeks, P. A. (1996). Collaborative staff development. *Innovative Higher Education, 21,* 101-111.

Seldin, P. (1995). *Improving college teaching.* Bolton, MA: Anker.

Smith, B. (1998). Adopting a strategic approach to managing change in learning and teaching. In D. DeZure & M. Kaplan (Eds.), *To improve the academy: Vol. 17. Resources for faculty, instructional, and organizational development* (pp. 225-242). Stillwater, OK: New Forums Press.

Smith, R. A., & Geis, G. L. (1996). Professors as clients for instructional development. In L. Richlin & D. DeZure (Eds.), *To improve the academy: Vol. 15. Resources for faculty, instructional, and organizational development* (pp. 129-153). Stillwater, OK: New Forums Press.

Stanley, C. A. (2000). Factors that contribute to the teaching development of faculty development center clientele: A case study of ten university professors. *Journal of Staff, Program, and Organizational Development, 17,* 155-169.

Stanley, C. A., Porter, M. E., & Szabo, B. L. (1997). An exploratory study of the faculty-client relationship. *Journal of Staff, Program, and Organization Development, 14,* 115-123.

Sweidel, G. B. (1996). Partners in pedagogy: Faculty development through the scholarship of teaching. In L. Richlin & D. DeZure (Eds.), *To improve the academy: Vol. 15. Resources for faculty, instructional, and organizational development* (pp. 267-274). Stillwater, OK: New Forums Press.

Taber, L. S. (1999). Faculty development for instructional technology: A priority for the new millennium. *Journal of Staff, Program, and Organization Development, 15,* 159-174.

Weimer, M. E. (1990). *Improving college teaching.* San Francisco, CA: Jossey-Bass.

Wildman, T. M., Hable, M. P., Preston, M. M., & Magliaro, S. G. (2000). Faculty study groups: Solving good problems through study, reflection, and collaboration. *Innovative Higher Education, 24,* 247-263.

Woods, J. Q. (1999). Establishing a teaching development culture. In R. J. Menges & Associates (Eds.), *Faculty in new jobs: A guide to settling in, becoming established, and building institutional support.* (pp. 268-290). San Francisco, CA: Jossey-Bass.

Wright, D. L. (1996). Moving toward a university environment which rewards teaching: The faculty developer's role. In L. Richlin & D. DeZure (Eds.), *To improve the academy: Vol. 15. Resources for faculty, instructional, and organizational development* (pp. 185-194). Stillwater, OK: New Forums Press.

Wright, D. L. (2000). Faculty development centers in research universities: A study of resources and programs. In M. Kaplan & D. Lieberman (Eds.), *To improve the academy: Vol. 18. Resources for faculty, instructional, and organizational development* (pp. 291-301). Bolton, MA: Anker.

Wright, W. A. (1995). *Teaching improvement practices: Successful strategies for higher education.* Bolton, MA: Anker.

Wright, W. A., & O'Neil, M. C. (1995). Teaching improvement practices: International perspectives. In W. A. Wright (Ed.), *Teaching improvement practices: successful strategies for higher education* (pp. 1-57). Bolton, MA: Anker.

Contact:

Kathleen McKinney
Center for the Advancement of Teaching
Box 3990
Illinois State University
Normal, IL 61790-3990
(309) 438-5943
Email: kmckinne@ilstu.edu

Kathleen McKinney is Professor of Sociology and Director of the Center for the Advancement of Teaching at Illinois State University. In addition, she supervises the university assessment office. Her current research interests include the scholarship of teaching and learning, sexual harassment in higher education, and personal relationships. McKinney is active in organizations and research related to both sociology and faculty development.

16

The Graphic Syllabus: Shedding a Visual Light on Course Organization

Linda B. Nilson
Clemson University

Students rarely understand how a course is organized from the week-by-week topical listing in traditional syllabi. This chapter explains a teaching tool called a graphic syllabus, which elucidates (and may improve) course design/organization and increases student retention of the material. It may resemble a flow chart or diagram or be designed around a graphic metaphor with another object. Included here are materials, experiences, and graphic syllabi from a workshop conducted several times on how to compose one (involving about 115 faculty and faculty developers). Graphic representations of text-based material appeal to the visual learning preferences of today's students and complement distance and computer-assisted learning as well as traditional classroom instruction.

INTRODUCTION

This chapter describes both a tool for enhancing student learning and the faculty workshop conducted to explain and enable faculty to use it. Winner of the Professional and Organizational Development Network's (POD) 2000 Bright Idea Award, this tool is called a graphic syllabus. In it simplest form, a graphic syllabus is a flow chart, diagram, or graphic organizer of the topical organization of a course. It is typically a one-page document included in a regular text syllabus, preferably right after the week-by-week (or class-by-class) list of course topics and assignments.

Since the graphic syllabus is a visual tool, it may be best understood inductively, intuitively, and holistically by viewing examples. So the workshop does not open with a definition. After considering some general syllabus advice (a three-page checklist of recommended information to include and some strategies for ensuring students read a syllabus at all), participants review a fairly simple graphic "syllabus" of the workshop itself, shown in Figure 16.1. This first illustration is done in MS Word, which is the software the participants use during the last hour of the three-hour workshop (see Appendix 16.1 for software options).

FIGURE 16.1
Graphic Syllabus of This Graphic Syllabus Workshop

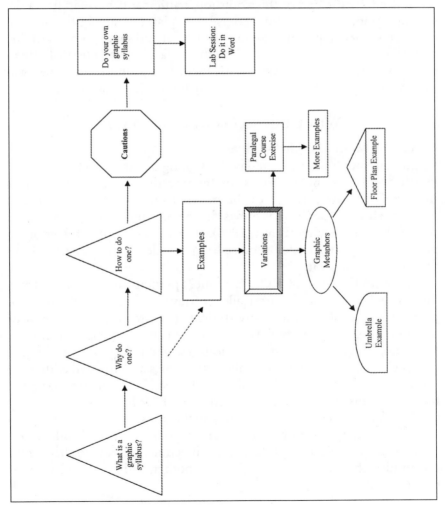

As participants are examining the figure, they are asked what patterns they detect in the graphics, such as the shape of the enclosures and the overall spatial layout. They quickly notice the relationship between the shapes (the medium) and the text inside them (the message), such as the triangles around questions (What? Why? How?), the stop sign around "Cautions," and the frame around "Variations." They also correctly identify the graphic metaphor as a more creative extension that may take on any structure or look. Finally, they see that the bulk of the workshop will be devoted to how to design a graphic syllabus, and that they will design their own.

Indeed, by the end of the workshop, participants have drafted a design of a graphic syllabus for a course they plan to teach in the near future. (This workshop is offered during summer and semester breaks.) The workshop announcement (posted on the all-faculty email list) asks them to bring a current text syllabus with them and promises that they will leave with at least a tentative graphic syllabus of their course.

WHY DESIGN A GRAPHIC SYLLABUS?

Reveal the Method to the Madness

Instructors spend hours, even days, designing a course, including pouring through different textbooks for the one that most closely mirrors their preferred organization of the material. In a sense, a syllabus is a piece of scholarship, one that brings the scholarship of integration to the scholarship of teaching (Boyer, 1990). It seems well worth the effort to present the organization of a course so that students can understand, appreciate, and follow it.

To begin the topic of "Why Do One?" participants are directed to a sample syllabus which whimsically portrays what a typical listing of course topics looks like to many students (e.g., week one: overview of something I gotta take; week two: the composition of apple peel; week three: introduction to giraffe consciousness, etc.). After all, on the first day of class, they know nothing about the issues a course will address or the organization of the field or subfield. At best, they notice repetition of technical terms and flag words like "continued." Why even read this part of the syllabus when the topical listing makes no sense? And it makes no sense because the topics bear no clear relationships to each other. Students might as well be reading written directions on how to drive from one unidentified, unconnected place to another, with no destination except the end.

Those who routinely review syllabi for faculty in other disciplines should be familiar with this feeling. It's like guessing from someone else's grocery list exactly what major meal he or she plans to prepare. How can students acquire and retain knowledge and abilities without having a valid, overarching structure in which to place them?

The workshop materials include the week-by-week listing of topics and assignments from a Social Stratification course I taught (Figure 16.2). The version in the workshop packet is more complete and true to life, cluttered by typical strings of reading assignments from various books and edited volumes, along with advice to students on how to read them. Participants are asked to explain the "organization" they discern in this sea of gray, and they find about as much as my students used to. Then they hear the story of how a graphic syllabus was conceived.

FIGURE 16.2
Week-by-Week Topics in Social Stratification Course

Sociology 123: Social Stratification
Dr. Linda B. Nilson
Department of Sociology, University of California, Los Angeles
Quarter System, circa 1980

Week-by-Week List of Topics

Weeks I & II:	What social stratification is—across species, through history, and according to consensus theory (functionalism), conflict theory, and Lenski's attempt at synthesis
Week III:	Inequalities in wealth and income (specialties of conflict theory)
Week IV:	Inequalities in power (specialties of conflict theory)
Week V:	Review and midterm
Week VI:	Inequalities in prestige; measurements of socioeconomic status (specialties of consensus theory)
Week VII:	Inequality of opportunity for wealth, income, power, and prestige: Social mobility and status attainment (specialties of consensus theory)

Weeks VIII & IX:	How modern stratification persists: The political system—wealthfare, welfare, and "pluralistic" representative democracy (specialties of conflict theory)
Week X:	How modern stratification persists: People's beliefs and subjective responses to stratification (specialties of both consensus and conflict theories, with influences from psychology)
Week XI:	Final examination

Like so many inventions, the idea was a response to frustration. With no good text available for this course, I developed my course organization from scratch. However, the organization seemed to be invisible to everyone but me. After teaching the course several times, I drew a flow chart of its substantive organization, shown in Figure 16.3, and handed it out to students. While there were no significant results, such as improvements in exam performance, students really studied the document, and some referred to it throughout the term as we moved from topic to topic. A few students in this very large class even commented that they liked it or better understood the course because of it, so I continued using it. At the time, it was very rare to assess a new teaching tool in any systematic way or to share it with colleagues.

Extending the two analogies above, a graphic syllabus is like a well-labeled map to supplement written driving directions or a cookbook picture of the complete planned meal, ordered from salad through dessert. Without word-laden explanations, it reveals exactly how and implicitly why a course is organized in a particular way. It makes the course's structure evident and shows the big picture: how the trees are arranged to create a forest.

Dual Code the Course Organization

Paivio (1971) forwarded the cognitive psychological theory that we have two long-term memories for the same information, the semantic (verbal) and the episodic (visual), the latter of which most people consider to be their better memory. This cognitive psychological theory has powerful implications for teaching and learning, yet it has received little mention in the college teaching literature (e.g., Tigner, 2000). One obvious implication is the wisdom of dual coding: that material received and processed

FIGURE 16.3
Graphic Syllabus of Social Stratification Course

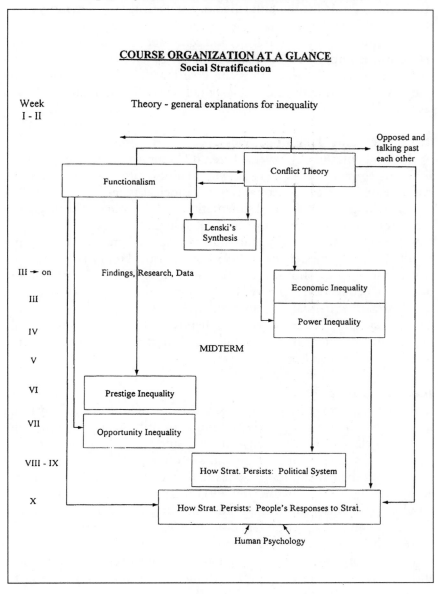

in both verbal and visual ways is likely to be retained better and longer than material received and processed in only one way. A standard syllabus engages only the semantic memory, if it engages any memory at all. A graphic syllabus ensures coding onto the episodic as well.

Students do not need to learn and remember a course syllabus in itself, but it is important that they retain the organization of the knowledge they acquired. Structure is the glue that holds knowledge in the mind. Without it, knowledge quickly falls away like so many irrelevant factoids.

Reach "Left Out" Learning Styles

At the moment, there are over a dozen different learning-style models in academic currency based on sensory modalities, information processing, multiple intelligences, personality/psychological types, cognitive styles, experiential preferences, and orientations to learning (Theall, 1997). Most of them posit at least one type or style that processes visually presented material more readily than the same material presented in another medium. These types/styles include visual, visual-kinesthetic, concrete, visual-spatial, global, holistic, artistic, intuitive-feeling, and diverger. As a rule, higher education is pitched to the more verbal, digital, rational, logical, abstract, sequential, and analytic types and styles, and so is the standard text syllabus. Adding a graphic syllabus levels the playing field, making the course design and scaffolding visible to those who need to see the plan before they can learn the pieces.

Teach a Learning Tool

Using the graphic syllabus as an illustration, instructors can quickly teach their classes the learning/study technique of mind-mapping, one quite likely to help the more visually-oriented students. (Concept maps and graphic organizers are based on the same idea.) This is assuming, of course, that the overall design is of the flow chart, diagram, or web/spider variety. Developed by Buzan (1991) and popularized by Ellis (2000), mind-mapping has proven useful to many students in outlining papers, taking class and reading notes, and organizing and summarizing material for tests. In-class activities where students fill in or develop concept maps and graphic organizers also make good classroom assessment techniques and test preparation exercises for both individual students and cooperative learning groups (Angelo & Cross, 1993).

For Oneself: Be Creative and Self-Critical

Faculty explore new venues during the graphic syllabus workshops. Some of the most seemingly reserved individuals release a surprising flood of metaphorical creativity and artistic flair. Before designing their own graphic syllabus for a real course, they try their hand at a fictitious one for Introduction to Law for the Paralegal, a real course at certain other universities but an area these participants know nothing about. Working with two or three colleagues, they manually draw their products on large newsprint paper using different colored markers. The different groups develop markedly disparate topical organizations and graphic designs, some using legal icons and metaphors (e.g., scales of justice, courthouse facades). While the graphic syllabi that individual faculty draft for their own real course show more restraint, they still display the participants' impressive abilities to recast abstract, verbal concepts and relationships in visual-spatial arrangements.

Faculty also report that, in the course of composing a graphic syllabus, they identify problems in their course organization and often decide to rearrange the topics. A few have even deleted units that, when viewed visually, actually lie outside the course flow.

HOW TO CREATE A GRAPHIC SYLLABUS

Workshop participants learn how to create a graphic syllabus first by viewing several examples. In addition to Figures 16.1 and 16.3, they examine those developed by other faculty, most of them from previous workshops (Figures 16.4 and 16.5). What these illustrations show is the tremendous potential for variation and creativity.

The possible variations include

- type size, face, and features (e.g., bolding, underlining, italics, software "art" options)

- connecting-line direction, length, thickness, color, and pattern (e.g., solid, broken, dotted)

- enclosure size, shape (e.g., square, rectangle, triangle, circle, oval, diamond, hexagon, parallelogram, star), shading, color, and borders

- general design and shape

For instance, though it is not evident in black-and-white print, Dr. Jan Williams Murdoch's graphic syllabus (Figure 16.4) reinforces her course's

FIGURE 16.4
Graphic Syllabus of Clinical Psychology Practicum Course

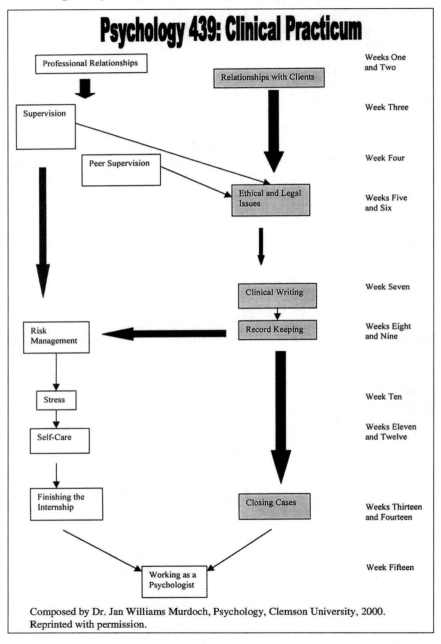

Composed by Dr. Jan Williams Murdoch, Psychology, Clemson University, 2000.
Reprinted with permission.

FIGURE 16.5
Graphic Syllabus of Conservation Ecology Course

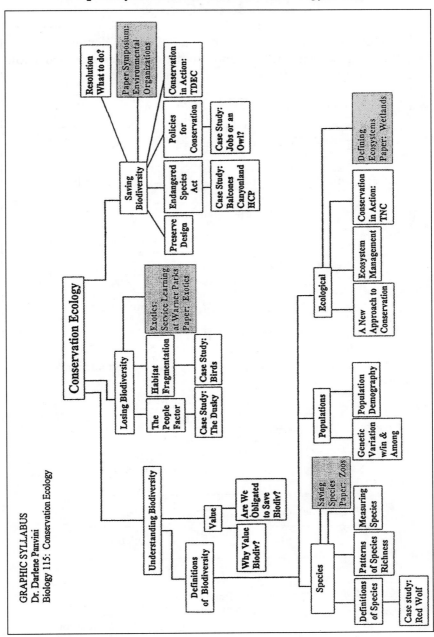

Reprinted with permission.

FIGURE 16.6
**Design Motifs for Visually Expressing Relationships
Among Several Concepts**

When properly implemented, the case method, problem-based learning (PBL), service-learning (SL), and simulations all teach students how to apply course material.

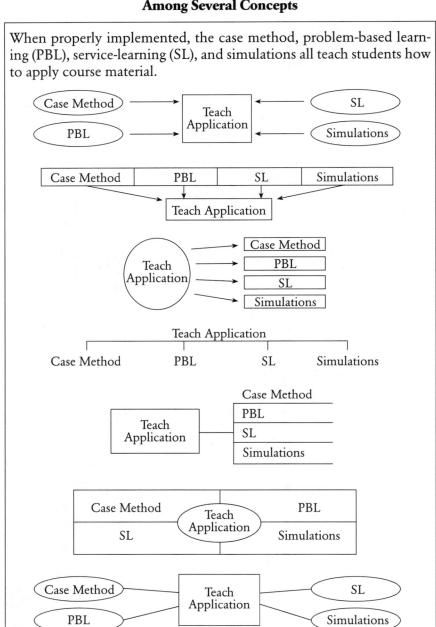

parallel coverage of "Professional Relationships" and "Relationships with Clients" with different colored boxes, as well as with their parallel spatial arrangement. Dr. Darlene Panvini's overall branching design suggests the ecological focus of her course, and she highlights her major assignments in shaded boxes (Figure 16.5). Both figures were done in MS Word.

After viewing these examples, participants study Figure 16.6, which shows a wide variety of design motifs for expressing a simple relationship among several concepts, a relationship stated verbally as "When properly implemented, the case method, problem-based learning (PBL), service learning (SL), and simulations all teach students how to apply course material." Cyrs and Conway (1997) formalized the idea of "constructing word pictures" of sentences and used these and other motifs as illustrations.

AN EXTENSION: THE GRAPHIC METAPHOR

A graphic metaphor is a type of graphic syllabus in which the design is based on an object or set of objects. The metaphorical object(s) may or may not be related to the course subject matter, but the metaphor is especially memorable when a relationship exists. (Recall how Dr. Panvini's graphic syllabus design "looks" somewhat biological or ecological, and as such it approaches a graphic metaphor.) Either way, however, the metaphor supplies a symbol, a kind of cognitive shorthand, of the course organization that should reinforce students' recall of the course material.

Compared to a standard graphic syllabus, a graphic metaphor has a distinct downside. As it is more of a drawing than a flow chart or diagram, only those familiar with sophisticated drawing or design software will be able to produce it on computer. For most faculty, the most realistic tools for composing most or all of a graphic metaphor will be the lowest-tech alternatives, such as pens, pencils, markers, crayons, rulers, triangles, T-squares, compasses, cut-outs, and tracing paper. If an electronic version is needed, the hand-drawn creation can always be scanned. A digital sender can even email it as an attachment.

Figures 16.7 and 16.8 show two graphic metaphors of the same course, Free Will and Determinism, a crossdisciplinary freshman seminar I have taught. Both metaphors are "overlaid" on the same visual arrangement of course topics and organizational dimensions (historical time from top to bottom and a philosophical continuum from left to right). They are worth showing here because both metaphors are flexible and adaptable to a variety of courses, whatever the discipline or subject

FIGURE 16.7
**"Umbrella" Graphic Metaphor for
Free Will and Determinism Course**

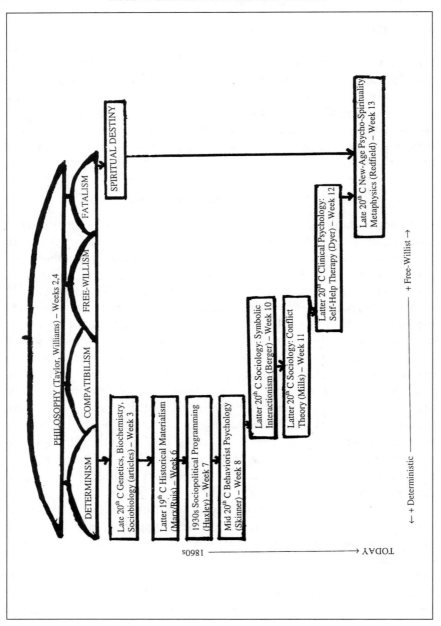

FIGURE 16.8
**"Floor Plan" Graphic Metaphor for
Free Will and Determinism Course**

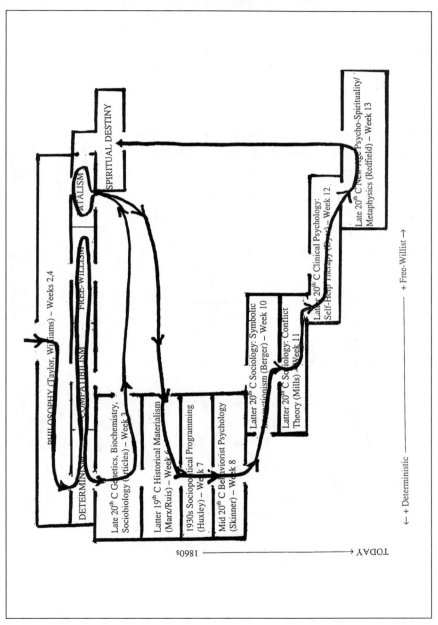

FIGURE 16.9
**"Corporate Site" Graphic Metaphor for
Budgeting and Executive Control Course**

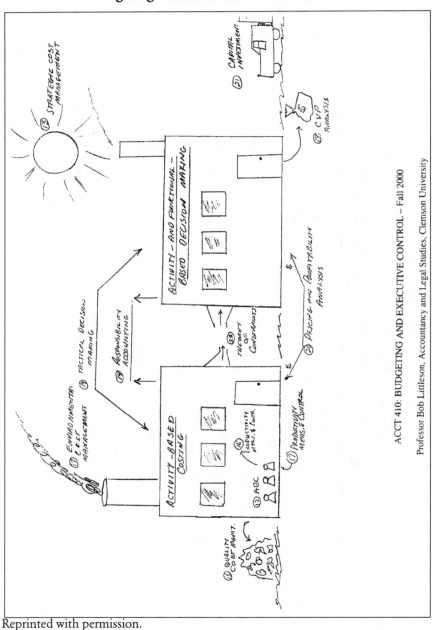

Reprinted with permission.

FIGURE 16.10
**"Engineering Graphics" Graphic Metaphor for
Engineering Graphics Course**

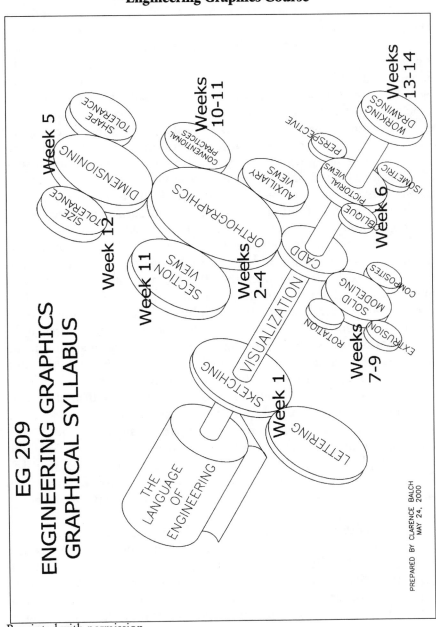

Reprinted with permission.

matter. They also allow for plenty of variation in type, color, and many other enclosure features.

The first metaphor (Figure 16.7) relies on the umbrella as its key object to illustrate how major topics and the various readings are related. Though crossdisciplinary, the entire course falls under the broadest umbrella, the field of philosophy, which also provides most of the early readings. Under philosophy are the major schools of thought involved in the determinism and free-will debate, which indeed has four sides rather than two. These schools, in turn, justify their own smaller umbrellas, with related readings falling under each one. Since occurrences defy explanation under fatalism, it has not inspired scientific study, utopian extrapolations, or clinical approaches, so it has no readings. But it has a popular stepchild, belief in spiritual destiny, which for the most part falls outside of philosophy (and into religion), as shown. Spiritual destiny has spawned many readings, however, including the assigned book. Any course organization built around different approaches, perspectives, or schools of thought may be amenable to the umbrella metaphor.

The second graphic metaphor (Figure 16.8) overlays a floor plan on the arrangement of topics, and the course follows the arrowed line, moving from one room (topic) to another. In fact, the course flow is the dominant graphic. Compared to the umbrella graphic metaphor, the floor plan more accurately reflects the week-by-week course organization. It clearly shows that the course actually backtracks, first visiting three of the four philosophical schools of thought (determinism, compatibilism, and free-willism), then going into late 20th-century genetics, biochemistry, and sociobiology, which exemplify modern scientific determinism. Then the course returns to the fourth school of thought, fatalism. There are good reasons for this turnaround, having to do with the background knowledge that students need for the first paper assignment and the historical chronology that the readings follow from week six on. The result may be graphically messy, but the students never found it confusing. The floor plan metaphor does restrict the enclosures to room-type shapes with cut-out doors, but it need not follow the standard layout of a house or office building.

In two additional examples, the graphic metaphor is related to the subject matter of the course. The first, for a corporate accounting course (Figure 16.9), is a whimsical hand-drawing of a corporate site, with a production facility on the left and an office building on the right. The main course topics appear as labels on the relationships between the two buildings (linking lines) and on the various icons (garbage heap, people, smoke from the smokestack, moneybag, incoming truck, and the sun). The numbers next to topics refer to the chapters in the text. Obviously the graphic doesn't "flow" with the course organization as a flow chart would; the course organization and reading assignments are not ordered from left to right or from top to bottom. But the picture shows very clearly how the major topics interrelate in corporate accounting operations.

The final graphic metaphor (Figure 16.10) is for an Engineering Graphics course. It is especially memorable because the metaphorical objects—strikingly drawn in three dimensions using engineering graphics software (AutoCAD)—mirror the subject matter, and their spatial arrangement reflects the relationships among topics. Again, however, the course flow is not easy to follow, as one week's topic may lie spatially distant from the next weeks.

CAUTIONS

The experience of conducting this workshop five times for over 115 faculty has taught me cautionary lessons. Some participants release so much creative energy and have so much fun while composing a graphic syllabus or metaphor, especially while working with colleagues on the fictitious paralegal course, that they seem to lose sight of the ultimate purpose, which is to clarify the course organization to the students. Participants seem to benefit from the following advice before tackling the real thing for a real course.

- Avoid overcomplexity, as in PowerPoint presentations and life in general. The graphics should be clean and simple so students focus on the course topics and flow.

- Since a course proceeds in predominantly one direction through the semester, so should a graphic syllabus. Instructors should carefully clarify any recursive relationships and double-arrowed lines to students (since time doesn't reverse itself).

- A graphic syllabus shows the structure of the course—not the field, not its major theoretical model, and not its history. Such graphic representations make superb teaching tools and student-learning aids, but none of them should be called a graphic syllabus. To do so will probably confuse students.

- An instructor should refer to a graphic syllabus frequently during the course, as one would to a road map on a trip.

CONCLUSION

Graphic representations of text material, such as the organization of a course, are likely to become more important and even expected components of courses, as distance education and computer-assisted classroom instruction grow more commonplace (Cyrs, 1997). Following the lead of primary and secondary education, higher education is taking on a more visual nature, both because web-based and television technologies foster it and because today's students are well adapted to it, perhaps better adapted to it than to extensive text. In fact, since graphic representations so concisely show the big picture, they make natural image maps and eye-appealing gateways to course information (readings, assignments, class activities, and details of course topics) and online sources of knowledge.

A graphic syllabus is just the beginning. As mentioned above, the organization of a discipline or a field of study, its history, and its theoretical models are ready candidates for recasting into flow charts, diagrams, and graphic organizers. So are many processes in the biological, physical, and behavioral sciences. The crucial elements of a plot or a case may also lend themselves to graphic representation.

Normally, a good syllabus includes a list of student-learning objectives (outcomes) for a course. In a truly comprehensive list, some of these are ultimate (end-of-semester) objectives while others are meditating— that is, objectives that students must meet by a certain time in the semester before they can meet one or more of the ultimate objectives. For example, in order to speak and write in the past tense of a foreign language, students must be able first to speak and write in the present tense. In order to write a research proposal, students must be able to do a great many other things beforehand, including formulate a viable hypothesis, conduct and write a cogent literature review, select an appropriate methodology, and write in a scholarly style. Students could better understand the structure of the course and their own learning as a cumulative, step-by-step process if an instructor laid out their learning objectives in a flow chart format, one showing earlier objectives as prerequisites linked to later ones.

The final suggestion is for academic departments to apply these principles in examining their curricula for possible revision. Faculty members can begin by asking the question, "What do we want our majors to be able to do by graduation?" Once they define these skills and abilities (and they usually have to for accreditation), they can work their way backwards in flow chart fashion to see how the department's various courses fit in and interrelate to equip students to meet the ultimate objectives for the major. Do the freshmen courses equip students for the sophomore courses, the sophomore courses for the junior courses, etc? Or are their faults in the flow? Are some basic knowledge and abilities not addressed until junior or senior years? Are juniors expected to know how to do something that most don't learn until senior year?

Such an exercise is neither for dysfunctional departments nor for faint-of-heart and insecure faculty. Visuals have a way of rendering the complex as simple as it really is, thus revealing the truth about structures and systems. They uncover sequencing problems, missing parts, and pieces that don't fit or aren't necessary.

REFERENCES

Angelo, T. A., & Cross, K. P. (1993). *Classroom assessment techniques.* San Francisco, CA: Jossey-Bass.

Boyer, E. L. (1990). *Scholarship reconsidered: Priorities of the professoriate.* Princeton, NJ: Carnegie Foundation for the Advancement of Teaching.

Buzan, T. (1991). *Using both sides of your brain.* New York, NY: Dutton.

Cyrs, T. E. (1997). *Teaching at a distance with the merging technologies: An instructional systems approach.* Las Cruces, NM: New Mexico State University, Center for Educational Development.

Cyrs, T. E., & Conway, E. D. (1997). *Beyond bullets: Let your students see what you are saying.* Session presented at the annual meeting of the Professional and Organization Development Network in Higher Education (POD), Haines City, FL.

Ellis, D. (2000). *Becoming a master student* (9th ed.). New York, NY: Houghton Mifflin.

Paivio, A. (1971). *Imagery and verbal processes.* New York, NY: Holt, Reinhart, and Winston.

Theall, M. (1997, May). *An overview of different approaches to teaching and learning styles.* Paper presented at Teaching and Learning Styles at a Distance, Central Illinois Higher Education Consortium Faculty Development Conference, Springfield, IL.

Tigner, R. B. (2000). Putting memory research to good use: Hints from cognitive psychology. *College Teaching, 48* (1), 149-152.

Contact:

Linda B. Nilson
Director
Office of Teaching Effectiveness and Innovation
445 Brackett Hall
Clemson University
Clemson, SC 29634
(864) 656-4542
(864) 656-0750 (Fax)
Email: nilson@clemson.edu

Linda B. Nilson is founding Director of Clemson University's Office of Teaching Effectiveness and Innovation and the author of *Teaching at Its Best: A Research-Based Resource for College Instructors* (Anker, 1998). She also conducts teaching workshops for faculty across the country. Previously, she directed teaching centers at Vanderbilt University and the University of California, Riverside and was a sociology professor at UCLA. She has recently held leadership positions in Toastmasters International, Mensa, and the Southern Regional Faculty and Instructional Development Consortium.

APPENDIX 16.1
SOFTWARE FOR COMPOSING A GRAPHIC SYLLABUS

Any graphic syllabus that resembles a flow chart—whatever its flow direction, enclosure shapes, colors, type variations, etc.—can be done in MS Word or PowerPoint. In Word, the graphic options are found on the Drawing Toolbar, which are also accessible by clicking on Insert, then Text Box, Symbols, and Picture. Under Picture, there is a wide array of graphics in AutoShape, ClipArt, and WordArt. (Adjustments can be made by clicking on Draw.) In PowerPoint, the key tool is Org Chart.

Commercial options in concept-mapping/graphic-organizing software are readily available. No software package actually designs a graphic; it is still the instructor's task either to design it from scratch or to select among templates. For instance, Inspiration, the most popular among academics and K–12 teachers of those listed below, transfers text from an outline to a flow chart, concept map, or web, and offers 35 templates to chose from. The instructor then "draws" the links and adds text to them. Generally, the more flexibility a package allows, the more complex and difficult it is to use. Educational prices vary from about $50 to over $200 (estimates only because some companies don't specify the educational discount), and most companies give a free, 30-day trial download. However, trial copies may not permit printing or saving. Here are some leading options.

- Inspiration: www.inspiration.com

- Pacestar: www.pacestar.com

- Magin: www.maginsoftware.com

- Desktop Brain: www.thebrain.com

- Enquire Within: www.EnquireWithin.co.nz/expertma.htm

- Decision Explorer: www.banxia.com/index.html

- VisiMap and InfoMap (Lite): www.coco.co.uk

- CorelDRAW: www.corel.com

17

Teaching Through Discussion as the Exercise of Disciplinary Power

Stephen D. Brookfield
University of St. Thomas

The French philosopher Michel Foucault spent much of his lifetime analyzing the way in which power flows through all human interactions, including those of discussion groups within higher education. His analysis of disciplinary power and surveillance is directly applicable to the practice of discussion-based teaching.

INTRODUCTION

Since 1998, one of the most frequent faculty development workshops I have facilitated has been on discussion as a way of teaching. I usually describe this as a hands-on introduction to some basic discussion techniques designed to get students talking. During the course of the workshop, participants usually raise questions about whether or not it is ever justified to call on students by name, whether teachers should ever give their opinion in direct response to a student's query (thus biasing subsequent conversation), and whether teachers have a responsibility to guide discussion away from what they judge are irrelevant side issues. In talking about these issues, the phenomenon of power rears its head. Sooner or later we come to face to face with the undeniable power of the discussion leader, and we start to discuss the way in which it can be exercised responsibly. During this moment in the workshop, I usually mention Michel Foucault and that he saw power as a circular flow, rather than as something either imposed from above or emerging as part of a groundswell of resistance from below. If there is one name and one book I'd like participants think about reading after the workshop it would be Foucault and his collection titled *Power/Knowledge* (1980). Reading Foucault makes us more circumspect, but more critically informed, regarding the ways discussion-based teaching equalizes power relations in the classroom and promotes truly participatory learning.

This chapter explores the relevance of Foucault's analysis of power for the conduct of discussion and examines common practices of discussion for the power relations they exhibit. To many university and college teachers, power is a Janus-like phenomenon, presenting two contradictory and mutually exclusive faces—repressive and liberatory. Repressive power is to be avoided if at all possible since it constrains and coerces, bending its subjects to its will. Liberatory power, on the other hand, is to be commended, since it activates and engages students, helping people take control of their lives. In the Professional and Organizational Development Network (POD) circles, it is the liberatory face of power that animates much of what we do. Faculty developers talk emphatically of empowerment as a process through which teachers help learners find their voices and develop the self-confidence to take control of their lives. The empowering urge is shared both by teachers who place themselves in the liberal-humanist tradition, and by those who see themselves as critical pedagogues. Empowering students is what we're about as teachers, and empowering teachers to be creative risk-takers is what we're about as faculty developers.

FOUCAULT AND POWER

A critique of the Janus-like dichotomy of power as being exercised for good or evil lies at the heart of the work of Michel Foucault, the French social theorist (Foucault, 1977, 1980, 1982). In his view, power is never unitary, and neither wholly good or wholly bad. Repression and liberation coexist to different degrees wherever power is present. Hence, "it would not be possible for power relations to exist without points of subordination which, by definition, are means of escape" (Foucault, 1982, p. 225). Foucault regards power as omnipresent, etched into the minutiae of our daily lives. We cannot avoid exercising the power that flows through a social situation, even when we claim to have left power at the door, as in a faculty retreat or departmental brainstorming session. Power moves around a room, whether this is an undergraduate class or departmental meeting. This is a decentralized view of the functioning of power that is in marked contrast to a view which sees power as possessed chiefly by a dominant elite, exercised from above and emanating from a central location that is clearly identifiable. To Foucault, "power reaches into the very grain of individuals, touches their bodies and inserts itself into their actions and attitudes, their discourses, learning processes and everyday lives" (1980, p. 39). Consequently, his study of power has concentrated on understanding its manifestation in everyday rituals and interactions. He studies power "at the extreme points of its exercise . . . where it installs itself and produces real effects" (Foucault, 1980, p. 197). In faculty development, the extreme points of exercise are the configurations of specific practices—peer review, teaching journals, self-designed developmental contracts, team teaching, and so on—often promoted by faculty developers as representing best student-centered practices.

Anyone guided by the philosophy of empowering teachers (in my experience a majority of those who identify themselves as faculty developers working within the field) benefit from reading Foucault. The fact that his writing is sometimes difficult to follow means it is easy to give up, but the struggle to understand and apply him is worth it. Without an appreciation of Foucault's ideas, faculty developers often end up with an incomplete and naïve understanding of how power manifests itself in college classrooms. His work is crucial in helping us learn to recognize the presence of power in our daily practices, particularly the false face of apparently beneficent power exercised to help teachers or learners realize their full potential. As faculty developers, we can never escape the contradictions of power, and it is dangerous to say we can ever be fully aware of exactly how power is flowing around our workshops, institutes, and training sessions. However, reading Foucault can bring us to a better understanding of some of the unanticipated consequences of our supposedly empowering practices.

DISCIPLINARY POWER

Foucault subsumed many of his most important ideas within a single concept, that of disciplinary power. Disciplinary power describes the processes by which we discipline ourselves to conform to an imagined ideal. For example, in a classroom discussion group, disciplinary power is exercised in practices such as the raising of hands to signify one wants to speak, the way eye contact is made between participants to signal to each other that they can speak, the preferred seating arrangement (usually a circle), and the form of speech and terminology that is approved. These things are rarely enshrined in some form of charter or formal class protocol. They are implicit, understood by participants as appropriate. In a professional development institute, disciplinary power might be seen in the way that junior faculty defer to senior faculty when the chance to contribute to a discussion occurs, or the way there's an unspoken agreement not to address anything too contentious.

Most people in the 20th century still think of power in sovereign terms; that is, as located in a clearly identifiable individual or political unit (the monarch, president, central committee of the party). Foucault believed this to be 200–300 years behind the times. In the 18th and 19th centuries, the economy of disciplinary power established "the circulation of effects of power through progressively finer channels, gaining access to individuals themselves, to their bodies, their gestures and all their daily actions" (Foucault, 1980, p. 152). Disciplinary power was in many ways more insidious, more sinister, than the workings of sovereign power, being based on "knowing the inside of people's minds" (Foucault, 1982, p. 214). At its heart were "procedures which allowed the effects of power to circulate in a manner at once continuous, uninterrupted, adopted and 'individualized' throughout the entire social body" (Foucault, 1980, p. 119). Disciplinary power exhibits an "attentive malevolence" (Foucault, 1977, p. 139) and is "a type of power which is constantly exercised by means of surveillance" (Foucault, 1980, p. 104). It is seen most explicitly in the functioning of prisons, but its mechanisms are also at play in schools, factories, social service agencies, and higher education. This form of power turns lifelong learning into a lifelong nightmare of "hierarchical surveillance, continuous registration, perpetual assessment and classification" (Foucault, 1977, p. 220).

Disciplinary power exhibits spatial and temporal dimensions. Learners are separated into individual cubicles and study carrels, or behind individual computer terminals, working on individual projects. Professional examinations are taken, essays written, and graduate theses submitted, as individual acts of intellectual labor. The collective learning represented by three or four students writing an essay together as a collaborative project, or two or three professors coauthoring scholarly articles, is discouraged as a plagiaristic diversion of the intellectually weak. Disciplinary power also breaks down time by arranging learning in a sequence of discrete stages. Training and professional practice are detached from each other, the curriculum is divided into elements for which predetermined amounts of time are allocated, and the timetable becomes the pivotal reference point for the organization of learners' and educators' activities.

A central mechanism of disciplinary power is the examination. The examination has "the triple function of showing whether the subject has reached the level required, of guaranteeing that each subject undergoes the same apprenticeship and of differentiating the abilities of each individual" (Foucault, 1977, p. 158). Those who go through a series of examinations have their lives fixed and recorded in documents. People are sorted, classified, and differentiated by the examination which functions as "a normalizing gaze, a surveillance that makes it possible to qualify, to classify and to punish" (Foucault, 1977, p. 184). When achievements and aptitudes are judged by exams then we enter "the age of examinatory justice" (Foucault, 1977, p. 305) in which "the judges of normality are present everywhere" (Foucault, 1977, p. 304).

DISCIPLINARY POWER AND THE DISCUSSION CIRCLE

Let us turn now to a consideration of the way disciplinary power is present in the smallest, apparently most inconsequential, human interactions. As we have seen, Foucault views power as something embedded in the everyday lives of citizens and in the everyday activities of learners and teachers. Power flows around the body politic and around the college classroom, rather than being located at one clearly discernible point. It is continually in use, always being renewed, altered, and challenged by all those individuals who exercise it. Foucault writes that "power is employed and exercised through a net-like organization. And not only do individuals circulate between its threads; they are always in the position of simultaneously undergoing and exercising this power...individuals are the vehicles of power" (Foucault, 1980, p. 98).

To Foucault, power relations are manifest in all higher education interactions; even those that seem the freest and most unconstrained. Students, just as much as teachers, are the vehicles of power. As an example, the circle is an educational practice that appears to equalize power relations, if not escape from them entirely. At POD conferences, it is almost compulsory for presenters (myself included) to arrive at the room early and move the chairs into a circle, space and content permitting. Whenever I have done this I assume I am demonstrating my commitment to honoring learners' voices and experiences, and to removing my own coercive power from the educational setting. To instructors who use discussion methods regularly in their own teaching, the circle is probably the room arrangement they instinctively prefer.

For many years, the circle has been so sacred and reified in my own teaching that I took it as an unchallengeable sign of my democratic purity and learner-centeredness. However, following Foucault, it is quite possible that participants may regard the discussion circle as an oppressive experience, as a situation in which the possibility of surveillance is dramatically heightened. Usher and Edwards write that while putting chairs in a circle "may create different discursive possibilities, it nonetheless simply reconfigures the regulation of students. They may not be so directly subject to the teacher/lecturer but they remain under the immediate scrutiny and surveillance of their peers.... Changing practices do not, then, do away with power but displace it and reconfigure it in different ways" (1994, p. 91). In a circle students know that their lack of participation, or their poorly articulated contribution, will be all the more evident to their peers.

Gore (1993) builds on Foucault's work to argue that beneath the circle's democratic veneer there may exist a much more troubling and ambivalent reality. For learners who are confident, loquacious, and used to academic culture, the circle holds relatively few terrors. It is an experience that is congenial, authentic, and liberating. For students who are shy, aware of their different skin color, physical appearance, or form of dress, unused to intellectual discourse, intimidated by disciplinary jargon, and the culture of academe, or conscious of their accent or lack of vocabulary, the circle can be a painful and humiliating experience. These learners have been stripped of their right to privacy. They are denied the chance to check educators out by watching them closely before deciding whether or not they can be trusted. This trust only develops over time as teachers are seen to act consistently, honestly, and fairly. Yet the circle, with its implicit pressure to participate and perform, may preclude the time and opportunity for this trust to develop. As such, it is a prime example of how apparently democratic educational practices exhibit power relations just as much as those labeled as autocratic or overly didactic.

So where does Foucault leave those of us who like the circle? Is the logic of his argument that we should abandon the circle and go back to the serried rows of earlier years? To me, this is not an either/or question. I continue to use the circle in my own practice but I hope in a more critically informed way. Foucault's analysis makes me aware of the circle's oppressive potential and reminds me that I must continually research how students experience it. Now I explain to students as they take their seats that I know the circle does not remove power relations from the group and that I realize the circle is often perceived as an oppressive mandating of participation. Sometimes this leads me to make a no-speech policy whereby I tell students that they have the right not to speak and that I will not interpret their silence as indicating apathy, hostility, or mental inertia. It may seem strange to suggest that you launch a discussion by advocating silence, but my experience has been that this puts diffident or introverted students at their ease.

The following is an example from my own teaching of a typical declaration I make to students at the start of a discussion-based course. It is intended to express my tolerance of silence and to inform students that participation in class discussion is entirely voluntary and should never be used to curry favor with me. It acknowledges that being in a circle increases the student's feeling of being under surveillance from peers as well as the teacher, and attempts to circumvent the performance anxiety this induces.

> I know that speaking in discussions is a nerve-wracking thing and that your fear of making public fools of yourselves can inhibit you to the point of nonparticipation. I, myself, feel very nervous as a discussion participant and spend a lot of my time carefully rehearsing my contributions so as not to look foolish when I finally speak. So please don't feel that you have to speak in order to gain my approval or to show me that you're a diligent student. It's quite acceptable to say nothing in the session, and there'll be no presumption of failure on your part. I don't equate silence with mental inertia. Obviously, I hope you will want to say something and speak up, but I don't want you to do this just for the sake of appearances. So let's be comfortable with a prolonged period of silence that might, or might not, be broken. When anyone feels like saying something, speak up.

I believe in the power of this kind of early declaration because I've seen how well it works. Students will often come up to me afterwards and say that by granting them public permission not to say anything I actually emboldened them to speak. By deliberately destroying the link between student speech and teacher approval the pressure on students to look smart in front of me—the performance anxiety that kills so much discussion participation—is much reduced. The autobiographical disclosure that as a discussion group participant I suffer from the same performance anxiety also seems to reassure students that my experience is not as far from theirs as they might imagine.

FOUCAULT AND DISCUSSION-BASED TEACHING

Many instructors either maintain that they have no power over others, or that they can choose when, and when not, to exercise it. Foucault views such confidence with amusement. He sketches out a theory of power as a circular flow that draws all into its currents. Choosing whether or not to exercise power is, in his eyes, an illusory choice. In reality, we are fated to exercise power. Using Foucault's analysis, it is revealing to examine common student-centered practices that are celebrated for their intent to avoid the exercise of power by involving all participants equally. We do not need Foucault to help us recognize the exercise of sovereign power in higher education. This is seen in the lecturer who treats a group of students as if they were ten-year olds, allowing few questions and no unauthorized interruptions. What Foucault helps us recognize is that another more subtle form of power—disciplinary power—is often present in practices that are usually thought of as democratic and participatory.

Discussion

One of the most democratic and participatory of all methods of teaching is that of discussion. Discussion is the methodological jewel in the crown of progressive-humanist education, designed to serve as an experimental laboratory for the learning of democratic habits. Yet, talking of the discussion method as if it were a single, integrated approach to facilitating learning that achieves broadly the same democratic consequences each time it is used is hopelessly naive and simplistic. Discussion is a problematic form of practice that is culturally situated. Its meaning and significance vary according to (amongst other things) the race, class, and gender of its participants, the institutional and cultural location of the speech acts that comprise discussion, and the ways in which the facilitator's behavior is interpreted. The purpose for which discussion is held—for example, to check whether students have properly understood concepts reviewed in readings and lectures, or to engage in ideology critique as a way of unmasking dominant cultural values—always represents a political stance, an ideological agenda.

The criteria underlying the evaluation of what counts as good discussion also spring from a particular sociopolitical milieu and represent the values of those who have managed to lever themselves into positions as professional gatekeepers. Not surprisingly, these values often accord with the prevailing values of laissez-faire capitalism. In fact, many teachers adopt a more or less conscious metaphor of the free market toward their practice, believing that the less interaction by the teacher, the better and more authentically student-centered the discussion. But intellectual exchanges in discussion never occur on a level playing field. Those who bring the greatest cultural capital to discussion find that participating in this activity ensures that they accrue yet more capital. Even the language teachers use to describe the outcomes they desire for discussion—getting students to "own" a concept or "buy into" an idea—buttress capitalist ideology.

Discussion groups in colleges and universities are not limpid; tranquil eddies cut off from the river of social, cultural, and political life. They are contested arenas—whirlpools containing the contradictory crosscurrents of the struggles for material superiority and ideological legitimacy that exist in the world outside. From a Foucaultian point of view, power is omnipresent in discussion. The flow of power can be named and redirected, and its seat can shift around the group, but it can never be denied or erased. Becoming aware of how the dynamics of power permeate and move among discussion group members helps us realize that forces present in the wider society always intrude into the classroom. Patterns of participation and deference based on race, class, and gender, unless deliberately named and challenged, invariably reproduce themselves as the natural order of things in the discussion.

Surveillance

Surveillance is one of the relations of power that lends itself to discussion. In a discussion group, we cannot be unobserved by staying silent. Our very silence draws attention to us. We may be unheard but we will not be unnoticed. Surveillance is the most important component of disciplinary power. In a society subject to disciplinary power, we discipline ourselves by watching others and ourselves. There is no need for the state to spend enormous amounts of time and money making sure we behave correctly since we are watching ourselves to make sure we don't step out of line. What makes us watch ourselves so assiduously is not an internal resolve to follow normal ways of thinking and acting, thereby avoiding a fall into disgrace. Instead, we watch ourselves because we sense that our attempt to stay close to the norm is itself being watched by another, all-seeing, presence. We carry within us the sense that "out there," in some hidden, undiscoverable location, "they" are constantly observing us. It is hard to deviate from the norm if you feel cameras hidden in every corner of your life are recording your thoughts and actions (figuratively and sometimes literally).

For Foucault, "the perfect disciplinary apparatus would make it possible for a single gaze to see everything constantly" (1977, p. 173), and for those being surveyed to be aware that at any time they may be subject to invisible scrutiny. "It is the fact of constantly being seen, of being able always to be seen, that maintains the disciplined individual in all his subjection" (Foucault, 1977, p. 187). Few methods of teaching in higher education are so suited to surveillance as discussion, inviting as it does surveillance by peers as well as teachers. Participants know their every word is heard, their every move seen, by someone in the group. This may help people focus on the issue at hand, but it may equally well deny them the reflective, relaxed pose, the time to glaze over and let ideas cogitate, and the silence necessary to understand and make connections between complex ideas. The norm of alertness, of showing that you're engaged in the discussion by making eye contact, nodding, and uttering "uh-huh," disallows all these things.

Discussion Leaders

Discussion as a way of learning that is quintessentially student-centered can be experienced by learners as performance theater. Students are actors in a loosely improvised drama, the broad outlines of which are implicitly agreed on in advance. Their performance as discussion participants is carefully watched by "the judges of normality" (Foucault, 1977, p. 304). These judges (discussion leaders) monitor the extent to which participants are participating in the conversation in a suitable manner. Foucault argues that "the universal reign of the normative" (1977, p. 304)— the standard prescription for how one should think and behave—means that each person "subjects to it his body, his gestures, his behavior, his aptitudes, his achievements" (1977, p. 304). Many discussion groups are certainly influenced by an unexpressed norm of what constitutes good discussion. This norm holds that such discussions are those in which everyone speaks intelligently and articulately for roughly equal amounts of time and all conversation is focused on the topic at hand. In this norm of the good discussion there is little silence. What conversation takes place focuses only on relevant issues with a suitably sophisticated level of discourse. Talk flows scintillatingly and seamlessly from topic to topic. Everyone listens attentively and respectfully to everyone else's contributions. People make their comments in a way that is informed, thoughtful, insightful, and unfailingly courteous. The Algonquin roundtable or Bloomsbury dinner parties are the exemplars the norm implies, and the one toward which participants direct their discussion performances.

Discussion leaders as judges of normality overtly reinforce the power of this norm by establishing criteria for participation that operationalize the norm's rules of conduct. Assigning part of a grade for participation, without defining what participation means, activates the norm's influence over participants. Learners immediately interpret participation as doing their best to exemplify this norm. They carefully rehearse stunningly insightful contributions that will make them sound like Cornel West or Gertrude Stein. Discussion teachers also covertly reinforce this norm by their subtle deployment of nonverbal behaviors signifying approval or disapproval of participants' efforts to exemplify the norm. Through nods, frowns, eye contact (or the lack of it), sighs of frustration or pity, grunts of agreement, disbelieving intakes of breath at the obvious stupidity of a particular comment, and a wide range of other gestures, discussion leaders communicate to the group when they are close to, or moving away from, the norm. Unless discussion leaders redefine criteria for discussion participation to challenge this norm, students will work assiduously to gear their behavior toward its realization.

THE UNAVOIDABLE EXERCISING OF POWER: THE PRACTICE OF DISCUSSION INFORMED BY FOUCAULT

I want to respond to the foregoing analysis by examining specific discussion practices and responsibilities, focusing particularly on the role of the teacher. As educators we cannot avoid taking action. The discussion leader cannot be a laissez-faire facilitator, exercising a minimum of control. Taking this stance only serves to allow patterns of inequity present in the wider society to reproduce themselves automatically in the classroom. Instead, the teacher must intervene to introduce a variety of practices— such as the circle of voices, periods when only those who have not spoken are allowed to speak, the ground rule that we can only speak about others' ideas (not our own), and the circular response technique (Brookfield & Preskill, 1999)—to ensure some sort of equity of participation.

Many teachers would like to believe either that they have no special power over students, or that any power mistakenly attributed to them by participants is an illusion that can quickly be dissolved by a refusal to dominate the group. But it is not that easy. No matter how much we protest our desire to be at one with learners there is a predictable flow of attention focused on us. While it is important to privilege learners' voices and to create multiple foci of attention in the classroom, it is disingenuous to pretend that as teachers we are the same as our learners. It is better to acknowledge publicly our position of power, to engage students in deconstructing that power, and to attempt to model a critical analysis of our own source of authority in front of them. This will sometimes involve us in becoming alert to, and publicly admitting, oppressive dimensions to practices that we had thought were neutral or even benevolent.

I know that I can never entirely escape the web of power relationships within which a discussion class operates. Structures of inequity existing outside the class frequently reproduce themselves within. I know, too, that a universal democratic purity of practice is an illusion, and that if I measure my work by whether or not I realize this I am doomed to perpetual guilt. But I know, too, that discussion groups can be more or less democratic, that the problematic nature of discussion can be continuously revealed, and that we can come to more informed and sophisticated understandings of how we are implicated in the unwitting maintenance of regimes of truth. The following are some of the steps I take to accomplish these ends. Others are described more fully in Brookfield and Preskill (1999).

Early in any discussion-based course, we can ensure that the group wrestle with creating what Bridges (1988) calls a moral culture for discourse—more prosaically, ground rules for conversation. These rules can be developed in several ways. The leader can suggest them, but that can seem a somewhat arbitrary exercise of teacher power. A better option is for students to generate these by reviewing their past autobiographical experiences as discussion participants to identify features they want to emphasize and avoid, and then generate specific procedures that encapsulate these preferences. Usually, these ground rules focus strongly on equalizing participation, guarding against behaviors such as hate speech, and preserving students' right to silence.

We can also make sure that the group's experience of discussion is constantly researched through a classroom assessment or action research approach such as the critical incident questionnaire (CIQ) (Brookfield, 1995) or discussion audit. In the CIQ, students write a weekly anonymous commentary on their experience of discussion, which is compiled and reported back to the class. The security that this instrument's anonymity affords emboldens students to make explicit the inequities of participation they observe, the imbalances in voice they notice, possible discrepancies between the group's espoused rules of conduct and its actual behavior, and any arbitrary abuses of power by the teacher or other group members. In the weekly reporting out of the previous week's CIQ data, the problematic nature of power relationships in the group becomes a matter for public discussion. The group learns to delve deeper and deeper in understanding how power is exercised and resisted at the specific site of a discussion-based course.

Any attempt to democratize discussion invariably raises the question whether or not teachers should require all students to participate in discussion, or whether this is a return to old-style sovereign power. Mandating participation seems like a repressive act that stands in direct contrast to the spirit of democratic conversation. However, hooks (1994) argues forcibly that there are occasions when it is justifiable to exercise power in this way. She requires students to read out paragraphs from their journals in class so that none feel invisible or silenced. To her, this is a responsible exercise of teacher power. Always allowing students the option to pass in discussion circles means that those who are shy and introverted, or uncomfortable because they perceive themselves as members of a minority race, gender, or class, end up not contributing. The longer this pattern of nonparticipation persists, the harder it is to break. In truly Foucaultian fashion, what seems like an empathic, benign action by the leader—allowing students the right to silence—serves to reinforce existing differences in status and power. Those used to holding forth will automatically speak, while those whose voices are rarely heard, will stay mute. In passing on the right to speak they ensure their continuing silence.

NOTE

Portions of this paper draw on an analysis of Foucault that first appeared in the *Canadian Journal for the Study of Adult Education,* Vol. 15, No, 1, 2001.

REFERENCES

Bridges, D. (1988). *Education, democracy, and discussion.* Lanham, MD: University Press of America.

Brookfield, S. D. (1995). *Becoming a critically reflective teacher.* San Francisco, CA: Jossey-Bass.

Brookfield, S. D., & Preskill, S. (1999). *Discussion as a way of teaching: Tools and techniques for democratic classrooms.* San Francisco, CA: Jossey-Bass.

Foucault, M. (1977). *Discipline and punish: The birth of the prison.* New York, NY: Vintage.

Foucault, M. (1980). *Power/knowledge: Selected interviews and other writings, 1972-1977.* New York, NY: Pantheon.

Foucault, M. (1982). The subject and power. In H. L. Dreyfus & P. Rabinow (Eds.), *Michel Foucault: Beyond structuralism and hermeneutics* (pp. 214-225). Chicago, IL: University of Chicago Press.

Gore, J. (1993). *The struggle for pedagogies: Critical and feminist discourses as regimes of truth.* New York, NY: Routledge.

hooks, bell. (1994). *Teaching to transgress: Education as the practice of freedom.* New York, NY: Routledge.

Usher, R., & Edwards, R. (1994). *Postmodernism and education: Different voices, different worlds.* London, England: Routledge.

Contact:

Stephen D. Brookfield
Mail #MOH 217
School of Education
University of St. Thomas
1000 LaSalle Avenue
Minneapolis, MN 55403-2009
(651) 962-4982
Email: sdbrookfield@stthomas.edu

Stephen Brookfield holds the title of Distinguished Professor at the University of St. Thomas. He is a three-time winner (1986, 1989, and 1996) of the Cyril O. Houle World Award for Literature in Adult Education and currently serves on the editorial boards of adult education journals in the United States, Canada, England, and Australia.

18

A Modified Microteaching Model: A Cross-Disciplinary Approach to Faculty Development

John P. Hertel
Barbara J. Millis
Robert K. Noyd
United States Air Force Academy

Three departments at the United States Air Force Academy successfully used a microteaching model to train new faculty. Like other models, its structured approach used videotaping and peer coaching. The model also contained several unique features, including a cross-disciplinary approach to supplement feedback from department members and focused small group feedback with built-in preparation time. Thus, this model results not only in enhanced teaching performance, but also in departmental and institutional collegiality.

INTRODUCTION

"At first I was fearful," confessed a new instructor in the management department at the United States Air Force Academy (USAFA). "Now I am convinced that microteaching truly influenced my classroom performance in a positive way." Three departments at USAFA—biology, law, and management—have integrated a microteaching component into their summer departmental orientations for new faculty members. The model used is a considerable modification of the original process, which has remained viable, particularly in graduate teaching assistant (GTA) training, since the 1960s. Involving both department faculty members and outside observers, the USAFA microteaching sessions result in rich feedback. Because of the opportunity not only for one-on-one feedback with a skilled facilitator, but also for carefully prepared feedback from small faculty groups, this model fosters collegiality and encourages the reflective insights needed for effective peer coaching and teaching enhancement.

WHAT IS MICROTEACHING?

Microteaching is defined by McKnight as "a scaled down realistic classroom training context in which teachers, both experienced and inexperienced, may acquire new teaching skills and refine old ones" (1980, p. 214). It was developed in the early and mid-1960s by Dwight W. Allen, Kevin Ryan (1969), and other colleagues at the Stanford Teacher Education Program. The Stanford model emphasized a teach, review and reflect, re-teach approach, using elementary school students as authentic audiences. It also focused on narrowly described skill sets. Videotaping a brief five- to ten-minute mini-lesson was a key component with considerable time devoted to the entire process.

Some subsequent modifications have eliminated the videotaping component altogether while maintaining an emphasis on a concentrated, focused form of feedback using role-playing peers, rather than actual students. Using faculty peers rather than actual students and allowing teachers to present skills of their own choosing during the mini-lesson results in a modification of microteaching which Tiberius (1997) calls laboratory teaching.

In the early models, often the peer audience and the instructor reviewed the videotape together after the mini-lesson, a tactic that was both time-consuming and repetitious. A more effective variation on this latter model, developed by Keesing and Daston (1979), eliminated the repetition by having the mini-lesson presenter and the facilitator review the tape privately while the peer audience prepared feedback emphasizing two skills specifically identified by the presenter.

Although many variations of microteaching exist, some basic premises behind the process remain constant.

- Microteaching is real teaching

- It lessens the complexities of normal classroom teaching in that class size, scope, and content are reduced

- It focuses on accomplishing specific tasks

- It organizes controlled, structured practice sessions

- It allows for immediate, focused feedback

- It promotes reflection on teaching approaches and on constructive feedback

THE USAFA MODEL

The USAFA microteaching model, based on the Keesing and Daston approach, grew from a fruitful collaboration between the director of faculty development in USAFA's Center for Educational Excellence (CEE), who was trained by Hugo Keesing in 1984, and two proactive faculty members responsible for faculty development in their respective departments of law and biology. In the summer of 1999, both departments involved their new faculty in microteaching activities and found the experience so positive that they repeated it with new faculty in 2000. Additionally, in 2000, the CEE faculty development expert and the law and biology specialists—now experienced microteaching facilitators—worked together to help the management department conduct microteaching sessions for an unusually high influx of new instructors, 14 in all.

The USAFA model contains several key steps.

Prior to the Microteaching Session

- Instructors plan a ten- to 15-minute mini-lesson, preferably on a topic that they will later use for a full 50-minute lesson. In the biology and management departments, the instructor selected the topic; the law department facilitator deliberately assigned a topic from an early lesson to help faculty prepare for early classes.

- Instructors, after reflection, complete a mini-lesson form (Appendices 18.2 and 18.3) indicating, among other things, the lesson title and objectives and teaching skills/abilities on which they wish specific feedback.

During the Microteaching Session

- After distributing their mini-lesson forms to the faculty participants, instructors teach the ten- to 15-minute mini-lesson before colleagues as it is videotaped. Time is called, as needed. The faculty observers, most from the department but some outside the discipline, serve as the pseudo students.

- The instructor and the microteaching facilitator spend the next ten minutes discussing the mini-lesson while they review the videotape. Special attention is paid to elements, such as mannerisms or movements, best captured by a camera.

- During this same ten minutes, colleagues in small groups discuss and plan a structured feedback session, emphasizing reinforcement of what went right and discussing how to lead the instructor toward positive changes. The roles of discussion leader, recorder, and spokesperson rotate within the small group.

- During the third ten-minute segment, the spokesperson for each group, representing the group's consensus, shares structured feedback with the instructor, concentrating on the specific feedback requested.

Typically, each small group offers, in turn, a positive comment—something the instructor should continue doing—and then each group, in turn, focuses on something the instructor might improve.

- A give-and-take discussion among all participants ensues, if time and inclinations permit.

- Participants make individual comments on their copy of the presenter's mini-lesson form, which are then returned to the new instructor.

THE CONTEXT FOR MICROTEACHING AT USAFA

All three USAFA departments were motivated to try a microteaching approach by an extrinsic factor: the dean of the faculty's requirement that all new faculty participate in practice teaching consisting of at least two classroom presentations with experienced faculty members observing in the role of students and providing constructive feedback. More importantly, though, all departments at USAFA are intrinsically motivated by a strongly perceived responsibility for training new instructors in methods specific to the discipline. All departments recognize the need to bring new faculty members—many of them young captains in the Air Force with master's degrees, but no teaching experience—up to speed in a relatively short period of time. With an average tour of approximately three years, USAFA military faculty members don't have the time to learn from their mistakes. Plus, teaching standards are exceptionally high: Like all USAFA faculty, newcomers are operating under institutional core values that emphasize "Excellence in All We Do." Thus, faculty development is a responsibility jointly shared by the CEE and by the individual departments. In addition to a weeklong orientation program organized by CEE for over 140 new and returning faculty, all departments offer a discipline-specific orientation.

The biology department, for example, offered six hours of teacher training that included classroom management, principles of learning and pedagogy, and professional development.

The law department provided sequenced orientation sessions. The first of these involved an informal one-on-one meeting between the department's faculty development specialist (who also served as the microteaching facilitator) and the new faculty member. During a subsequent welcome by the department head, which included all the department members, the microteaching facilitator explained the microteaching procedures in greater detail, distributed the ten-minute mini-lesson plan form (Appendix 18.3) and the microteaching guidelines (Appendix 18.4). During a third meeting, the individual responsible for the core law course taught by all new instructors discussed how the microteaching topics assigned to new faculty fit into a full lesson and into the course. This orientation helped new faculty members appreciate the relevance of the microteaching lesson and also determined the level of detail they should present during the microteaching session. The microteaching sessions prior to the start of classes were followed by 50-minute presentations with focused feedback. After the semester began, all new faculty also received structured classroom observations.

The management department, working with the CEE, scheduled over a week of half-day orientation events for new faculty. Sessions included "Lesson Planning and the First Day of Class," "Active Learning: Quick Ways to Engage Cadets," "Testing and Grading: The Agony and the Ecstasy," "Using the Web Effectively," and culminated with two mornings of microteaching.

This context is essential. The microteaching sessions become more meaningful when placed within the broader context of an orientation to effective teaching at the Air Force Academy. Furthermore, by establishing a collegial context for sharing teaching ideas, new instructors are more likely to seek help with teaching later in the term. There is a tendency, as Kinsella notes, to avoid such consultations: "Novice and veteran professors alike may feel that to actively seek advice on curriculum, instruction or classroom management is admitting a lack of competence and a potential threat to their professional reputation and status within the department" (1995, p. 110). The emphasis on formative evaluation—

feedback intended to strengthen teaching, not to evaluate faculty for administrative decisions—during this microteaching process allows faculty to experiment in a relatively risk-free environment.

FACTORS CONTRIBUTING TO THE SUCCESS OF THE MICROTEACHING EXPERIENCE

In addition to the positive context, several features of the USAFA microteaching model contributed to its success in all three departments. These features could be replicated in virtually any other academic setting.

Structured Guidelines

Faculty new to a department need to develop confidence in the department's policies and procedures, as well as in the people who will become working colleagues. Having a well-structured orientation program that addresses as many professional and personal issues as possible will promote a sense of belonging to a competent, caring institution. The law department's orientation, for example, included detailed discussions about the microteaching presentations, including their purpose and procedures. Discussing the actual forms used in the microteaching process overcame much of the new instructor's initial anxiety (see Appendices 18.1, 18.2, 18.3, and 18.4).

Departmental Involvement

Having as many department members as possible participate in the microteaching sessions adds a dimension of collegiality and caring. Teachers with different levels of experience made for rich discussions within the small groups. During the mini-lesson, participants acted as typical students by asking and answering clarifying questions and, in a few cases, exhibiting real types of student behavior. The new faculty demonstrated a wonderful variety of teaching techniques—an added benefit to all participants, new and experienced. The value of reflection on teaching cannot be emphasized enough. As Killen notes, "There is a limit to how much you can learn from self-analysis. The benefits of reflection can be greatly enhanced if the process involves a sharing of ideas with a colleague" (1995, p. 129). Involving an entire department—or at least a large segment of it—results in rich, productive conversations about teaching and learning and engenders trust and collegiality.

Small Group Feedback Opportunities

Most importantly, having the small groups of participant-observers prepare the feedback was tremendously valuable. The comments from each group typically reinforced important points and allowed for in-depth commentary. Multiple groups also offered different perspectives and permitted additional issues to emerge. On more than one occasion, one of the groups reacted one way to an instructor's technique while another group reacted exactly the opposite. Rather than providing confusing feedback, these occasions highlighted the fact that the technique employed was likely to produce similarly mixed reactions in students—a valuable lesson learned. Because the groups were deliberately small—four to five faculty members—there was ample opportunity for all voices to contribute. The discussions about teaching were rich and intimate, reinforcing Kinsella's emphasis on "a context that is supportive, non-evaluative, and intellectually stimulating.... This willingness and ability to take risks to teach more effectively, and to constantly monitor and adjust goals and strategies, can only be fostered within a trusting, collaborative environment" (1995, p. 109).

Cross-Disciplinary Involvement

Similarly, it was helpful to include participants who were not from the presenter's department and who did not have special knowledge of the topic presented. More than once, either during the mini-lesson itself or during the group discussions, these participants raised issues that the others did not see, perhaps because the subject matter experts had unconsciously filled in the blanks in the instructor's presentation. During the law department's microteaching sessions, two visiting nonlaw professors from a large state university and a nonteaching spouse of a faculty member added insightful comments and differing perspectives. While these last participants were unplanned (as visitors, they had expressed an interest in the microteaching procedures), they proved especially helpful. The three outside facilitators from biology, law, and English critiqued the management department's microteaching sessions.

In addition to these external insights, input from members of the department who are familiar with the lessons being taught is critical. These content expert participants are best able to determine whether the instructor is presenting the material at an appropriate level and in a way consistent with the department objectives.

Length of the Mini-Lesson

Faculty new to a department, an institution, and a community have a myriad of demands on their time. Thus, new faculty appreciated the fact that they could teach an abbreviated lesson. Some found that a ten-minute session was not intimidating, and a new faculty member also mentioned that the ten- to 15-minute session allowed him to "work through a lesson plan, albeit abbreviated, which helped me establish a format for such plans that I'm still using."

Videotaping

Although some microteaching models omit the videotape portion, viewing the tape one-on-one with a facilitator had several important benefits. One was to provide feedback to the presenter on presentation mechanics such as voice, body position and movements, hand gestures, and eye contact, as well as recognizing student responses to the lesson. A second benefit was to allow the presenters to review, more as outsiders, how they presented the lesson. This previewing feature became beneficial during the group feedback sessions, since the instructors had observed their teaching before receiving feedback from the group, rather than being limited to memory. Davis also recognizes the value of videotaping: "Watching a videotape of yourself is an extremely valuable experience. Videotaping allows you to view and listen to the class as your students do . . . " (1993, p. 355).

Another important function of the video review was to provide the participants time to synthesize and prioritize their observations and construct meaningful feedback. Immediate feedback from individual observers often prompts idiosyncratic comments or even criticisms without reasoned recommendations for improvement. Also, during immediate feedback sessions a single comment often carries too much significance, particularly if it is negative. When small group discussions filtered and focused these individual criticisms, group consensus allowed for a more balanced perspective during the feedback to the presenter. Without fail, the group comments became more constructive.

FEEDBACK FROM NEW FACULTY

Approximately two months into the fall semester, all 18 of the new instructors from the management and law departments received the opportunity to provide feedback on this microteaching model. Nine of them responded, either with written email replies to questions asking for comments or in small group sessions with the authors. These comments, which were collected and examined, reinforced several key points.

The new instructors emphasized, first of all, that preparation for the microteaching process was essential. The mini-lesson forms were only useful where there was a discussion beforehand on how they would be used. Several faculty members indicated that more preparation would have been helpful. Secondly, the management instructors were allowed to select whatever topic they wanted from the courses they were to teach. While this choice put them into a comfort zone, several recommended that assigned topics would let them experiment with presentations, which they then could perfect before teaching their first real class. One commented, "The [assigned] lesson should be a new topic to show any weakness."

All of the presentations were videotaped, and the faculty presenters overwhelmingly considered the videotaping experiences very effective. One instructor commented, "You never know how your teaching comes off. This gives you a chance to be a fly on the wall and to be critical of yourself." More than one instructor agreed that seeing the videotape caused them to be less defensive during the group feedback sessions and allowed them to better understand and even agree with many of the comments, especially the negative ones.

All of the instructors agreed that it was essential for the participant groups to have time to compose their feedback, outside the presence of the presenter. And they agreed that the preparation/consensus-building time changed how the feedback was presented. One new faculty member wanted more "hardball" feedback. He felt that the comments from his colleagues were too kind: "Just tell me where I went wrong; where I blew it," he said. At the same time, he appreciated the value of constructive feedback, including the recommended improvements—"as long as [they] identify the shortcomings."

When asked what—besides more instruction on the microteaching process—they recommended most, there was clear consensus that new faculty members wanted more follow-up. Fortunately, this follow-up occurred because in all three departments routine classroom observations for new faculty are the norm. All agreed that the microteaching experience prepared them well for these multiple follow-up visits and encouraged them to pursue further conversations about teaching and learning.

"This is like a lab," one instructor commented. "It's where you're supposed to make mistakes in order to learn." Another remarked, "I got some good feedback... some things to put in my toolbox to use later."

CONCLUSION

Because of its flexibility and efficiency, virtually any department can adapt this microteaching model. It is effective not only because it focuses attention on good teaching practices, but also because it promotes collegiality. This model requires minimal preparation for both the facilitator and the new faculty member. It allows neophyte teachers both rehearsal and feedback before entering an actual classroom. Once in the classroom, because they are accustomed to collegial peer review, they feel comfortable welcoming subsequent observations. This combination of microteaching and formative classroom observations—established practice at the Air Force Academy through the CEE and departmental initiatives—is a viable model for virtually any institution.

REFERENCES

Allen, D. W., & Ryan, K. (1969). *Microteaching.* Reading, MA: Addison-Wesley.

Davis, B. G. (1993). *Tools for teaching.* San Francisco, CA: Jossey-Bass.

Keesing, H. A., & Daston, M. (1979). *How to run a microteaching workshop.* College Park, MD: University of Maryland University College Faculty Development Program.

Killen, R. (1995). Improving teaching through reflective partnerships. In E. Neal (Ed.), *To improve the academy: Vol. 14. Resources for faculty, instructional, and organizational development* (pp. 125-141). Stillwater, OK: New Forums Press.

Kinsella, K. (1995). Peers coaching teaching: Colleagues supporting professional growth across the disciplines. In E. Neal (Ed.), *To improve the academy: Vol. 14. Resources for faculty, instructional, and organizational development* (pp. 107-123). Stillwater, OK: New Forums Press.

McKnight, P. C. (1980). Microteaching: Development from 1968-1978. *British Journal of Teacher Education, 6,* 214-227.

Sahu, A. R. (1985). An introduction of microteaching: A systems approach. *International Journal of Math, Education, Science, and Technology, 16,* 25-31.

Tiberius, R. (1997). Microteaching, teaching laboratory, and alliances for change. In K. T. Brinko & R. J. Menges (Eds.), *Practically speaking: A sourcebook for instructional consultants in higher education.* (pp. 131-137). Stillwater, OK: New Forums Press.

Contact:

John P. Hertel
Assistant Professor of Law
HQ USAFA/DFL
2354 Fairchild Drive, Suite 1J-116
USAF Academy, CO 80840-6248
(719) 333-2950
(719) 333-9165 (Fax)
Email: John.hertel@usafa.af.mil

Barbara J. Millis
Director of Faculty Development
HQ USAF/DFE
2354 Fairchild Drive, Suite 4K25
USAFA Academy, CO 80840-6220
(719) 333-2549
Email: Barbara.millis@usafa.af.mil

Robert K. Noyd
Associate Professor of Biology
HQUSAFA/DFL
2354 Fairchild Drive
USAF Academy, CO 80840
(719) 333-2720
Email: Bob.Noyd@usafa.af.mil

John P. Hertel is Assistant Professor of Law at the United States Air Force Academy. For the past two years, he has directed the law department's New Faculty Orientation Program and has worked with the academy's Center for Educational Excellence to assist new faculty from other departments to prepare to teach.

Barbara J. Millis is Director of Faculty Development at the United States Air Force Academy, frequently offers workshops at professional conferences (American Association for Higher Education (AAHE), Lilly Teaching Conference, Council of Independent Colleges, etc.) and for various colleges and universities. She publishes articles on a range of faculty development topics and co-authored with Philip Cottell, *Cooperative Learning for Higher Education Faculty,* Oryx Press (now Greenwood). Her interests include cooperative learning, peer review, critical thinking, and writing for learning. After the Association of American Colleges and Universities (AAC&U) selected the United States Air Force Academy as a Leadership Institution in Undergraduate Education, she began serving as the liaison to the AAC&U's Great Expectations Consortium on Quality Education.

Robert K. Noyd is Associate Professor of Biology at the United States Air Force Academy. He teaches a variety of biology courses, conducts scientific research, directs the department's curriculum development activities, and presents teaching workshops for academy faculty.

APPENDIX 18.1
THE MINI-LESSON: A COMPONENT SKILLS APPROACH

Department of Biology, USAFA

Each new instructor will present a mini-lesson of 15 minutes to the faculty for assistance in improving their teaching skills.

Mini-Lesson Components

1) Lesson plan (see below) to provide context for the mini-lesson

2) Required teaching skills to present:

• Warm up or preparing student for lesson/activity

• Concept development

• Present a single concept

• Illustrating

• Closure or transition (if appropriate)

3) Include one of the following in your presentation

• Stimulus variation

• Questioning

• Silence and nonverbal cues

• Verbal reinforcement

• Recognizing student behaviors

Topic

Any topic from a general biology course. Select one that you can open and transition/close within a 15-minute time frame. Please complete the mini-lesson plan attached.

DFB Faculty Role

To give feedback and play the role of cadets by answering questions. *Unless you are asked, please do not exhibit contrived student behaviors.*

Feedback Session

The mini-lesson will be videotaped. For 10 minutes following the mini-lesson:

- I will play back and go over the videotape with the instructor.
- DFB faculty will break up into small groups and give feedback on the required and selected teaching skills presented. Each group will give the instructor the three most important things they did effectively or can do to improve.

For the next 15 minutes, the instructor will receive feedback.

APPENDIX 18.2
MINI-LESSON PLAN

Department of Biology, USAFA

New instructors, please complete this form and make 15 copies

Instructor: _____

Course: _____

Lesson No: _____

Title: _____

Time frame within content block: beginning   middle   end

Previous lesson title: _____

What have students been asked to do in preparation?

_____

Lesson Objectives/Goals:	**Teaching Methods to Achieve Goal**

Specific learning obstacles anticipated?
(lack of student interest, background, time in semester, etc.)

_____

Feedback: An area in which I particularly want feedback is . . .

Colleague comments:

Warm Up: _____Concept Development:

Other areas:

APPENDIX 18.3
TEN-MINUTE MINI-LESSON PLAN

Department of Law, USAFA

Instructors, please bring ten copies of this form with the first four items completed.

Instructor:

Lesson title:

Lesson objectives:

Two ability areas on which I particularly want feedback:

Colleague comments:

APPENDIX 18.4
MICROTEACHING GUIDELINES

Prepared by B. Millis and distributed to law department faculty
participating in microteaching sessions

A supportive, positive atmosphere characterizes microteaching sessions
with an emphasis on supportive feedback and mutual reflection and discussion. The various participants assume different roles.

The **INSTRUCTOR PRESENTING THE MINI-LESSON** is in an
active teaching role.

Prior to the microteaching session, you will prepare your ten-minute
mini-lesson and complete the information form on which colleagues will
write comments. You have several decisions to make, including your
topic, your lesson objectives, and the teaching abilities on which you
want specific feedback. If you choose a tried and true topic and request
feedback on skills you already suspect are effective, then you will obviously perform well in front of your colleagues, a worthy goal to build
confidence. On the other hand, such a polished presentation may not
help your future teaching. A workshop such as this should involve risk-
taking, with deliberate exposures resulting in professional growth. Try to
prepare a mini-lesson that will most benefit you and your future students. Select a topic that you expect to re-teach as a full 50-minute session. Remember also to select a topic and an approach that will interest
your workshop colleagues.

During the session, before beginning your mini-lesson, rearrange the
furniture (if possible) to provide a congenial classroom atmosphere.
Keep your objectives in mind, also, so that if student participation is a
concern, for example, the arrangement of the desks will not only encourage student-teacher or student-student interaction, but will also
allow the cameraperson to capture the exchanges. Put material on the
board or overhead or pass out handouts prior to or during the mini-lesson, just as you would do during a regular class session.

Immediately prior to the taping of your mini-lesson, you will review
with the other workshop participants the information you have recorded
on the form. During this review, keep two critical points in mind: 1) You
must clearly identify the two skills/abilities you want feedback on so that
your colleagues can concentrate selectively during your presentation,
and 2) be certain not to confuse your pre-taping discussion of objectives

with the objectives you might re-identify as part of the mini-lesson itself. As soon as the camera clicks on and the lesson begins, your fellow participants become students who are approaching your mini-lesson with fresh eyes. To be certain that you clearly separate your introduction for colleagues from the actual mini-lesson, pre-arrange a given signal with the cameraperson. A definite pause and a nod should indicate the beginning of the mini-lesson to both your audience and the cameraperson. After that, relax and enjoy your teaching.

Ideally, every mini-lesson will conclude in the allotted ten minutes. In actual practice, however, many instructors are still presenting material when the ten minutes elapse. Please do not be offended when the workshop facilitator signals both you and the cameraperson to stop. This practice may seem rude, particularly if you are in an unusually dynamic segment of the lesson, such as the conclusion. Frustrating as it may be, adhering to the ten-minute limit is the only way to ensure equal participation. Plus, running out of time is a realistic classroom concern. Unless you identified closure as one of the two teaching skills you were concentrating on, a ten-minute tape of an incomplete lesson will provide sufficient material for effective feedback.

The **STUDENTS**, including those who are offering mini-lessons, act as interested observers.

Perhaps one of the most consistent comments about the microteaching experience concerns the difficulty of playing the roles of both student and analyst. There is no easy solution to this duality other than a flexible willing suspension of disbelief coupled with as natural a classroom setting as possible. This means for example, that you may want to ask questions about material that you already know, but students may not. Please remember, however, that this is not a role-playing situation where you might, for instance, deliberately cause classroom disruptions to watch the instructor's response. Your questions, comments, and body language should help instructors anticipate what their students might actually experience during a similar lesson. At the same time you are reacting as a student, you must keep your critical faculties attuned to what is occurring in the simulated classroom. You'll want to make notes on the mini-lesson form the instructor distributed, remembering to comment specifically on those areas where feedback was requested.

The **DISCUSSION LEADER** channels discussion constructively as the student/analysts prepare for the feedback session.

When guiding the discussion, be certain that the group focuses initially on the two specific skills the instructor wants feedback on. Keep the tone positive and constructive, perhaps asking questions such as, "How do we provide X with the most help?" "Do we really want to tell X that if she cannot do anything to change this behavior?" "How do we phrase these comments to get X to reflect on possible changes?" Try to draw out all the members of the group, including those who will also be offering mini-lessons.

Watch the time carefully so that the group can take the final few minutes to prepare the final feedback.

The **RECORDER** accurately paraphrases and summarizes the group's comments.

When preparing your summary, remember you are aiming for the gist of an idea, not exact phrasing. If the discussion is as animated as it should be, you won't have time in any case to copy verbatim comments during the ten-minute period. Because you are reflecting the opinions of a group, you will want to use phrasing such as "Most of us felt..." or "A few people suffering from math anxiety indicated...." Just prior to your feedback session, work out with the group the best way to get the instructor thinking about possible areas of improvement. Decide, for example, when a question might be more helpful than a direct statement. Instead of "Some of us felt the material was too simple," try asking, "Did you deliberately simplify your presentation because you were targeting a basic psychology class?"

Organize the group's ideas under the two teaching skills/abilities you are providing feedback for, not in the order that the comments arose. You are providing a summary, not a transcript. Alternatively, each group might want to organize the feedback by giving one positive comment (something the person should continue doing) and one negative comment (something the person could improve or alter).

The **SPOKESPERSON** diplomatically presents the group's ideas to the instructor giving the mini-lesson.

When presenting your group's summary to the instructor, remember to be as positive as possible, perhaps beginning with the strong points about the mini-lesson. When noting negative points, use phrases such as "We wondered..." or "A couple of us became confused because...." Definitely include the other group members in your presentation, perhaps asking some of them to clarify points. As you talk with the instructor, include your colleagues also through your glances at the group members to verify the accuracy of your summary. With a constructive, supportive tone, your presentation should result in a friendly exchange of ideas, stimulating instructors to continue doing positive things and to reflect on possible changes.

The **CAMERAPERSON** captures everything of importance during the mini-lesson, including pseudo students' responses.

Bibliography

Aitken N., & Sorcinelli, M. D. (1994). Academic leaders and faculty developers: Creating an institutional culture that values teaching. In C. Wadsworth (Ed.), *To improve the academy: Vol. 13. Resources for faculty, instructional, and organizational development* (pp. 63-78). Stillwater, OK: New Forums Press.

Allen, D. W., & Ryan, K. (1969). *Microteaching.* Reading, MA: Addison-Wesley.

Anderson, L. E., & Carta-Falsa, J. S. (1996). Reshaping faculty interaction: Peer mentoring groups. *Journal of Staff, Program, and Organization Development, 14,* 71-75.

Angelo, T. A. (1991). Ten easy pieces: Assessing higher learning in four dimensions. *New Directions for Teaching and Learning, No. 46.* San Francisco, CA: Jossey-Bass.

Angelo, T. A. (2001). Doing faculty development as if we value learning most: Transformative guidelines from research to practice. In D. Lieberman & C. Wehlburg (Eds.), *To improve the academy: Vol. 19. Resources for faculty, instructional, and organizational development* (pp. 97-112). Bolton, MA: Anker.

Angelo, T. A., & Cross, K. P. (1993). *Classroom assessment techniques.* San Francisco, CA: Jossey-Bass.

Arons, A. B. (1979). Some thoughts on reasoning capacities implicitly expected on College Students. In J. Lockhead & J. Clement (Eds.), *Cognitive process instruction: Research on teaching thinking skills* (pp. 209-215). Philadelphia, PA: Franklin Institute Press.

Australian Vice Chancellors Committee. (1963). *Teaching methods in Australian universities* (Report). Melbourne, Australia: UNSW Press.

Bain, K. (1998). *What do the best teachers do?* Evanston, IL: Northwestern University, Searle Center for Teaching Excellence.

Baldwin, J. (2000). Why we still need liberal arts learning in the new millennium. *Education Digest, 66* (4), 4-9.

Banks, C. A. M., & Banks, J. A. (1995). Equity pedagogy: An essential component of multicultural education. *Theory into Practice, 34* (3), 152-158.

Banks, J. A. (1993). Multicultural education: Development, dimensions, and challenges. *Phi Delta Kappan, 75* (1), 22-28.

Banks, J. A. (1998). The lives and values of researchers: Implications for educating citizens in a multicultural society. *Educational Researcher, 27* (7), 4-17.

Banner, J. M., & Cannon, H. C. (1997). The personal qualities of teaching: What teachers do cannot be distinguished from who they are. *Change, 29,* 40-43.

Barr, R. B., & Tagg, J. (1995, November/December). From teaching to learning: A new paradigm for undergraduate education. *Change,* 13-25.

Bass, R. (1999, February). The scholarship of teaching: What's the problem? *Invention: Creative thinking about learning and teaching, 1* (1), 1-10.

Beard, R. M. (1970). *Teaching and learning in higher education.* Harmondsworth, England: Penguin.

Bernstein, D. J., Jonson, J., & Smith, K. (2000). An examination of the implementation of peer review of teaching. *New Directions for Teaching and Learning, No. 83.* San Francisco, CA: Jossey-Bass.

Bess, J., & Associates. (2000). *Teaching alone, teaching together: Transforming the structure of teams for teaching.* San Francisco, CA: Jossey-Bass.

Black, B. (1998). Using the SGID method for a variety of purposes. In D. DeZure & M. Kaplan (Eds.), *To improve the academy: Vol. 17. Resources for faculty, instructional, and organizational development* (pp. 245-262). Stillwater, OK: New Forums Press.

Bligh, D. (1972). *What's the use of lectures?* (3rd ed.). Hertfordshire, England: Penguin.

Bonwell, C. C., & Eison, J. A. (1991). *Active learning: Creating excitement in the classroom.* San Francisco, CA: Jossey-Bass.

Boyer, E. (1990). *Scholarship reconsidered: Priorities of the professoriate.* Princeton, NJ: Carnegie Foundation for the Advancement of Teaching.

Braxton, J. M., Milem, J. F., & Sullivan, A. S. (2000). The influence of active learning on the college student departure process: Toward a revision of Tinto's theory. *Journal of Higher Education, 71,* 569-590.

Bridges, D. (1988). *Education, democracy, and discussion.* Lanham, MD: University Press of America.

Brinko, K. T., & Menges, R. J. (1997). *Practically speaking: A sourcebook for instructional consultants in higher education.*

Stillwater, OK: New Forums Press/Professional and Organizational Development Network in Higher Education.

Brookfield, S. D. (1995). *Becoming a critically reflective teacher.* San Francisco, CA: Jossey-Bass.

Brookfield, S. D., & Preskill, S. (1999). *Discussion as a way of teaching: Tools and techniques for democratic classrooms.* San Francisco, CA: Jossey-Bass.

Brown, J. S., Collins, A., & Duguid, P. (1989). Situated cognition and the culture of learning. *Educational Researcher, 13,* 32-41.

Buber, M. (1947). *Between man and man.* London, England: Collins.

Bulik, R. (2000). Issues, challenges and changing metaphors: Teaching and learning in the virtual classroom. *Journal for the Art of Teaching, 7* (1), 17-34.

Buxton, C. (1956). *College teaching: A psychologist's view.* New York, NY: Harcourt Brace.

Buzan, T. (1991). *Using both sides of your brain.* New York, NY: Dutton.

Caffarella, R. S., & Zinn, L. F. (1999). Professional development for faculty: A conceptual framework of barriers and supports. *Innovative Higher Education, 23,* 241-254.

Center for Instructional Development and Research (Producer). (1991). *Teaching in the Diverse Classroom* [Video]. (Available from Anker Publishing Company, Inc., P. O. Box 249, Bolton, MA 01740-0249)

Centra, J. A. (1976). *Faculty development practices in U.S. colleges and universities.* Princeton, NJ: Educational Testing Service.

Cerbin, W. (1992). How to improve teaching with learner centered evaluation. *National Teaching and Learning Forum, 1* (6), 6-8.

Chickering, A., & Gamson, Z. (1987). Seven principles for good practice. *AAHE Bulletin, 39,* 3-7.

Chism, N. V. N., & Szabo, B. (1996). Who uses faculty development services? In L. Richlin & D. DeZure (Eds.), *To improve the academy: Vol. 15. Resources for faculty, instructional, and organizational development* (pp. 115-128). Stillwater, OK: New Forums Press.

Chism, N. V. N., & Szabo, B. (1997). How faculty development programs evaluate their services. *Journal of Staff, Program, and Organization Development, 15,* 55-62.

Coffing, R. T. (1973). *Identification of client demand for public services: Development of a methodology.* Unpublished doctoral dissertation, University of Massachusetts.

Cooper, R. (1958). *The two ends of the log: Learning and teaching in today's college.* Minneapolis, MN: University of Minnesota Press.

Covington, M. (1996). *Motivation, achievement, and self-worth.* Presentation at the 4th annual Faculty Seminar on Teaching with GSIs, University of California, Berkeley.

Cox, M. (2001). Faculty learning communities: Change agents for transforming institutions into learning organizations. In D. Lieberman & C. Wehlburg (Eds.), *To improve the academy: Vol. 19. Resources for faculty, instructional, and organizational development* (pp. 69-93). Bolton, MA: Anker.

Cross, K. P. (1994). *How to professionally develop GSIs for today's world of higher education.* Presentation at the 2nd annual Faculty Seminar on Teaching with GSIs, University of California, Berkeley.

Cross, K. P., & Steadman, M. (1996). *Classroom research.* San Francisco, CA: Jossey Bass.

Cuban, L. (1999). *How scholars trumped teachers: Change without reform in university curriculum, teaching, and research, 1890-1990.* New York, NY: Teacher's College Press.

Cyrs, T. E. (1997). *Teaching at a distance with the merging technologies: An instructional systems approach.* Las Cruces, NM: New Mexico State University, Center for Educational Development.

Cyrs, T. E., & Conway, E. D. (1997). *Beyond bullets: Let your students see what you are saying.* Session presented at the annual meeting of the Professional and Organization Development Network in Higher Education (POD), Haines City, FL.

Davis, B. G. (1993). *Tools for teaching.* San Francisco, CA: Jossey-Bass.

Deming, W. E. (1986). *Out of the crisis.* Cambridge, MA: Massachusetts Institute of Technology.

Detterman, D. K., & Sternberg, R. J. (Eds.). (1993). *Transfer on trial: Intelligence, cognition, and instruction.* Norwood, NJ: Ablex.

Dewey, J. (1902). *The child and the curriculum: The school and society.* Chicago, IL: University of Chicago Press.

DeZure, D. (1996). Closer to the disciplines: A model for improving teaching within departments. *AAHE Bulletin, 48* (6), 9-12.

Diamond, N. (1988). S.G.I.D. (Small group instructional diagnosis): Tapping student perceptions of teaching. In E. C. Wadsworth (Ed.), *A handbook for new practitioners* (pp. 89-93). Stillwater, OK: New Forums Press.

Dormant, D. (1986). *Introduction to performance technology.* Washington, DC: National Society for Performance and Instruction.

Eggan, P., & Kauchak, D. (1997). *Educational psychology: Windows on classrooms* (3rd ed.). Upper Saddle River, NJ: Prentice-Hall.

Eisler, D. (2000). *Dave's web page* (Online). Available: http://weber.edu/deisler/portal_content.htm

Eison, J., & Stevens, E. (1995). Faculty development workshops and institutes. In W. Alan Wright (Ed.), *Teaching improvement practices: Successful strategies for higher education* (pp. 206-227). Bolton, MA: Anker.

Eleser, C. B., & Chauvin, S. W. (1998). Professional development how to's: Strategies for surveying faculty preferences. *Innovative Higher Education, 22,* 181-201.

Ellis, D. (2000). *Becoming a master student* (9th ed.). New York, NY: Houghton Mifflin.

Emery, L. J. (1997). Interest in teaching improvement: Differences for junior faculty. *The Journal of Staff, Program, and Organization Development, 15,* 29-34.

Ertmer, P. A. (1999). Addressing first and second order barriers to change: Strategies for technology integration. *Educational Technology Research & Development, 47* (4), 47-61.

Falk, B., & Dow, K. L. (1971). *The assessment of university teaching.* London, England: Society for Research into Higher Education.

Farmer, D. (1999). Course-embedded assessment: A catalyst for realizing the paradigm shift from teaching to learning. *Journal of Staff, Program, and Organization Development, 16,* 199-211.

Farmer, D. W., & Mech, T. F. (1992). Information literacy: Developing students as independent learners. *New Directions for Higher Education, No. 78.* San Francisco, CA: Jossey-Bass.

Farrell, C. (1999). Loans for college don't have to crush grads. *Business Week, 3637,* 147.

Feldman, K. A., & Paulsen, M. B. (1999). Faculty motivation: The role of a supportive teaching culture. *New Directions for Teaching and Learning, No. 78.* San Francisco, CA: Jossey-Bass.

Fernstermacher, G. D. (1986). Philosophy of research on teaching: Three aspects. In M. C. Wittrock (Ed.), *Handbook of research on teaching* (3rd ed.) (pp. 37-49). New York, NY: Macmillan.

Foucault, M. (1977). *Discipline and punish: The birth of the prison.* New York, NY: Vintage.

Foucault, M. (1980). *Power/knowledge: Selected interviews and other writings, 1972-1977.* New York, NY: Pantheon.

Foucault, M. (1982). The subject and power. In H. L. Dreyfus & P. Rabinow (Eds.), *Michel Foucault: Beyond structuralism and hermeneutics* (pp. 214-225). Chicago, IL: University of Chicago Press.

Fox, D. (1983). Personal theories of teaching. *Studies in Higher Education, 8* (2), 151-163.

Franklin, U. (1990). *The real world of technology.* Toronto, Canada: CBC Enterprises.

Freire, P. (1971). *Pedagogy of the oppressed.* New York, NY: Herder & Herder.

Fulton, C., & Licklider, B. L. (1998). Supporting faculty development in an era of change. In D. DeZure & M. Kaplan (Eds.), *To improve the academy: Vol. 17. Resources for faculty, instructional, and organizational development* (pp. 51-66). Stillwater, OK: New Forums Press.

Gabelnick, F., MacGregor, J., Matthews, R., & Smith, B. L. (1990). Learning communities: Creating connections among students, faculty, and disciplines. *New Directions for Teaching and Learning, No. 41.* San Francisco, CA: Jossey-Bass.

Gaff, J. G. (1975). *Toward faculty renewal: Advances in faculty, instructional, and organizational development.* San Francisco, CA: Jossey-Bass.

Gage, N. L. (Ed.). (1963). *Handbook of research on teaching.* Chicago, IL: Rand McNally.

Gay, G. (1994). *A synthesis of scholarship in multicultural education: Urban monograph series.* Oak Brook, IL: North Central Regional Educational Laboratory.

Gay, G. (2000). *Culturally responsive teaching.* New York, NY: Teachers College Press.

Gilbert, S. (2000a). *Realizing the vision: Scaling online education from the classroom to the institution.* Presentation at the Blackboard Summit 2000, Washington, DC.

Gilbert, S. (2000b). *Virtual teaching, learning, and technology centers: Meeting the rising expectations for information technology* (Online). Available: http://webct.com/ecolloquia/viewpage?name=ecolloquia_event_10

Gillespie, K. H. (2000). The challenge and test of our values: An essay of collective experience. In M. Kaplan & D. Lieberman (Eds.), *To improve the academy: Vol. 18. Resources for faculty, instructional, and organizational development* (pp. 27-37). Bolton, MA: Anker.

Goodwin, L. D., Stevens, E. A., Goodwin, W. L., & Hagood, E. A. (2000). The meaning of faculty mentoring. *Journal of Staff, Program, and Organization Development, 17,* 17-30.

Gore, J. (1993). *The struggle for pedagogies: Critical and feminist discourses as regimes of truth.* New York, NY: Routledge.

Gose, B. (2000). Measuring the value of an ivy degree. *Chronicle of Higher Education, 46* (19), A52-A53.

Groundswell. (2000). *Groundswell Hawaii surf company* (Online). Available: http://www.groundswell.com

Grunert, J. (1997). *The course syllabus: A learning-centered approach.* Bolton, MA: Anker.

Hall, G. E., & Hord, S. M. (1987). *Change in schools: Facilitating the process.* Albany, NY: State University of New York Press.

Hallowell, E. (1999). *Connect.* New York, NY: Pantheon.

Handy, C. (1998). A proper education. *Change, 30* (5), 13-19.

Hargreaves, A., & Dawe, R. (1989). Paths of professional development: Contrived collegiality, collaborative culture, and the case of peer coaching. *Teaching and Teacher Education, 6* (3), 227-241.

Havelock, R.G. (1995). *The change agent's guide to innovation in education.* Englewood Cliffs, NJ: Educational Technology Publications.

Holdaway, E., et al. (1991, Fall). Program reviews: Practices and lessons. *Canadian Society for the Study of Higher Education, 9,* 2-11.

hooks, bell. (1994). *Teaching to transgress: Education as the practice of freedom.* New York, NY: Routledge.

Horton, M. (1990). *The long haul.* New York, NY: Doubleday.

Huczynski, A. A. (1978). Approaches to the problems of learning transfer. *Journal of European Industrial Training, 2* (1), 26-31.

Huczynski, A. A., & Lewis, J. W. (1980). An empirical study into the learning transfer process in management training. *Journal of Management Studies, 17,* 227-240.

Hutchings, P. (1996). The peer review of teaching: Progress, issues and prospects. *Innovative Higher Education, 20* (4), 221-234.

Hutchings, P. (Ed.). (1998). *The course portfolio.* Washington, DC: American Association for Higher Education.

Hutchings, P. (2000). Promoting a culture of teaching and learning. In D. DeZure (Ed.), *Learning from* Change: *Landmarks in teaching and learning in higher education from* Change *Magazine 1969-1999* (pp. 1-4). Sterling, VA: Stylus.

Hutchings, P., & Cambridge, B. (2001). The Carnegie Academy for the Scholarship of Teaching and Learning (CASTL). Projects and initiatives that influence the environment for CASTL's work. Paper presented at the Annual Forum on Faculty Roles and Rewards, Tampa, FL.

Janowitz, M. (1970). *Political conflict: Essays in political sociology.* Chicago, IL: Quadrangle.

Java in Administration Special Interest Group (JA-SIG) Clearinghouse. (2000). *Portal framework project* (Online). Available: http://www.mis2.udel.edu/jasig/portal.html

Kardia, D. (1998). Becoming a multicultural faculty developer: Reflections from the field. In D. DeZure & M. Kaplan (Eds.), *To improve the academy: Vol. 17. Resources for faculty, instructional, and organizational development* (pp. 15-33). Stillwater, OK: New Forums Press.

Keesing, H. A., & Daston, M. (1979). *How to run a microteaching workshop.* College Park, MD: University of Maryland University College Faculty Development Program.

Kegan, R. (1994). *In over our heads: The mental demands of modern life.* Cambridge, MA: Harvard University Press.

Kemp, J. E. (1996). School restructuring: Your school can do it. *Techtrends, 41* (1), 12-15.

Killen, R. (1995). Improving teaching through reflective partnerships. In E. Neal (Ed.), *To improve the academy: Vol. 14. Resources for faculty, instructional, and organizational development* (pp. 125-141). Stillwater, OK: New Forums Press.

Kinsella, K. (1995). Peers coaching teaching: Colleagues supporting professional growth across the disciplines. In E. Neal (Ed.), *To improve the academy: Vol. 14. Resources for faculty, instructional, and organizational development* (pp. 107-123). Stillwater, OK: New Forums Press.

Kirr, S. T. (1996). Visions of sugarplums: The future of technology, education, and the schools. In S. T. Kirr (Ed.), *Technology and the future of schooling: Ninety-fifth yearbook of the National Society for the Study of Education* (pp. 1-27). Chicago, IL: University of Chicago Press.

Kitano, M. K., Dodge, B. J., Harrison, P. J., & Lewis, R. B. (1998). Faculty development in technology applications to university instruction: An evaluation. In D. DeZure & M. Kaplan (Eds.), *To improve the academy: Vol. 17. Resources for faculty, instructional, and organizational development* (pp. 263-290). Stillwater, OK: New Forums Press.

Kotter, J. (1995, March/April). Leading change: Why transformation efforts fail. *Harvard Business Review*, 59-67.

Lambert, L. M., & Tice, S. L. (1993). *Preparing graduate students to teach*. Washington, DC: American Association for Higher Education.

Lave, J. (1988). *Cognition and practice: Mind, mathematics and culture in everyday life*. Cambridge, MA: Cambridge University Press.

Laylock, M. (2000). QILT: An approach to faculty development and institutional self-improvement. In M. Kaplan & D. Lieberman (Eds.), *To improve the academy: Vol. 18. Resources for faculty, instructional, and organizational development* (pp. 69-82). Bolton, MA: Anker.

Levine, A. (2000a). *The remaking of the American university*. Presentation at the Blackboard Summit 2000, Washington, DC.

Levine, A. (2000b, October 27). The future of colleges: Nine inevitable changes. *The Chronicle of Higher Education*, p. B10.

Lewis, K. G. (1996). Faculty development in the United States: A brief history. *The International Journal of Academic Development, 1* (2), 26-33.

Licklider, B. L., Schnelker, D. L., & Fulton, C. (1997). Revisioning faculty development for changing times: The foundation and framework. *Journal of Staff, Program, and Organization Development, 15*, 121-133.

Lieberman, D. A., & Rueter, J. (1996). Designing, implementing and assessing a university technology-pedagogy institute. In L. Richlin & D. DeZure (Eds.), *To improve the academy: Vol. 15. Resources for faculty, instructional, and organizational development* (pp. 231-249). Stillwater, OK: New Forums Press.

Many, W. A., Ellis, J. R., & Abrams, P. (1969, Spring). In-service education in American senior colleges and universities: A status report. *Illinois School Research,* 46-51.

Marchesani, L., & Adams, M. (1992). Dynamics of diversity in the teaching-learning process. *New Directions in Teaching and Learning, No. 52.* San Francisco, CA: Jossey-Bass.

Marincovich, M., Prostko, J., & Stout, F. (Eds.). (1998). *The professional development of graduate teaching assistants.* Bolton, MA: Anker.

McKeachie, W. J. (1951). *Teaching tips: A guidebook for the beginning college teacher.* Lexington, MA: D. C. Heath.

McKeachie, W. J. (1969). *Teaching tips: A guidebook for the beginning college teacher* (7th ed.). Lexington, MA: D. C. Heath.

McKeachie, W. J. (1978). *Teaching tips: A guidebook for the beginning college teacher* (8th ed.). Lexington, MA: D. C. Heath.

McKeachie, W. (1999). *Teaching tips: A guidebook for the beginning college teacher* (10th ed.). Boston, MA: Houghton Mifflin.

McKnight, P. C. (1980). Microteaching: Development from 1968-1978. *British Journal of Teacher Education, 6,* 214-227.

McNeil, L. M. (2000). Creating new inequalities: Contradictions of reform. *Phi Delta Kappan, 80,* 728-734.

Menges, R. J. (1997). Fostering faculty motivation to teach: Approaches to faculty development. In J. L. Bess (Ed.), *Teaching well and liking it* (pp. 407-423). Baltimore, MD: Johns Hopkins University.

Meyers, C., & Jones, T. (1993). *Promoting active learning: Strategies for the college classroom.* San Francisco, CA: Jossey-Bass.

Middendorf, J. (2000). Finding key faculty to influence change. In M. Kaplan & D. Lieberman (Eds.), *To improve the academy: Vol. 18. Resources for faculty, instructional, and organizational development* (pp. 83-93). Bolton, MA: Anker.

Middendorf, J. (2001). Getting administrative support for your project. In D. Lieberman & C. Wehlburg (Eds.), *To improve the academy: Vol. 19. Resources for faculty, instructional, and organizational development* (pp. 346-359). Bolton, MA: Anker.

Middendorf, J. K. (1998). A case study in getting faculty to change. In D. DeZure & M. Kaplan (Eds.), *To improve the academy: Vol. 17. Resources for faculty, instructional, and organizational development* (pp. 203-224). Stillwater, OK: New Forums Press.

Miles, M. B. (1959). *Learning to work in groups: A program guide for educational leaders*. New York, NY: Teachers College, Columbia University.

Mintz, J. (1997). *Mentoring supervisors of postgraduate students*. Presentation at the University of Strathclyde, Glasgow, Scotland.

Mintz, J., & von Hoene, L. (1997). *Mentoring for (a) change: Working with faculty to rethink the role of teaching in graduate education*. Presentation at the 5th national TA Conference, Minneapolis, MN.

Mintz, J., von Hoene, L., Duggan, J., & Reimer, J. (1995). *Teaching with teaching assistants: A cross-disciplinary dialogue with faculty*. Presentation at the 4th national TA Conference, Boulder, CO.

Mintz, J., von Hoene, L., & Reimer, J. (1998). *Pedagogical mentorship: The role of faculty in preparing graduate students to teach*. Presentation at the American Association for Higher Education Conference on Faculty Roles and Rewards, Orlando, FL.

Monett, M. L. (1977). The concept of educational need: An analysis of selected literature. *Adult Education, 27* (2), 116-127.

Moore, S., & Mizuba, K. (1968). Innovation diffusion: A study in credibility. *The Educational Forum, 33* (1), 181-185.

Morrison, D. (1997). Overview of instructional consultation in North America. In K. T. Brinko & R. T. Menges (Eds.), *Practically speaking: A sourcebook for instructional consultants in higher education* (pp. 121-130). Stillwater, OK: New Forums Press.

National Center for Public Policy and Higher Education. (2000). *Measuring up 2000: The state-by-state report card for higher education*. Washington, DC: Author.

Noe, R. A. (1986). Trainees' attributes and attitudes: Neglected influences on training effectiveness. *Academy of Management Review, 11* (4), 736-749.

Noffke, S. (1995). Action research and democratic schooling: Problematics and potentials. In S. Noffke & R. Stevenson (Eds.), *Educational action research: Becoming practically critical* (pp. 1-10). New York, NY: Teachers College Press.

Norman, M. (2000). Portal technology: In the looking glass. *Converge* (Online). Available: http://www.convergemag.com/SpecialPubs/Portal/portal.shtm

Notarianni-Girard, D. (1999, Spring). Transfer of training in teaching assistant programs. *Journal of Graduate Teaching Assistant Development, 6* (3), 119-147.

Nyquist, J., & Wulff, W. (1988). Consultation using a research perspective. In E. C. Wadsworth (Ed.), *A handbook for new practitioners* (pp. 82-88). Stillwater, OK: New Forums Press.

Olsen, F. (2000). Institutions collaborate on development of free portal software. *The Chronicle of Higher Education* (Online). Available: www.chronicle.com/free/2000/05/2000050501t.htm

Orme, M. (1977). *Effective teaching techniques* (video). Toronto, Canada: Ryerson TV Studios.

Paivio, A. (1971). *Imagery and verbal processes.* New York, NY: Holt, Reinhart, and Winston.

Palmer, P. J. (1997). The heart of a teacher: Identity and integrity in teaching. *Change, 29,* 15-21.

Patrick, S. K., & Fletcher, J. J. (1998). Faculty developers and change agents: Transforming colleges and universities into learning organizations In D. DeZure & M. Kaplan (Eds.), *To improve the academy: Vol. 17. Resources for faculty, instructional, and organizational development* (pp. 155-170). Stillwater, OK: New Forums Press.

Paulsen, M. B., & Feldman, K. A. (1995). Taking teaching seriously: Meeting the challenge of instructional improvement. *ASHE-ERIC Educational Report No. 2.* Washington, DC: The George Washington School of Education and Human Development.

Perry, R. P. (1992). Teaching in higher education. *Teaching and Teacher Education, 8* (3), 311-317.

Perry, W. (1970). *Forms of ethical and intellectual development in the college years.* New York, NY: Holt, Rinehart, and Winston.

Piccinin, S. (1999). How individual consultation affects teaching. In C. Knapper & S. Piccinin (Eds.), *Using consultants to improve teaching* (pp. 71-83). New Directions for Teaching and Learning, No. 79. San Francisco, CA: Jossey-Bass.

Pittinsky, M. (1999). Campus and course portals in 2015. *Converge* (Online). Available: http://www.convergemag.com/Publications/CNVGOct99/Possibilities/Possibilities.shtm

Pratt, D. D., & Associates. (1998). *Five perspectives on teaching in adult and higher education.* Malabar, FL: Krieger.

Prochaska, J. O., DiClemente, C. C., & Norcross, J. C. (1992). In search of how people change. *American Psychologist, 47,* 1102-1114.

Ramsden, P. (1992). *Learning to teach in higher education*. London, England: Routledge.

Rando, W., & Menges, R. (1991). How practice is shaped by personal theories. *New Directions for Teaching and Learning, No. 45*. San Francisco, CA: Jossey-Bass.

Rauton, J. T. (1996). A home-grown faculty development program. *Journal of Staff, Program, and Organization Development, 14*, 5-9.

Reich, R. B. (2000). How selective colleges heighten inequality. *Chronicle of Higher Education, 47* (3), B7-B10.

Robertson, D. L. (1996). Facilitating transformative learning: Attending to the dynamics of the educational helping relationship. *Adult Education Quarterly, 47* (1), 43-53.

Robertson, D. L. (1999). Professors' perspectives on their teaching: A new construct and developmental model. *Innovative Higher Education, 23*, 271-294.

Rogers, E. M. (1995). *Diffusion of innovation* (4th ed.). New York, NY: Free Press.

Sahu, A. R. (1985). An introduction of microteaching: A systems approach. *International Journal of Math, Education, Science, and Technology, 16*, 25-31.

Saint Meinrad School of Theology. (1995). *Proposal for a campus network and technology empowerment project*. Unpublished manuscript, Saint Meinrad School of Theology, St. Meinrad, IN.

Saint Meinrad School of Theology. (1996). *Strategic plan for the Saint Meinrad development program 1996-2001*. Unpublished manuscript, Saint Meinrad School of Theology, St. Meinrad, IN.

Saint Meinrad School of Theology. (1997). *Information technology for theological teaching implementation grant*. Unpublished manuscript, Saint Meinrad School of Theology, St. Meinrad, IN.

Saint Meinrad School of Theology. (1998). *Integrating technology in instruction: Needs analysis project at Saint Meinrad School of Theology*. Unpublished manuscript, Saint Meinrad School of Theology, St. Meinrad, IN.

Sanders, K., Carlson-Dakes, C., Dettinger, K., Hajnal, C., Laedtke, M., & Squire, L. (1997). A new starting point for faculty development in higher education: Creating a collaborative learning environment. In D. DeZure (Ed.), *To improve the academy: Vol. 16. Resources for faculty, instructional, and organizational development* (pp. 117-150). Stillwater, OK: New Forums Press.

Sandy, L. R., Meyer, S., Goodnough, G. E., & Rogers, A. T. (2000). Faculty perceptions of the importance of pedagogy as faculty development. *Journal of Staff, Program, and Organization Development, 17,* 39-50.

Sax, L. J., Astin, A. W., Korn, W. S., & Gilmartin, S. K. (1999). *The American college teacher: National norms for the 1998-99 HERI faculty survey.* Los Angeles, CA: University of California, Los Angeles, Higher Education Research Institute.

Schilling, K. M., & Schilling, K. L. (1999). Increasing expectations for student effort. *About Campus, 4* (2), 4-10.

Schön, D. A. (1995, November/December). The new scholarship requires a new epistemology. *Change,* 27-34.

Scott, D. C., & Weeks, P. A. (1996). Collaborative staff development. *Innovative Higher Education, 21,* 101-111.

Seldin, P. (1995). *Improving college teaching.* Bolton, MA: Anker.

Senge, P. (1990). *The fifth discipline.* New York, NY: Currency Doubleday.

Sherer, P., & Shea, T. (in press). Designing courses outside the classroom: New opportunities with the electronic delivery toolkit. *College Teaching.*

Showers, B., Joyce, B., & Bennett, B. (1987). Synthesis of research in staff development: A framework for future study. *Educational Leadership, 45,* 77-87.

Shulman, L. S. (1993). Teaching as community property. *Change, 25,* 6-7.

Silberman, M. (1996). *Active learning: 101 strategies to teach any subject.* Boston, MA: Allyn and Bacon.

Smith, B. (1998). Adopting a strategic approach to managing change in learning and teaching. In D. DeZure & M. Kaplan (Eds.), *To improve the academy: Vol. 17. Resources for faculty, instructional, and organizational development* (pp. 225-242). Stillwater, OK: New Forums Press.

Smith, K. (1996). Cooperative learning: Making "groupwork" work. *New Directions for Teaching and Learning, No. 67.* San Francisco, CA: Jossey-Bass.

Smith, R. A., & Geis, G. L. (1996). Professors as clients for instructional development. In L. Richlin & D. DeZure (Eds.), *To improve the academy: Vol. 15. Resources for faculty, instructional, and organizational development* (pp. 129-153). Stillwater, OK: New Forums Press.

Sorcinelli, M. D. (1991). Research findings on the seven principles. *New Directions for Teaching and Learning, No. 47.* San Francisco, CA: Jossey-Bass.

Sorcinelli, M. D. (1997). The teaching improvement process. In K. T. Brinko & R. T. Menges (Eds.), *Practically speaking: A sourcebook for instructional consultants in higher education* (pp. 157-158). Stillwater, OK: New Forums Press.

Stanley, C. A. (2000). Factors that contribute to the teaching development of faculty development center clientele: A case study of ten university professors. *Journal of Staff, Program, and Organizational Development, 17,* 155-169.

Stanley, C. A., Porter, M. E., & Szabo, B. L. (1997). An exploratory study of the faculty-client relationship. *Journal of Staff, Program, and Organization Development, 14,* 115-123.

Stern School of Business. (1996). *Stern teaching effectiveness program (STEP).* Unpublished report, New York University, Stern School Teaching Effectiveness Committee.

Stern School of Business. (1999). *Stern teaching effectiveness program activities report: Academic year 1998-99.* Unpublished report, New York University.

Strebel, P. (1998). *Harvard business review on change.* Boston, MA: Harvard Business School.

Sullivan, L. L. (1983). Faculty development: A movement on the brink. *College Board Review, 127,* 20-21, 29-31.

Sutherland, T. E., & Bonwell, C. (1996). Using active learning in college classes: A range of options for faculty. *New Directions for Teaching and Learning, No. 67.* San Francisco, CA: Jossey-Bass.

Sweidel, G. B. (1996). Partners in pedagogy: Faculty development through the scholarship of teaching. In L. Richlin & D. DeZure (Eds.), *To improve the academy: Vol. 15. Resources for faculty, instructional, and organizational development* (pp. 267-274). Stillwater, OK: New Forums Press.

Taber, L. S. (1999). Faculty development for instructional technology: A priority for the new millennium. *Journal of Staff, Program, and Organization Development, 15,* 159-174.

Tafoya, W. L. (1983). Needs assessment: Key to organizational change. *Journal of Police Science Administration, 11* (3), 303-310.

Theall, M. (1997, May). *An overview of different approaches to teaching and learning styles.* Paper presented at Teaching and Learning Styles at a Distance, Central Illinois Higher Education Consortium Faculty Development Conference, Springfield, IL.

Tiberius, R. G. (1986). Metaphors underlying the improvement of teaching and learning. *British Journal of Educational Technology, 17* (2), 144-156.

Tiberius, R. (1997). Microteaching, teaching laboratory, and alliances for change. In K. T. Brinko & R. J. Menges (Eds.), *Practically speaking: A sourcebook for instructional consultants in higher education.* (pp. 131-137). Stillwater, OK: New Forums Press.

Tigner, R. B. (2000). Putting memory research to good use: Hints from cognitive psychology. *College Teaching, 48* (1), 149-152.

Tinto, V., Love, A. G., & Russo, P. (1993). Building community. *Liberal Education, 79,* 16-21.

Tobias, S. (1992). Disciplinary cultures and general education: What can we learn from our learners? *Teaching Excellence, 4* (6).

Usher, R., & Edwards, R. (1994). *Postmodernism and education: Different voices, different worlds.* London, England: Routledge.

Vigotsky, L. (1986). *Thought and language.* Cambridge, MA: MIT Press.

Wadsworth, E. C. (Ed.). (1988). *A handbook for new practitioners.* Stillwater, OK: New Forums Press/Professional and Organizational Development Network in Higher Education.

Watkins, K. E., & Marsick, V. J. (1993). *Sculpting the learning organization.* San Francisco, CA: Jossey-Bass.

Wechsler, H., Lee, J., Kuo, M., & Lee, H. (2000). College binge drinking in the 1990s: A continuing problem. *Journal of American College Health, 48* (10), 219-226.

Weimer, M. E. (1990). *Improving college teaching.* San Francisco, CA: Jossey-Bass.

Weiss, C. H. (1977). Research for policy's sake: The enlightenment function of social research. *Policy Analysis, 3,* 531-545.

Wildman, T. M., Hable, M. P., Preston, M. M., & Magliaro, S. G. (2000). Faculty study groups: Solving good problems through study, reflection, and collaboration. *Innovative Higher Education, 24,* 247-263.

Wilkerson, L. (1988). Classroom observation: The observer as collaborator. In E. C. Wadsworth (Ed.), *A handbook for new practitioners* (pp. 95-98). Stillwater, OK: New Forums Press.

Woods, J. Q. (1999). Establishing a teaching development culture. In R. J. Menges & Associates (Eds.), *Faculty in new jobs: A guide to settling in, becoming established, and building institutional support.* (pp. 268-290). San Francisco, CA: Jossey-Bass.

Wright, D. L. (1996). Moving toward a university environment which rewards teaching: The faculty developer's role. In L. Richlin & D. DeZure (Eds.), *To improve the academy: Vol. 15. Resources for faculty, instructional, and organizational development* (pp. 185-194). Stillwater, OK: New Forums Press.

Wright, D. L. (2000). Faculty development centers in research universities: A study of resources and programs. In M. Kaplan & D. Lieberman (Eds.), *To improve the academy: Vol. 18. Resources for faculty, instructional, and organizational development* (pp. 291-301). Bolton, MA: Anker.

Wright, W. A. (1995). *Teaching improvement practices: Successful strategies for higher education.* Bolton, MA: Anker.

Wright, W. A., & O'Neil, M. C. (1995). Teaching improvement practices: International perspectives. In W. A. Wright (Ed.), *Teaching improvement practices: successful strategies for higher education* (pp. 1-57). Bolton, MA: Anker.